LADY OF FRANCE

The Biography of Gabrielle d'Estrées
Mistress of Henry the Great

Noel B. Gerson

SAPERE
BOOKS

LADY OF FRANCE

Published by Sapere Books.

20 Windermere Drive, Leeds, England, LS17 7UZ,
United Kingdom

saperebooks.com

ISBN: 978-1-80055-495-5.

For Beulah Harris

TABLE OF CONTENTS

PREFACE — 9

1: THE FIRST MEETING: NOVEMBER 1590 — 13

2: THE EARLY YEARS: 1573–90 — 31

3: HENRY THE GREAT — 49

4: RENDEZVOUS AT CHARTRES, 1591 — 63

5: MARRIAGE, 1592 — 69

6: THE LOVE GAME, 1592–93 — 84

7: THE POWER BEHIND THE THRONE, 1593 — 100

8: THE CONVERSION, 1593 — 111

9: PARIS IN THE SPRINGTIME, 1594 — 123

10: THE DIVORCE, 1594 — 135

11: THE LADY AND THE POPE, 1595 — 152

12: THE LADY DIPLOMAT, 1595–96 — 164

13: KEEPER OF THE KEYS, 1596 — 180

14: THE CRUCIBLE, 1597 — 198

15: THE SILKEN GLOVE, 1597–98 — 220

16: THE EDICT OF NANTES, 1598 — 235

17: A KING, A QUEEN, AND A PAWN, 1598 — 249

18: LADY OF FRANCE, 1598–99 — 266

19: THE DEATH OF GABRIELLE, 1599 — 281

20: AFTERMATH — 291

NOTES — 302

BIBLIOGRAPHY — 313

A NOTE TO THE READER — 316

PREFACE

Gabrielle d'Estrées, Duchess de Beaufort, Duchess d'Étampes, Marquise de Monceaux, Royal Administrator of the Duchy of Vendôme, Dame de Liencourt, and Dame de Vandeuil has enjoyed a not altogether undeserved notoriety for the better part of four hundred years.

She is one of history's most bewilderingly complex and contradictory women. She was an amoral woman who fell in love but once in her life, and thereafter was a model of fidelity. She inspired similar fidelity in a man who, for centuries, has been noted for his profligacy. A product of an age in which bigotry was virtually universal, she developed and practiced almost unprecedented tolerance. She received no training in the art of statesmanship, but became a diplomat of the first magnitude.

A member of the aristocracy, she earned the love of the common people, about whom she had known nothing. A great beauty, she learned that surface attractiveness was meaningless. Indolent and careless from early childhood, she became zealous, hard-working, and prompt. Almost shockingly greedy, she changed overnight and willingly sacrificed a great fortune.

The daughter of a woman who was murdered because of her scandalous behavior, Gabrielle started to follow in her mother's footsteps, but became transformed by love, and was a devoted, self-sacrificing mistress and mother. Then tragedy struck at the very moment she was about to achieve her greatest triumph, the acquisition of respectability.

Gabrielle would have been a minor figure in history, a mere footnote, had she not become the mistress of one of the most illustrious of French monarchs, Henry IV, whose popularity among his countrymen, down to the present day, has been second only to that of Napoleon. Henry the Great was an ugly, battle-scarred veteran, two decades Gabrielle's senior, who fell in love with her at first sight and did not look at another woman as long as she lived. That she should have inspired such constancy is astonishing, for Henry had, at one time or another, fifty-five other known mistresses.

He could have married any princess in Christendom, but chose to make Gabrielle his bride, braving the displeasure of the Pope, of the allies who had supported him through decades of turmoil, and of the enemies who, with Gabrielle's help, he had recently pacified. He could afford to ignore the ugly rumors that surrounded her, for he alone knew the truth about her. Yet it is odd that Henry, who never trusted any other woman, should have shown such blind faith in one who he knew had betrayed him. On second thought, he was wise: he did not trust her until she had earned his complete approval.

It is obvious that Henry the Great was the most important single influence that molded and strengthened the character of Gabrielle d'Estrées. What is less apparent, but far more significant, is that Gabrielle changed Henry.

The biographer of Gabrielle cannot and does not argue that Henry would have been any less towering a figure had he never met Gabrielle. There is no evidence to suggest that she played a role in his modernization of the French tax structure, in his land reforms, in his campaigns to introduce industry into France, in his sweeping modernization of the army and navy, or in his encouragement of New World exploration.

The part she played was, with one notable exception, too subtle to be subjected to broad generalization. However, the hard facts that emerge from the mists of the late sixteenth century are startling, and suggest that history would have been far different had Gabrielle not been Henry's mistress. It was she, acting as a self-appointed agent, who brought about a reconciliation between Henry and the great nobles who had bled France dry to prevent him from acquiring the crown that was rightfully his. It was Gabrielle, acting decisively in a moment of national peril, who supplied the funds that enabled Henry's army to defeat the most persistent of his foes, the legions of Philip II of Spain.

And, above all, it was Gabrielle, boldly moving out of the shadows and stepping into the spotlight, who shares with Henry the everlasting glory of promulgating the Edict of Nantes, one of the Western world's foundation stones of religious tolerance. It is likely that the Edict would have been issued had Gabrielle never lived, but Henry could not have written and signed the decree when he did and in the way he did without her help. Acting voluntarily, with her intuition as her guide and her own unique background as her cushion, she was the living bridge between Catholics and Protestants.

It is not accidental that both factions rightly considered her their good friend, and this at a time when France, like so many other European nations, was being torn by religious struggles that rivaled the Cold War in their intensity. Perhaps we can most accurately define the role Gabrielle played in this fight by use of a modern example. Let the reader imagine that there exists today some person who enjoys the absolute trust of both the White House and the Kremlin, and that both the United States and Russia freely grant this individual the right to negotiate on their behalf. Such was Gabrielle d'Estrées' position in the bitter religious feud that was resolved when Henry the Great published his Edict. Both groups were satisfied, and both were grateful to her.

Gabrielle's achievement is all the more unusual if we keep in mind that Henry, the Protestant champion, had resisted conversion to Catholicism — and thus prolonged the struggle for the throne of France — until Gabrielle entered his life. Protestants called him a turncoat when he became a Catholic, and Catholics suspected that political expediency had dictated his change of heart. But no one condemned Gabrielle, and it was in the years following his conversion that she worked so long and hard for the reconciliation of faiths that eventually produced the Edict of Nantes.

Gabrielle d'Estrées was, finally, a woman who loved life. She was neither a brilliant intellectual like Diane de Poitiers, a sober reformer like Françoise de Maintenon, nor a sly schemer like Jeanne du Barry. Those ladies loved power for its own sake, but Gabrielle loved only Henry. Her single-minded simplicity was the source of her strength, and of her influence. As a girl she had been vain and clever; as an adult she was neither, and her enemies freely blackened her name.

Lady of France has been written in the hope that it will help to restore Gabrielle d'Estrées to her rightful place in history.

Paul Lewis
New York City

1: THE FIRST MEETING: NOVEMBER 1590

A surprisingly hot sun, bright and clear, burned away the autumn haze of early morning that blanketed the fields surrounding the castle of Coeuvres, a few miles southeast of the town of Soissons. The peasants of Picardy claimed that their gently rolling valleys remained green longer than those found in any other part of France, but throughout the nation the earth was scorched, an ugly reminder of the civil war that had raged in the country almost unceasingly for more than twenty years.

Sentries armed with ceremonial pikes and more practical, muzzle-loading arquebuses paced up and down the high ramparts of the castle, neither pausing nor glancing off toward the south, where cannon were thundering. The master of Coeuvres, Antoine d'Estrées, was nominally loyal to the legal heir to the throne, Henry of Navarre, who had been calling himself Henry IV since he had succeeded his relative and ally, Henry III, the preceding year. But troops under the command of the Duke of Mayenne, head of the threateningly powerful house of Guise and Captain-General of the Catholic League, were operating in the vicinity, and the Marquis de Coeuvres was a hard-headed realist.

If the Spanish and Flemish legions of Mayenne came to his gates, he would allow their commander entry, but would forbid access to knights and common soldiers. He had done the same when Henry's German and English forces had been in the neighborhood, and his stratagem had been successful. Antoine d'Estrées was a prudent man who wanted, above all, to save his own property.

It was well worth saving. Inside the high walls stood the great manor house, a magnificent Renaissance structure of gray sculptured stone, raised on vaulted arches. The four corners of the high protective wall that shielded the house, its huge stables, inner court and kitchens, servants' quarters and artisans' workshops were flanked with square turrets which jutted out over the water-filled moat. The main entrance stood behind a drawbridge on the north side of the castle, facing the little town of Coeuvres. The turret on the northeast side was used as a chapel; the other three contained apartments and were utilized as living quarters by the six daughters and two sons of the prolific marquis. The turret on the southeast side, which had its own cluster of servants' outbuildings, was the apartment of eighteen-year-old Diane d'Estrées and her sister, Gabrielle, one year younger.

The freshly erupted civil war had made living conditions in Paris even more hazardous than they were in the country, so the two girls, both of whom enjoyed reputations as great beauties, had returned from their father's town house to his country estate the preceding year. Their social activities were limited at Coeuvres, but they had every comfort. The windows of their spacious tower apartment were ornamented with sculptures, and rococo lead figures decorated the ridges on the slate roof that hid the gutters. The main part of the building faced toward the east, and from their private sitting room the sisters could see clipped trees and hedges, an expanse of neatly trimmed lawn, and a pond on which their brothers skated in cold weather, on their double-bladed wooden skates.

The great hall was located in the principal building of the château, of course, and was unusually spacious and elegant. A gallery surrounded it, giving access to two other rooms on the ground floor, and there were two flights of broad stone steps leading from the great hall to the upper portion of the manor house. In all, the property surrounded by the protective stone wall was seventy meters long and sixty-four wide, a spacious compound whose residents lived graciously if not luxuriously.

The routine of daily life at the castle was fixed, and remained unchanged even when Henry of Navarre and his Protestant regiments were fighting the armies of the League in the vicinity. Antoine d'Estrées ate breakfast in the great hall with his sons, François-Louis, who was in training for a military career, and François-Annibal, who was studying for the priesthood. Sometimes the younger daughters of the household joined them and, infrequently, the children's maternal aunt came to the table.

The presence in the household of Isabelle Babou de Sourdis, wife of the former governor of Chartres and mistress of Armand de Chiverny, Henry of Navarre's legal adviser, was odd, to say the least. Her sister, Françoise, Antoine d'Estrées' wife, was conspicuously absent and her name was never mentioned. She had eloped with a neighbor, taking the youngest of her daughters with her, and subsequently had given birth to still another daughter, who was illegitimate. The scandal had rocked France, even diverting warriors of the opposing armies, and Antoine d'Estrées was determined that his daughters should not follow in their mother's footsteps.

History offers no logical explanation of his reasons for allowing his sister-in-law, the worldly Isabelle de Sourdis, to spend the better part of her time under his roof. It was true that she held no official position, but she helped with the household management and acted as chaperone for Diane and Gabrielle, while Antoine spent most of his mornings working on his ledgers and his afternoons riding through the fields of peasants who were obligated by law to give him three-quarters of their produce.

It was Madame de Sourdis who made out the daily marketing and shopping lists, and who often accompanied the major domo on his visits to the food stalls and artisans' shops in Coeuvres. Everyone accepted her as a fixture, and apparently no one was disturbed when her husband or her lover occasionally appeared and took her away for a few days.

François-Annibal, who subsequently had a distinguished career, living to the age of ninety-eight under Louis XIV after accumulating the baton of a marshal of France and the golden sash of a duke, offered a strong hint regarding his aunt in his *Memoirs*. "Madame de Sourdis," he wrote, "was as much inclined to the life of a voluptuary as my mother and their other sisters. But Madame de Sourdis was endowed with an intelligence lacking in her sisters. She knew she had passed the peak of her own beauty, and saw in Gabrielle and Diane the tools through which she could acquire power. Her influence over my father was great, but I know not why he tolerated her. He was opposed to all that she believed, and espoused all that she rejected."

The two boys were required to spend the better part of their time studying. François-Louis practiced swordsmanship with the master-at-arms and jousted with the knights; François-Annibal should have been reading ecclesiastical history in Latin, but was far more interested in sneaking off to join his brother.

The younger girls spent the mornings with their tutor, as Antoine, far ahead of his time, held the unusual theory that females should read and write. Their governess took charge of them in the afternoons, which were devoted to needlework and the staple of French high society, gossip.

The heavy silk draperies that shut sunlight out of the bedchambers in the southeast tower remained closed until early afternoon. Diane, later to become the second wife of the Marshal de Balagny, describes the routine she and Gabrielle followed. Writing in her *Memorial to Gabrielle, Duchess de Beaufort*, she says: "Hunger awakened me when the afternoon shadows appeared. I usually went to my sister's room and shook her awake. Gabrielle, in those days, would have slept until dusk if allowed to rest undisturbed."

Lunch for the sisters was usually a light repast of grilled fish, roasted chicken, and a smoking joint of beef, ox, or lamb, washed down with a chilled wine. Their appetites temporarily curbed, they spent the afternoons at their cosmetics tables, interrupting their labors only for visits from dressmakers. If they hurried, they were able to join the rest of the family in the great hall for dinner, which was served at sundown. Antoine tolerated no nonsense, and any of his children who failed to appear on time for the evening meal went without food.

The household rule irked Gabrielle, who complained that she had no chance to finish arranging her hair. "She often remarked," Diane declares, "that she would as soon sit down to dinner in her shift. But our father would not compromise, no matter how incomplete our toilet, and necessity compelled me to abide by his regulations. Gabrielle, more indolent than I, yet more strong-willed, was ever in rebellion, and had she not been famished, would have absented herself from the table in order to spite him."

Girls who had grown accustomed to the excitement of life in Paris found very little other than sleep to occupy them at Coeuvres. Diane indicates in her *Memorial* that she and

Gabrielle spent the better part of the previous year 1589 at the Hôtel d'Estrées in the city, prior to the death of Henry III, with the indefatigable Isabelle de Sourdis as their chaperone. There is reason to believe they also spent portions of 1587 and 1588 in Paris.

It was during this period, presumably, that Gabrielle met the dashing Roger de Saint-Larry, Duke of Bellegarde, a handsome and engaging rake about eleven or twelve years her senior. Regardless of when they met, she soon became involved in an affair with him. Of all the many lovers with whom she is alleged to have been intimate before she entered Henry's life, only Bellegarde actually had relations with her.

Adrien Desclozeaux, whose monograph, *Gabrielle d'Estrées*, has been the authoritative document on the lady since its first publication, in Paris, in 1887, states flatly that Bellegarde was her only lover, other than Henry.

That she and the young duke were intimate has been denied by no one. Henry bitterly discussed the subject at length in some of his early letters to her. Diane takes for granted in her *Memorial* that everyone who read her book was familiar with the open secret. François-Annibal bluntly states that his sister was Bellegarde's mistress. And Bellegarde himself, telling his story in thinly disguised novel form early in the seventeenth century, in a remarkable volume entitled *Amours du Grand Alcandre*, happily boasts that Gabrielle had been his mistress.

Details are lacking. When Gabrielle and the young duke became involved with each other, how long the affair lasted, and the nature of their love can only be guessed. Bellegarde claims, in the *Amours*, that he and Gabrielle intended to be married. No other authority substantiates this, although it is true that the duke had free access to the castle at Coeuvres, and Antoine d'Estrées was not a man who would allow any noble, regardless of his rank, to stain the honor of a d'Estrées daughter.

The importance of Bellegarde is not his affair with Gabrielle, but his relationship with Henry. The duke was one of many prominent Catholic noblemen whose patriotism induced him to support the direct descendant of St. Louis in his claim to the throne, regardless of Henry's Protestantism. Presumably, Bellegarde had become acquainted with the prince from Navarre at the court of Henry III, and possibly they had served together in the field. In any event, when Henry took up arms in 1589 in his climactic struggle against the Catholic League, Bellegarde joined him and soon became his chief equerry, a post comparable to that of personal aide-de-camp in later times.

Bellegarde was a young man of many virtues, but discretion was not one of them. He boasted of his mistress' beauty so loudly, so frequently, and in such glowing terms that Henry's curiosity was finally aroused. The ladies of France, it was said, were less safe than the generals of the League when Henry decided to attack, and the reports were valid.

Long separated from his wife, the dissolute Marguerite de Valois, who was known throughout Europe as "Margot the Wanton," Henry made strenuous efforts to prove that his prowess in the bedchamber was as overpowering as his generalship in the field. He succeeded. Princesses and duchesses gladly sacrificed their good names to go to bed with him, and a red-haired Norman camp follower, about whom nothing is known except that she had come from the Isle of Jersey, attained a dubious immortality by refusing payment from him for her services.

Henry, then, was not one to listen idly to talk of a glorious Venus. On either November 8 or November 10, 1590, he accompanied Bellegarde to the castle at Coeuvres in order to see this paragon of beauty and make his own judgment.

The visit was a miserable failure.

"Gabrielle," François-Annibal says in his *Memoirs*, "had eyes at this time only for Bellegarde."

Bellegarde goes into greater detail, confusing this occasion with subsequent events, and the *Amours*, in which he habitually refers to himself in the third person, bristle with righteous, inaccurate indignation. "She who did not love the King, and who had given all her affection to Bellegarde, fell into a great rage with Henry, swearing that she would never love him and reproaching him for preventing her from marrying Bellegarde, as she desired. Henry meekly accepted her rebuke and retired from the competition. The sister of the lady offered him solace, and he found a few hours of repose in her arms."

It is impossible to determine what threads of truth are woven into this fairy tale. No young woman, meeting Henry for the first time, would have dared to "fall into a great rage with him." He was noted for his calm disposition, but when he became aroused, his temper was the most ferocious in Christendom. He was a civilized man, but he was also the product of his times, and would not have hesitated to throw an impertinent girl into a dungeon had she ranted at him.

Diane's account of the incident, related in her *Memorial* with modest brevity, probably indicates what really happened. "Gabrielle," she says, "showed in deed and in word that she preferred the company of Bellegarde to that of the King. If Henry was vexed, he did not show his displeasure, but conversed with me on many subjects. He spoke freely of his ambition to win the whole of his kingdom to his cause, and he discoursed learnedly on many another matter, proving to my

taking faith in
religous heresay

satisfaction that he was not the heretical barbarian pictured by the Leaguers."

Another source must be regarded as somewhat less than reliable. Agrippa d'Aubigné had been Henry's closest boyhood friend and companion in Navarre; they had studied together in Paris, and together had escaped the knives of assassins in the frightful St. Bartholomew's Day Massacre of August 23–24, 1572, when thousands of Huguenots were murdered at the instigation of the Queen Mother, Catherine de Medici, and the Duc de Guise. D'Aubigné served for many years as Henry's confidential secretary, and on the surface at least, remained loyal to his monarch. But his *Letters*, many of them written to his relatives, were circulated after Henry's death in 1610, and in them d'Aubigné revealed his secret disgust with a companion who had allowed himself to become converted to Catholicism.

"The Béarnais," d'Aubigné states harshly, "was rejected by the fair Gabrielle. Unable to tolerate the insult to his manhood, he bedded the ravishing Diane."

Madame de Sourdis, who was present, undoubtedly would have encouraged either of the sisters to become intimate with Henry. But Antoine d'Estrées was also at home, and officially received the King. In the light of Antoine's later conduct, it is inconceivable that either Bellegarde or Henry succeeded in creeping off to one or the other of the bedchambers in the southeast tower. No one knew better than the badly burned marquis that the flesh of man was weak and that of woman even weaker, and it stands to reason that he kept a sharp watch on his guests — and his daughters.

Bellegarde was writing to salvage his injured ego, d'Aubigné was venting his spleen on a monarch who had betrayed religious principles in which both men had believed, but the comments of Diane and François-Annibal to the effect that

Gabrielle preferred Bellegarde must be accepted as the most accurate. It is unlikely that Diane would have remained silent in her *Memorial* had she entertained Henry in her bedroom. She wrote long after the death of both Gabrielle and the King, and she was not reluctant to mention her many other affairs, one of them with a cardinal who was her husband's favorite nephew. The daughters of Françoise Babou enjoyed keeping a tally of their conquests, and Diane was not the sort who would have hesitated to let the world know that her sister had not been the only member of the family with whom Henry had been intimate.

One fact that cannot be questioned arises out of the welter of bedchamber claims and counterclaims. Scores of slanders to the contrary notwithstanding, it seems certain that Henry and Gabrielle did not leap into bed together at their first meeting.

But the serene beauty of the seventeen-year-old intrigued Henry, who found her far more attractive than her livelier sister and paid a second visit to Coeuvres at some time during the winter of 1590–91. The circumstances are outlined in detail by Bellegarde in the *Amours*, although he was not present. They also appear at length in another "novel," that written by Mademoiselle Louise de Guise, later the Princesse de Conti.

This lovely, intelligent, and amiable young woman was in a position to speak with authority, having become, eventually, the close friend and confidante of Gabrielle. A member of the semiroyal house of Guise and niece of Mayenne, she was courted briefly by Henry, who toyed with the idea of marrying her for political reasons. However, he was much in love with Gabrielle at the time, and Louise was far too wise to become embroiled in a situation from which she could not extricate herself with honor. When Gabrielle freely told her intimate details of her life, Louise listened with sympathy and

22

understanding, then retired to make copious notes. She amused herself by writing, and published her chronicle, the *Adventures de la Cour de Perse*, a year after Henry's death. Virtually everything she says about Gabrielle is substantiated by other sources, so there is no reason to doubt her account of the King's second visit to Coeuvres.

It is one of history's most romantic stories, and Bellegarde, who lost the affections of Gabrielle to his master, had no cause to repeat it if it had been false.

Only the date is missing from both the *Adventures* and the *Amours*. M. Desclozeaux speculates that it may have taken place in December 1590, during the siege of nearby Saint-Quentin, or on January 13, 1591, when the King was traveling to neighboring Chauny.

In any event, the forces of the League were occupying the town of Coeuvres, and held all of the surrounding territory. The young Duke de Guise, still a schoolboy, had just concluded a two-day visit to Antoine d'Estrées' castle as the representative of his uncle, Mayenne, and there were fifteen thousand Spanish, Austrian, and Papal State troops in the vicinity.

One afternoon the drawbridge of the castle was lowered so that Madame de Sourdis and the major domo could ride into town, and before it could be raised again, a woodcutter appeared out of a nearby forest and requested the right to enter. The sentries on duty tried to turn him away, but he persisted. They argued bitterly, and so loudly that François-Annibal and the marquis' almoner, who were nearby, came out to see what was causing the commotion.

They took one quick look at the "woodcutter" and quickly led him into the great hall, where each dropped to one knee and touched his forehead to the man's dusty boots.

Henry threw off his ragged cloak, revealing himself in clothes that were scarcely in better repair. His doublet was worn, his breeches were threadbare, and his knee-high boots were badly scuffed. His short, square-cut beard, which he wore in the style that was universal among the leaders of Europe's Protestant sects, was streaked with gray, as was his hair. His prominent nose and long face gave him a lugubrious appearance, and he was almost painfully thin. As always, he lacked funds, and his purse contained few silver coins and still fewer of gold.

Until he began to speak, he was an unprepossessing man, but asserted himself immediately in the company of others. His energy was boundless, and was matched only by his aggressive, penetrating intellect. He was invariably in high spirits, and the wit which so many of his contemporaries admired is seen throughout his enormous correspondence. Obsessed with the desire to become a great monarch, minor details, among them his appearance, meant nothing to him.

His dangerous trip through enemy lines in disguise was commonplace, and his generals, Henry, Duke of Montmorency, later to become Constable of France, and Charles, Duke of Biron, who became both an admiral and marshal, knew he was an incorrigible daredevil. He needlessly exposed himself in battle, leading charges that should have been left to subordinates, and he relished the name he had acquired for personal valor. "I would rather lose my crown than be branded a coward," he announced at the siege of Amiens shortly before the turn of the century, and lived his whole life according to that principle.

Gabrielle d'Estrées was less than impressed with this human dynamo, however. Her father and older brother attended the King in the great hall, but Gabrielle calmly continued to apply her creams and lotions, ignoring the pleas of her relatives to hurry down from her suite.

Madame de Sourdis, frantically summoned from her shopping trip into town, had other ideas. Gabrielle's golden hair was brushed, cosmetics were scrubbed from her face to emphasize her clear complexion, she was dressed in a green velvet gown, and pushed down to the great hall. Displaying a composure remarkable in a seventeen-year-old, Gabrielle indifferently greeted the King who had risked his life to visit her.

Her tranquility was no pose, although she was less serene under ordinary circumstances. It must be remembered that at this time she was immersed in her first love, and hoped to become the Duchess of Bellegarde. The thirty-seven-year-old monarch, whose chances of winning all France appeared slim, was not an impressive figure. Diane noted in her *Memorial* that he was so poor he could ill afford a change of linen, and Gabrielle was a girl who craved luxury.

She was flattered by his attention, of course, and conducted herself with a natural dignity that she retained to the end of her life. The personality that enabled her to win so many friends in opposing political and religious camps helped her on this occasion, too, and Henry was charmed by her sweet, placid grace.

Diane was also present that evening, and when a response was required, it was usually the older sister who spoke. Gabrielle sat in a chair on the King's right, smiling at him, encouraging him with nods but saying almost nothing. There seems to be no truth in the allegation, which appears only in Bellegarde's *Amours*, that Gabrielle became so bored that she retired, leaving Diane to entertain Henry. Common sense would indicate, too, that the charge was false; even though more than half of France had not accepted Henry as its monarch, he was a king. No girl in her right mind would have defied him by walking out of the room. And certainly Gabrielle was aware of the rumor to the effect that one of his former mistresses, Adrienne d'Arcy, had literally been whipped into submission when she had resisted his advances. Although there was no basis in fact for the canard, everyone in France believed it, and the lovely Gabrielle surely prized her beauty much too highly to run any risks of being scarred by this imperious man. English nobles paid tribute to the forceful Henry IV by describing him as even more ruthless than their own great Queen Elizabeth.

Henry spent one or two nights at Coeuvres and then disappeared again, successfully making his way through the bivouacs of the Leaguers to his own headquarters. There is no evidence to suggest that Gabrielle became his mistress during this visit. On the contrary, there is every reason to believe that she found it difficult to be more than polite to him. He, however, was infatuated, and made no secret of his feelings. Biron and d'Aubigné both noted in their correspondence that the King, who seldom spoke of matters other than military problems, praised Gabrielle at every meal.

If the more important members of the royal entourage dismissed their master's latest love with a shrug, Bellegarde was less fortunate. Henry "suggested" that his equerry find another interest. "There are many hundreds of young ladies of quality in France," the young duke reports Henry as saying in the *Amours*. "Disport yourself with one of them. I believe that the lovely d'Estrées has learned to care only for me."

Bellegarde had reason to believe otherwise. Gabrielle assured him of her love in brief letters, and in more positive form when he sneaked away from the King's camp-court on several occasions to see her. But he adopted the wise policy of keeping his mouth shut in Henry's presence. Biron or Montmorency might argue with the King on military policy, and Maximilien de Bethune, Baron de Rosny, later the Duke of Sully, exercised a power over Henry in financial affairs that was tantamount to a veto. But these great lords were near-equals to whom Henry of Navarre had granted the right to express disapproval. Bellegarde was little more than a noble lackey, and obviously realized he would not win royal approbation if he continued to woo Gabrielle openly.

One of the most common falsehoods about the relationship between Henry and Gabrielle is that the King persuaded Antoine d'Estrées to bring both of his daughters to Compiègne, where the court was temporarily residing, in March 1591. It is said that the marquis obeyed the summons, that Henry publicly proclaimed his love for Gabrielle, and that she lived with him from that time forward.

According to another story, Madame de Sourdis accompanied her nieces to Compiègne. Neither account is correct. The marquis, who thoroughly disapproved of Henry's attention to Gabrielle, was busily making other plans for her at the time. And he permitted neither Isabelle de Sourdis nor anyone else to take the girl off for another meeting with a man who, with good cause, had acquired a blazing reputation as a lecher.

What did happen at Compiègne is related by Bellegarde, who had no reason to dissemble on this phase of the subject. M. Desclozeaux is inclined to accept his statement at face value. It was quite a statement: "No task is too hard, might it but bring me a kingdom, yet my passion is dearer to me than all the crowns in the world."

Bellegarde, given no real choice, promised to give up Gabrielle. Unfortunately for him — and for her — he was not prepared to keep his word. Perhaps he had seen too many ladies of dubious virtue entering and leaving the château, town house, or tent that was Henry's headquarters for a night at the court-without-women.

In all justice to Bellegarde, it was as difficult for him as it was for other members of the King's entourage to take Henry's protestations of love for Gabrielle seriously. Montmorency, writing to his uncle in Languedoc, graphically described the life that the uncrowned ruler of France and his staff were living:

"Nearly one half of France is now enrolled under Henry's banner, and if we can, with God's help, defeat Farnese and Mayenne in the months to come, there surely will be a ceremony of consecration with Holy Oil at Reims. Yet Henry remains his old self, and there is scarce a change in him, so that we who have lived with him long might think ourselves still in Navarre. He travels like a modest gentleman of small means, scorns an honor guard and protests when Biron, who is now charged with the safety of his person, disposes a company of arquebuses to watch over him.

"We ride in a small band, numbering five to twenty, sometimes in the van of our regiments, sometimes following after, and where we halt at sundown, there do we make our court for the night. Surely Henry is the only monarch in the world who sleeps without complaint, often do I think gladly, on a mean pallet of straw or feather ticking thrown upon the floor of a house that knows no permanent occupants.

"Rosny is often vexed and would have the King ride in a style fitting to his station, so that his subjects will know him for what he is. But Henry jests, for his people know and love him all the more because he is one of them. Rosny saves the gold which his tax collectors gather in such small harvests, so none are truly sad that we travel like gypsy mountebanks.

"Only in private is Henry careless with gold, spewing it in nightly showers on the sluts who warm the royal pallet. He uses new trollops more often than he changes his hose. One sleeps with him for a fortnight, another for a month, and all are amiable, merry harlots. She who is now in favor is an English slut who lived long at the court of Elizabeth, and the King knows she was sent by her who is his friend and ally to spy him out. But he pays her less gold than he does the others, and with each bag of money he saves, he sends still another knight into the tournament with the battalions of the Pope. No man knows what seethes in his mind, and he confides in no woman, so the English trickery will not win Calais."

In other words, at the very time that Henry was proclaiming his love for Gabrielle, he was traveling incessantly, sleeping in dwellings unsuitable for a monarch, and taking camp followers into his bed. It is small wonder, then, that Bellegarde found it difficult to believe that his master was really interested in the lovely young lady from Coeuvres.

Gabrielle could not have been ignorant of Henry's way of life, either. The French nobility had little to think about except the latest scandals, particularly the affairs enjoyed by the leaders of the opposing camps. When Alexander Farnese, Duke of Parma, the military genius who was Mayenne's field commander, spent a night at the château of a still-handsome widow, tongues wagged from the English Channel to the Pyrenees mountains. And news of every move made by Henry was circulated by busy letter writers.

A young lady not yet eighteen years of age, much in love and hoping to marry a duke, would have found it impossible to imagine that Henry was in love with her. And if she mistakenly supposed that the King's intentions were honorable, her father and Madame de Sourdis were on hand to disillusion her. It is not surprising to find no shred of evidence indicating that Gabrielle wasted one moment of her self-centered life thinking about the impoverished, middle-aged monarch who was trying to win his kingdom.

But Henry was a man who hated waste, particularly that of his own time and energies. He had made up his mind that Gabrielle would be his, and in his own mind the issue was settled. He was content to wait for the right occasion, and the possibility that Gabrielle, her father, and Bellegarde all had other ideas was irrelevant. He was right, as usual, but his preoccupation with his enemies created complications that proved to be almost beyond even his ability to solve.

2: THE EARLY YEARS: 1573–90

No one knows precisely when or where Gabrielle d'Estrées was born, but the information supplied in two obscure but widely quoted documents on the subject is false. Both claim the château at la Bourdaisière as her birthplace, and both assert that she was born in 1565. These statements were generally accepted until M. Desclozeaux presented evidence to the contrary in his monograph. La Bourdaisière, which is not far from Tours in the province of Touraine, was in fact the home of Gabrielle's mother and aunts, and an older sister who died early in childhood was born there in 1565.

No documents relating to Gabrielle's birth have survived, but according to the testimony she herself gave in her divorce suit in 1594, she was born at Coeuvres, in Picardy, late in 1573. François-Annibal and Diane both support this view in their own writings, and Louise de Guise gives an exact date, December 23, 1573, in her *Adventures*. So it is reasonably safe to assume, as does M. Desclozeaux, that she was seventeen when she first met King Henry.

Gabrielle's mother, Françoise Babou de la Bourdaisière, Dame d'Estrées, and Marquise de Coeuvres, was born at the château near Tours, which had been built in 1520. The family first gained prominence when one Philibert Babou married a young lady named Marie Gaudin, who soon became the mistress of Francis I. King Francis built the château for her at the same time the palaces of Chambord and Saint-Germain were constructed, and it was a splendid edifice whose residents rarely lived up to its grandeur.

The most important member of the family was Gabrielle's grandfather, Jean Babou, who was a prominent soldier, politician, and diplomat in the reign of Henry II. He had two sons, both of whom fought with valor, vigor, and obstinacy against Henry of Navarre as generals serving under the banner of the League. Françoise was one of seven sisters, all of them beautiful, all of them immoral. All married, all were unfaithful to their husbands, and all loved to play intricate games of intrigue.

"The sisters Babou," Voltaire declared, "were the seven deadly sins."

His witticism was not original. He was merely repeating an observation commonly made during the reign of Henry III, when the many affairs of the entrancing sisters kept the nobility of France agog. By all odds, Françoise was the most beautiful of the sisters, and was by far the most depraved.

She took a series of lovers soon after her marriage to Antoine d'Estrées, and he seems to have been the only man in France unaware of her infidelities. Then, for ten years she was faithful to him, giving birth to a child punctually in the early winter of each year. She repeated the procedure nine times, and eight of the children lived. Then, tiring of motherhood, she eloped with a man many years her junior, Antoine, Marquis de Tourzel-Alègre. In 1583, when she was more than forty, she accompanied her lover to his château, lived with him openly, and bore him a daughter.

Parisians were accustomed to the romantic peccadilloes of the aristocracy, but countryfolk were strait-laced, and Françoise was regarded as the living symbol of sin by most of the peasants of Picardy. No one mourned her passing when she and her lover were murdered in June 1592, during the very week that Gabrielle was married. The incident created a sensation, but none of the dead woman's children were affected. They had dismissed her from their minds when Françoise had abandoned them, and not one of them wept. Isabelle de Sourdis, their mother's ambitious sister, had become the guardian of their persons, if not of their morals.

Gabrielle's family on her father's side was as distinguished as it was ancient. One of the most notable was her grandfather, Jean d'Estrées, about whom Henry IV wrote: "Still fresh in our memory are the services rendered by the Sieur d'Estrées, the grandsire of our beloved, who served without intermission under the four kings preceding us, in all the wars they waged, fighting in all their battles and taking part in every noteworthy achievement, and always receiving some special notice for his bravery. After holding many important and honorable offices, he was appointed Grand Master of the Artillery, a post which he filled for many years so worthily that even by foreigners he was considered the greatest and the wisest that had ever held that office."

Jean's son, Antoine, was less than distinguished. A faithful follower of Henry IV, in spite of provocation that might have thrown him into the arms of the League, he was an absentminded man who occasionally compensated for his neglect of his children by setting almost impossibly strict standards for them to follow. Perhaps his greatest mistake — apart from his marriage to Françoise Babou — was his carelessness in allowing his greedy sister-in-law, Isabelle de Sourdis, to rear his children.

Gabrielle and Diane, whom Isabelle nurtured, never became models of propriety. A third sister, Françoise, Baroness de Mouchi, enjoyed many affairs. A fourth, Angélique, was even more depraved than her mother, despite the fact that she became a nun and eventually was made abbess of the important Convent of Maubisson, where many girls and women belonging to the oldest French nobility were members of her order.

Angélique probably would have escaped with a mere reprimand from her bishop had she confined her activity to taking lovers. Members of the Church hierarchy in France were inclined to treat abbesses of noble descent leniently if their behavior was reasonably discreet. But Angélique was not content with her own pleasure, and it became her special delight to persuade young nuns to take lovers, too. When, early in the seventeenth century, her stunned bishop learned what was happening, he reported his findings to a board of cardinals. The brazen Angélique tried to defy them, and was removed to a convent that was a Renaissance equivalent of a home for delinquents. She remained there, under close supervision, for the rest of her life.

The notorious exploits of Angélique were virtually forgotten in the years immediately following the death of Henry IV in 1610, when the name of Gabrielle was vilified by scandalmongers who had not dared to speak while her lover was still alive. She was presented as one of the most evil women who had ever lived, and stories circulated in letters and pamphlets written by former League adherents were believed for more than two hundred years.

One of the most common lies told about her is that her mother sold her to the lascivious Henry III when she was fifteen, using the services of the notorious Duc d'Epernon for the purpose, the duke supposedly being the lover of Diane. The truth is that Gabrielle did not set eyes on her mother from the time she ran away from Coeuvres, when her daughter was ten; Gabrielle was only fifteen at the time of Henry III's death, and the King had been impotent for at least three years.

Another story relates that Gabrielle was also sold to Louis Zamet, a wealthy Swiss financier and sixteenth-century playboy who maintained a palatial residence in Paris. Zamet often provided his more important clients with personal services, and the canard about Gabrielle is easy to trace. It was originated by the Duke of Sully, who developed an intense hatred toward her in his senile later years, as he was afraid that her fame would dim his own. Sully had been in charge of state finances during the better part of Henry the Great's reign, but the King had followed the unique practice of separating his private purse and the public treasury. Zamet had been his personal banker and had also been custodian of Gabrielle's funds, so Sully, in his dotage, tried to smear two birds with one mudball by linking their names.

Cardinal de Guise, whom Gabrielle did not meet until she was a mature woman, was also one of the alleged lovers of her pre-Henry days, and so were a number of nobles who owned estates in the neighborhood of Coeuvres. Two of them, men named Stenay and Brunet, are remembered only because of their supposed affairs with her. Several of the scurrilous pamphlets charging her with having lived as the mistress of these gentlemen are still extant: they offer no details, no proof, and are totally lacking in substance. corrupt

Had Gabrielle lived such a debauched life prior to her long and intimate relationship with Henry, it would have been known during her lifetime, and would have influenced many who became her close friends. Agrippa d'Aubigné, Henry's boyhood companion, who broke with his master on religious grounds, chanted Gabrielle's praises at the top of his stern Huguenot voice:

"The d'Estrées is a miracle of sweet beauty and feminine charm. How one who is so gentle, so simple and so modest can bear to tolerate the embraces of a turncoat who has loved many women surpasses all understanding. But one cannot point the finger of blame at her for falling prey to her seducer's wiles.

"Would that he marries her within the year. Papist though she may be, she will become France as a Queen of great dignity, and surely she will save us all from being crushed under the boot of one whose tyranny ever mounts.

"I do not believe in miracles; I leave such to the credulity of the Papists. Yet I have with my own eyes seen a near-miracle. The d'Estrées possesses a beauty so great that all who see her, men and women alike, fall under her spell. There is no touch of the sensual, no hint of the carnal in that beauty. She is pure, as the dewdrop that clings to a thorn is pure. May her beauty and purity soften the sting of the thorn who sits upon the throne of France. All who love our country and our God join me in this silent prayer."

Others were less lyrical than d'Aubigné, but no less sincere in their friendship for Gabrielle. Heading the list was Catherine of Navarre, the King's only sister. "Madame," as she was known, was a devout Protestant, a lady whose moral standards were so high that even the most fanatical Leaguers could find no fault in her. Princess Catherine became Gabrielle's intimate friend, and when they were not together they corresponded regularly. Gabrielle's only daughter was named after Catherine, who became the child's godmother.

It is significant that, in 1597, when Henry was being urged to marry one or another of Europe's royal heiresses, he received a brief note from his sister. Like all of her correspondence with him, it was crisp and businesslike:

April 12, 1597

My dear King:

Once again rumors spread, when you are absent from Paris, that you will soon take a Queen. The Papal Ambassador and our cousin, Cardinal de Bourbon, are the most assiduous in this regard, and insinuate that you have agreed to make the de Medici your bride. Those who favor the causes of the Spanish Infanta and the Duchess of Savoy are no less diligent in pressing their claims.

I do not pretend to know what high policy of state may require you to take one of these great ladies into your apartment at the Louvre. But I, who have the welfare of France, your own happiness and that of her who loves you at heart, beg you not to look for a wife in foreign places.

Much though it grieves me to know that your queen will be one who espouses the Catholic faith and bows her head in submission to omnipotent Rome, I am reconciled to this necessity if only you will wed her who is already your Queen in all but name.

She is loyal to you beyond all loyalty, sincere beyond all sincerity, loving beyond all loving, and asks for nothing but your love, which you have already given her in ample measure. Your people know her to be true and virtuous, as does your sister and subject,

Catherine

Several other ladies of high rank were also Gabrielle's champions, and not the least of the group was the frail, morally immaculate widow of Henry III, Louise of Lorraine. Queen Louise had been untouched by corruption or scandal, even though she had lived at one of the most debauched of courts, and long before her husband's death had become a symbol of decency. Queen Louise went to great lengths to demonstrate her friendship for Gabrielle, often riding through the streets of Paris with her in the same coach or litter, and frequently entertaining her at the château of Chenonceaux, where only the virtuous and just were admitted across the drawbridge.

The Dowager Princess of Orange, Louise de Coligny, who was one of the first Protestant ladies of Europe, was another of Gabrielle's intimate companions, and was often seen in public with her. The Princess was enormously popular with the people of France because of the heroic exploits of her father, Gaspard de Châtillon, Count Coligny, who had been Admiral of France. Louise's brother, François, was one of the most devoted of Henry's followers, and one of the King's first acts after becoming master of his realm was to give the young sailor his father's post of Admiral.

Louise, who feared no man and freely criticized those of whom she did not approve, was a blunt, forthright woman. She suspected that Biron was more interested in feathering his own nest than in making Henry's crown secure and refused to receive the general or members of his family at the Hôtel de Coligny, in spite of the fact that Biron was one of the most influential of Henry's advisers.

She had no doubts about Gabrielle, however, and often embraced her in public, much to the chagrin of those who were trying to advance the cause of Marie de Medici. In 1598, when Marie's supporters were campaigning desperately for their favorite, the Princess of Orange paid a visit to the Louvre in Gabrielle's company and spent an entire afternoon showing her marked attention in the presence of the entire diplomatic corps. And on at least two occasions she is known to have visited Henry privately in order to urge him to marry his mistress.

The most surprising of Gabrielle's friendships was with Louise de Guise. This regal young beauty was the favorite in the royal sweepstakes, and in 1591 Henry was seriously considering marrying her. His Catholic supporters repeatedly urged him to take such a step, knowing that this one bold stroke would end his feud with the house of Guise and cause the collapse of the League.

The handsome young Louise was willing to enter into such an alliance, as she freely admits in her *Adventures*. "At that time I had not yet made the acquaintance of the King," she writes, "and all who knew him called him bestial, crude, and vulgar. But I had my own view of a man who fought with such pertinacity for his kingdom, and I had no reluctance to share his throne with him.

"It was my fate to lose him. Discreet discussions were being held between members of my family and his representatives, and he had been supplied with four of my miniatures, all of which I had myself selected with great care for his perusal. It was at this time that the beautiful Gabrielle was presented to him, and all thoughts of a marriage to another faded at once from his mind. I do allow that I conceived a great jealous rage which consumed me, for not many women come as close as I to wearing the Lilies of France, only to have them snatched away.

"My distemper was short-lived, and vanished on the day when Gabrielle and I met. None who knew her could fail to love her, and her modesty was as becoming as it was refreshing. I tried to make my obedience, as was proper, before the King's Favorite. But she snatched my hand, raised me up, and cried that it was the duty of a mere d'Estrées to show courtesy to the house of Guise. Prettily, and in the presence of the King, she curtsied before me, and instantly won my heart."

In the years that followed, Louise de Guise became, in effect, Gabrielle's chief lady-in-waiting, and considered it an honor to arrange the hair of the royal mistress, to stand behind her place at royal banquets and serve her wine, and, on the nights when Gabrielle slept alone, to tuck her into bed. Inasmuch as Henry was as dependent on the Guises as they were on him, at least during the early years of his reign, Louise certainly was not trying to win his favor by humbling herself. She was, after Madame de Sourdis, Gabrielle's closest friend and companion, and the two young beauties were usually seen together.

It pleased them, when on holidays in the country, to dress in identical gowns, to arrange their hair in similar styles, and to eat from the same dish. "The de Guise," Sully declares in his sour, senile *Memoirs*, "tried valiantly to worm her way into the royal featherbed by entwining her life with that of the d'Estrées."

No facts confirm this opinion, and it is unlikely that Louise, a great lady in her own right, would have been willing to become Henry's part-time mistress when she had almost succeeded in being his Queen. It is significant, too, that Louise de Guise disappeared from the court of the Béarnais for several years after Gabrielle's death. She spent much of this time at her estate near Amiens, writing at least a portion of the *Adventures*, and returned to the court some time prior to her marriage in 1605 to François, Prince de Conti. What she herself says in a volume originally intended for no eyes except her own must be accepted at face value: her feeling of friendship for Gabrielle was genuine.

Nothing in Gabrielle's childhood indicated that she would become, in Henry's words, "a woman of wonderful beauty," someone who would inspire feelings of conjugal love and fidelity in a king whose whole life had been spent in pursuit of many women. Nor was there any hint of the qualities that the most important ladies of the period found so entrancing.

"Our father," Diane writes in her *Memorial*, "insisted that his daughters learn their letters and sums, and our tutors were as strict with us as with our brothers. Françoise and I took naturally to learning, and were good pupils. Gabrielle did not like to exercise her mind, and found many excuses to avoid the work that was imposed on us. Her indisposition often infuriated our father, and often he threatened to cane her with the same rod of birch that had instilled discipline in the backside of our illustrious grandfather. Only her sex saved her from this humiliation.

"Angélique was even more indolent than Gabrielle, and our tutors frequently wept because she vexed them, obdurately refusing to read either French or Latin. Her influence on Gabrielle was poor, and when the hour of recitation arrived, a search was conducted for the truants, who were usually found riding their ponies in the fields, watching the knights at practice in the jousts, or chattering like crows with the scullions in the kitchen.

"A change for the better transformed Gabrielle when we were left alone in 1583. She made consistent efforts to conquer her indolence, and was not always successful in these attempts, but her natural ebullience more than compensated for the bad habits she had acquired earlier in her childhood. When goaded, she was my peer, and proved herself far superior to Françoise."

Diane was being discreetly loyal to a sister whom she loved. François-Annibal, however, felt no strong ties, even though Gabrielle was responsible for his first steps up the ladder; without her help he might have remained an obscure country gentleman, like his father. After the death of his older brother in battle, in 1595, he resigned the bishopric to which Henry had assigned him, and overnight became a prominent member of the court.

In his *Memoirs* he is aware of his debt to Gabrielle, but she had been dead for many years, and the crusty old soldier believed in expressing his recollections candidly. "Of my sisters," he writes, "Diane was the liveliest, Françoise the most considerate, Angélique the most wicked, and Gabrielle the laziest.

"It has been my observation that beautiful women are ever thus. My father's knights fawned upon Gabrielle from the time she was scarcely out of swaddling clothes, and even the most ferocious visiting warriors thawed when she smiled at them. She learned the value of a smile early in her life, and never forgot the lesson. With that smile she gained the ability to set armies in motion, and not until she began to return the love of the King did she know that it is simpler to begin a war than to halt one.

"Gabrielle was a strange young woman. I do not believe that a serious thought passed through her head from the day of her birth until some mystical moment long after she became the mistress of King Henry. What happened to her at that time, I cannot explain. I can only add my observation to that of so many others, that she became a new woman, as it were, in the course of a single day. When one reflects upon the influence she exerted on King Henry, it would not be impertinent to reflect that the change in her character took place in the course of a night rather than of a day.

"Henry aroused a quality in her that had been asleep. Some who knew her have written that she became transformed after the birth of her first child. I have heard Caesar himself discourse on this proposition, but he is a vain youth, much given to posturing, and he is mistaken. Gabrielle shook off her sloth long before the birth of Caesar.

"I remember the first occasion upon which I became aware of the transformation. I had been given command of a regiment of dragoons, and called on King Henry to take leave of him before joining my troops. The King asked me to wait for a few moments, as he said Gabrielle wished to bid me farewell, too. I remonstrated with him that my men were awaiting me in the village of Montmartre, and that I could ill afford to be tardy on this, my introduction to them.

"'Fear not,' he told me, 'Gabrielle will join us at four o'clock.'

"I dared not reply that Gabrielle was never punctual, and that many hours would elapse after four o'clock before she appeared. But King Henry was right, and I was mistaken, for as the old clock presented to Charles IX by the clockmakers' guild began to chime the fourth hour, Gabrielle presented herself in the King's apartment.

"From that time forward I never knew her to be tardy in anything, and she came to resemble Henry, who usually appeared at a given place before the appointed time of his arrival, much to the consternation of those who had assembled to greet him.

"It is to Henry that credit must be given for the remarkable alteration in the character of Gabrielle. A soldier is taught discipline in the field, a cleric learns the same behind the walls of a cloister, but a beautiful woman can respond only to the instruction of a man whom she loves.

"I have pondered, when I have heard the praises of Gabrielle sung by those who did not really know her, what might have become of her had she remained married to d'Amerval and not become the mistress of King Henry. Her beauty had become a legend before she reached her eighteenth birth date, and she was herself immersed in the story. Only one as ferocious as King Henry had the power to arouse her from her slumber. France may be grateful to him in this, as in many things, for all made greater the glory of his reign."

It is unlikely that François-Annibal was deliberately deprecating his sister. His view was one commonly held in the seventeenth century, that women were incapable of achieving anything on their own initiatives, and required assistance from a man in order to become whole human beings. In Gabrielle's case, the belief of three hundred years ago seems accurate, for there is no indication that she was anything other than beautiful and lazy, depraved and indolent, before her blazing affair with the King.

At some time prior to Gabrielle's sixteenth birthday, Antoine d'Estrées took his daughters to his town house in Paris, the Hôtel d'Estrées, located on the Rue des Bons-Enfants. The marquis attended to his business affairs, leaving his ubiquitous sister-in-law, Isabelle de Sourdis, to present Diane and Gabrielle at court. Both of the sisters are mentioned in various journals and memoirs, which list them among the beauties who were in attendance on King Henry III and Queen Louise. But neither made a lasting impression, and neither became involved in scandal, notwithstanding later gossip about Gabrielle.

The girls paid their respects to Queen Louise at the Louvre on Tuesdays and Saturdays, when the royal family received members of the nobility. Presumably they met Henry III from time to time, whenever that ineffectual, harried monarch had an opportunity to forget the problems that created so much unrest in his turbulent realm.

The people of Paris revolted in 1588, and Henry III fled to Chartres with a few followers, but most nobles remained in Paris, and it is probable that Antoine d'Estrées, like so many of his contemporaries, was not frightened into leaving the capital. Civil war had become an almost normal state of affairs for most Frenchmen, and everyone assumed that Henry III and his wily mother, Catherine de Medici, who was not only the power behind the throne, but on occasion actually sat on her son's throne, would find some way to reconcile the burning conflicts between Catholics and Huguenots.

Henry of Navarre spent at least part of 1588 in Paris, which was something of a neutral meeting ground for the opposing religious forces whose armies were making a shambles of the provinces. The League had put a price on the head of the heir to the throne, but he boldly ignored his enemies, riding through the city with a small company of companions and daring members of the house of Guise, the League's leaders, to molest him.

He and Gabrielle did not meet during this period. When Henry came to the capital, his sole purpose was to secure the support of the vacillating Henry III and obtain funds to continue his struggle in the field against the Catholic adherents of the League who were determined to keep him from the throne. At no time did he appear at the social functions of the court, and he kept his distance from the Queen Mother. Catherine de Medici had organized the St. Bartholomew's Day Massacre, and he had never forgotten his narrow escape from the knives of her assassins.

Bellegarde, who had not yet become his equerry, was in Paris in 1587, 1588, and the first months of 1589, so it must be assumed that the young duke met Gabrielle either at court or at the town house of a fellow member of the nobility, The beginning of their affairs is wrapped in a curious silence. Gabrielle herself wrote no letters and kept no diary or other record during this period. Diane and François-Annibal say nothing about their celebrated sister's meeting with Bellegarde, and the duke himself is a model of discretion in his *Amours*.

All that can be said with certainty is that they were in love by the autumn of 1590.

They had little chance of seeing each other in the capital during 1588 or most of 1589. The conflict between Catholics and Protestants had become a full-fledged war soon after Henry III had arranged the murder of the head of the house of Guise, Duke Henry, shortly before Christmas 1588. Catherine de Medici had died the following month, and although her son had cried, "At last I am King," the country had been leaderless for a time.

Then Mayenne, the youngest of the Guise brothers, had taken charge of the League's destinies, and Henry of Navarre had rallied both Huguenots and those Catholics who were opposed to foreign intervention in the affairs of France. Mayenne had begun to prepare Paris for a siege, and as soon as the ground dried after the spring rains, enabling the carriages of nobles to travel on the rutted roads, Antoine d'Estrées decided that the air at Coeuvres was healthier than that of the city.

Henry of Navarre, aided by the weakling King, was preparing his siege of the capital when Gabrielle and Diane returned to Picardy to enjoy the dubious pleasures of a bucolic life.

Gabrielle, whose chief concerns were her toilet, wardrobe, and beauty sleep, has left no record of her reactions to this sudden change. Diane, however, discusses the move frankly in her *Memorial*, and admits that daily existence was confining and dull.

"I felt a bewildering sense of loss when we returned to the home of our childhood," she writes, "and begged our father to reconsider. But he replied that only those who had risen in open rebellion against the legitimate Crown remained in Paris, and our Aunt de Sourdis shared his opinion, so I tried to make the best of our lot.

"Gabrielle made no attempt to accept the life with which we had been so familiar in times past, and it was obvious she believed she had been cheated. When we were alone in our rooms she expressed bitter thoughts, and often wept for the grandeur and excitements of Paris. But she said no word in the presence of others, preferring to maintain a dignified silence.

"She kept up the habits we had acquired in Paris, dressing each day in one of her court gowns and arranging her hair in styles favored by the great ladies of the city. Our father often lost patience with her, and even the children knew she was contemptuous of Picardy and its ways, but her melancholy became deeper when our brothers and sisters tried to cheer her.

"Then, late in the summer, we learned news that made me realize the policy of our father had been right. Two couriers arrived at Coeuvres on the same day, I recall not the precise date, one wearing the livery of the League, the other in a shabby doublet and threadbare hose.

"Albeit their appearance was different, their tidings were the same. Both carried the shocking word that the last King of the Valois was dead, and had been murdered by lackeys in the pay of the house of Guise. Henry of Navarre, whom most of our countrymen feared, was now the King, and all had cause to believe that there would be a long and terrible war.

"Our father was gloomy, and our Aunt de Sourdis, who went straight away to join her husband, was of the same view. Both said they would support the cause of him who had become Henry IV, and I, too, signed the pledge of fealty they sent to him by the courier who had been dispatched from his headquarters outside of Paris.

"Gabrielle would sign no paper, and cried that she wanted peace so she could taste the joys of Paris which were being denied her. For two days she sulked in our rooms, and in vain our father begged her to join us at table. When she would not, he directed that no viands be served to her in her chamber, and a young groom who disobeyed him was whipped by Sieur Paul le Blanc, the captain of knights, in the presence of all.

"I comment on these events, long past, not to hold up my sister to ridicule nor to parade her ignorance, but to show how marked is the contrast between her thinking in those days and in the times that followed. It is scarcely credible that she who cared nothing of the world populated by kings should have become the most powerful woman in France, showing a strength of purpose exceeded only by that of the King, and a subtlety in political maneuvers equaled by none."

Diane's cool estimate is, in the light of subsequent events, both fair and accurate. Gabrielle was a petulant, spoiled, and lazy young beauty who lived only for her own selfish pleasure, gave no thought to the great events taking place around her, and demonstrated neither intelligence nor wit. Her metamorphosis was due to her relationship with the galvanic Henry, and consequently it is impossible to know her without understanding the extraordinary man responsible for her transformation.

3: HENRY THE GREAT

When Henry of Navarre was born in the little town of Pau in the Pyrenees on December 14, 1553, the event was considered minor outside the immediate family circle. His father, Antoine de Bourbon, was the Duke of Vendôme and head of the junior branch of the Bourbon family. Henry was descended from the thirteenth-century monarch Louis IX, who had been canonized nine years after his death in 1270, but no bonfires were lighted in French towns and villages in 1553. After all, the direct ancestor of Antoine de Bourbon and his son had been St. Louis' sixth son, Robert of Clermont.

There was more cause for rejoicing on the distaff side. Henry's mother was Jeanne d'Albret, Queen of Navarre, and the child became king of his own realm at birth, under a regency headed by his parents. The predominant religion of the little country's nobility was Protestant, so it was taken for granted that he would be raised in the reformed faith, although his father, being a Bourbon, was Catholic.

Navarre was a country with frontiers that changed from generation to generation, and owed its independence to the more or less permanent feud between France and Spain. It was a small area located at the southeastern end of the Bay of Biscay, where France and Spain meet, and was composed, in the main, of provinces of those two nations that remain Basque down to the present day. Then, as now, its people were characterized by a fierce pride, a determined sense of independence, and a tradition of individual courage, honor, and decency. In Henry's day Navarre was closer to France than to Spain, and had enjoyed this relationship for several generations. Its nobility was usually educated in Protestant Switzerland, the eldest sons of prominent families taking instructions from tutors at the theological seminaries in Bern.

Antoine de Bourbon was a self-centered man, but Queen Jeanne was enormously ambitious for her son, and Henry paid glowing tributes to her later in his life, saying that she was responsible for his own zeal.

His parents took him to the court of Henry II at Amiens when he was four years old, but he attracted little notice there. The family of the reigning monarch was large, and three of his sons eventually succeeded to the throne, Francis II, Charles IX, and Henry III. It was at the court of the King that Henry met his future wife, Marguerite de Valois, the younger daughter of Henry II and Catherine de Medici.

Queen Jeanne placed her son in the College of Navarre, in Paris, and he studied there for four years, from 1561 to 1565, at which time he was sent to a seminary in Bern. His grades were excellent, and he began to show signs of the driving ambition that later characterized his whole life. When he wrote a theme or report, he was never satisfied with a paper that was less than perfect.

His studies were interrupted when the so-called "Third War of Religion" broke out in France in 1568. His mother sent him to join the Protestant army commanded by Gaspard de Coligny, and the next year, at the age of sixteen, he distinguished himself in action at the battle of Arnay-le-Duc in Burgundy, displaying an instinctive grasp of both strategy and tactics. It was at this time that he began taking mistresses, a practice he was to follow throughout his life.

Students of psychology need not search too hard for his reasons. His mother, who constantly goaded him in the hope that he would become a great man, demonstrated little affection; she was a cold woman who was incapable of giving love to anyone. Henry, as a consequence, felt a desperate emptiness that was not filled until his affair with Gabrielle.

The year 1572 was climactic in Henry's life. His mother died early in the year, and he succeeded to the crown of Navarre in fact as well as in name. His marriage to Princess Marguerite, whose brother, Charles IX, was then sitting on the throne of France, followed shortly.

The ceremony was curiously drab, even though a king was marrying the sister of a king. Catherine de Medici, who ruled her sons with the same iron hand with which she had ruled her husband, wanted the alliance for political purposes, but did not relish the presence of a Huguenot heretic in the family. Therefore, the guest list was small and there was a marked absence of pomp. The ceremony was held at the Louvre, as the Church would not allow Henry to take part in a service at Notre Dame.

Reports of Henry's relations with his bride are many and varied. According to some, he discovered on their wedding night that she was not a virgin and refused to take her to bed. Most of these accounts have been written by Huguenots. Sully, in his *Memoirs*, indicates that Henry and Margot conceived a great passion for each other. But Sully is not a reliable source of information. In any event, Henry and his wife lived under the same roof, in Paris, for several months.

It is useless, but fascinating, to speculate, in the light of latter-day medical knowledge, that Henry and Margot should have made a perfectly matched couple. Both had strong sexual drives, both were inclined to indulge in erotic practices, and both threw themselves enthusiastically into games of love. But history remains maddeningly silent, and if they wrote love letters to each other, none has survived.

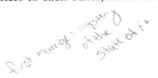

51

Henry himself was lucky to survive the year. He was marked for murder in the St. Bartholomew's Day Massacre, which was carefully planned by Catherine de Medici and several of the older members of the house of Guise. The Queen Mother and her son-in-law had conceived a strong mutual dislike for each other, and Catherine needed no other reason to wish Henry of Navarre exterminated. But far more important reasons did exist: Henry was a Protestant who was displaying a natural talent for leadership, and, after her own sons, was heir to the throne of France.

There is no evidence to suggest that King Charles, who had some notion of his mother's over-all plans, realized Henry was on the list of those who were to be killed. And, later Huguenot charges to the contrary, Margot was kept in the dark. Henry never forgave those who took part in the butchery, and the mere fact that Margot lived for many years is proof that she did not conspire against her husband. Henry would not have hesitated to order her executed in later years, had he even suspected that she had been an accomplice.

The Massacre began on August 23, 1572, and continued through the following day. Coligny was murdered in cold blood, and mobs raced through the streets of Paris killing Protestants. Most of those who managed to go into hiding for periods ranging from several days to two months, eventually were ferreted out and murdered.

Henry and his friend, Agrippa d'Aubigné, were walking near Notre Dame at the time the Massacre began, and the young King of Navarre demonstrated remarkable presence of mind. He and his friend darted into the cathedral, and there Henry stripped off his fur-trimmed cape, silver spurs, and other signs of high rank. Snatching a prayer book from a startled young priest, he ran out into the street again, closely followed by d'Aubigné. The participation of troops in the uprising made it obvious that this was no ordinary riot, and Henry realized the danger of his own position when, unrecognized, he heard officers shout orders to conduct a search for him.

He knew that immediate escape from Paris was impossible, so he chose to follow a bold course. Prominently displaying the stolen prayer book, he strolled through the streets to the Louvre, where the Queen Mother was directing the grisly operation. No one molested him, and when he reached the palace, he immediately dispatched a servant to the Hôtel de Navarre, his official residence, and requested Margot to join him at once.

She arrived within the hour, and accompanied him to the private apartment of King Charles. Not even Catherine de Medici dared to flout public opinion by allowing her son-in-law to be murdered in the dwelling place of the King and in the presence of Margot. For the moment, Henry was relatively safe.

But he suffered no false illusions regarding his safety, and that evening he and d'Aubigné ate nothing, fearing their food might be poisoned. They barricaded themselves in a room, and it was there that Henry developed his long-term strategy. He realized that for the moment he was powerless to help his fellow Huguenots; though tempted to take a bold stand, he had no weapons.

Early in the morning he and d'Aubigné feigned abjuration and pretended to embrace Catholicism. King Charles was relieved, and so was Margot, but the device did not fool Catherine, who kept her thoughts to herself.

Meanwhile, the slaughter in Paris continued. No accurate figures are available, but reports to the effect that one hundred thousand Huguenots had been killed were a gross exaggeration. It is estimated that approximately seven to ten thousand persons lost their lives, and Catherine is known to have exclaimed, "The cause of Protestantism in France is dead!"

A wave of horror swept through the Protestant nations of Europe, but Philip II of Spain laughed aloud when he heard the news, and Pope Gregory XIII, an enlightened man who did much to reform the Church from within, made the mistake of allowing zealous partisans to strike a medal bearing his name, in honor of the Massacre. Religious hatreds throughout all of Europe were intensified, and the opposing camps prepared for a final, conclusive battle.

That battle was long delayed because the man who overnight became the symbol of Protestantism in France was literally a prisoner in the palace of his mother-in-law. Armed guards were attached to the person of Henry of Navarre, allegedly to protect him, but as he discovered, when he tested them by riding to the north gate of the city, he was not allowed to leave Paris.

The St. Bartholomew's Day Massacre was a temporary victory for a cruel and bigoted woman, but a great man emerged from the holocaust. Henry of Navarre formed new ambitions and new goals after the terrible tragedy, and his cool reasoning was a miracle of intellectual discipline. He knew that protracted religious wars would ruin France and that if the nation hoped to survive, it would be essential for Protestants and Catholics to work together.

He realized that the Catholic faction would not surrender its power voluntarily, and it followed that the Huguenots, therefore, would have to force them to make concessions. The only language men understood was that of the battlefield; hence, he planned to lead a mighty Protestant force into the war for peace?

field. When he conquered, he would compel both sides to work peacefully together.

Since a king of Navarre could not force Frenchmen to do his bidding, Henry decided to become the monarch of France.

His reasoning on the subject was elementary. Charles was in poor health and his younger brother, Henry of Anjou, who later became Henry III, was a weakling. Henry of Navarre despised his young brother-in-law, who had helped Catherine de Medici plan the Massacre, but he kept his opinions to himself. It was enough, for the moment, that he knew his own mind.

Catherine kept him under close watch for many months, and it is likely that the bad feeling which finally separated Henry and Margot began to develop during this time. Even a man who thought in long-range terms undoubtedly found it difficult to remain attached to his wife when her mother was holding him prisoner.

In 1573 King Charles died, and Catherine immediately summoned her third son back to Paris from Warsaw, where he had been crowned King of Poland. France was the heart of Catherine's universe, and the dissipated youth who ascended the throne of lilies was closest to his mother's heart. Henry III was a monarch of France completely dominated by his mother.

And Henry of Navarre, brooding in a Louvre apartment that was watched night and day by troops who shared the Queen Mother's fanaticism, occasionally amused himself by writing "Henry IV" on a sheet of paper, which he then carefully threw into the flames of his hearth. He spent most of his time reading political and military treatises, studying maps, and, when he was alone, exercising to keep fit.

He made several attempts to escape from Paris, but each time Catherine intercepted him and he was forced to return to the Louvre. But he did not lose heart, and neither did his followers. Agrippa d'Aubigné slipped out of the city and carried the good word to Huguenot nobles that their leader was awaiting the chance to join them.

Finally, after three and a half years of virtual imprisonment, Henry managed to elude his warders at sundown on February 2, 1576, and rode unchallenged through the gates of Paris. He was the only man in France who was not startled by the warmth and size of the support he received everywhere. It was not surprising to find Huguenots hurrying to join him, but Henry III and his mother were dismayed to discover that large numbers of Catholic leaders who were tired of Catherine de Medici's cruel excesses and mismanagement were also enlisting under the banner of the King of Navarre.

Catherine's worst fears were confirmed. Henry formed a mighty army, and his foes were not prepared for him. The Queen Mother was forced to accept humiliating peace terms in the Treaty of Beaulieu. Henry was made Lieutenant General of the huge southern province of Guienne, which adjoined his own kingdom of Navarre, and for all practical purposes he added it to his personal realm.

Now he had a powerful base of operations, and could strengthen his forces. The League, which had fought Protestant dissidents in the past, was revived to oppose him, but he continued to hold the upper hand, and in 1577 he used the threat of his army to compel Henry III to sign the Treaty of Bergerac, which revoked the worst of the anti-Huguenot discriminatory laws.

 Henry was the most powerful Protestant leader on the European Continent. He traveled incessantly, gaining supporters throughout France, but refused Catherine's repeated invitations to confer in Paris. Margot had joined her husband at the time the Treaty of Bergerac was signed, and Henry lived with her for the next three years. The rupture in their domestic relations that occurred in 1580 has been cited as the cause of the so-called Seventh War of Religion, but was at most a minor contributing factor.

Henry never made the mistake of confusing political policy with bedchamber frolics. Gabrielle was the only one of his many mistresses who became involved in affairs of state, and her sole motive was to promote his aims. The others were content to make themselves available when he wanted distraction.

But Margot, too imperious to accept the fact that her husband would tolerate no interference, was further encouraged by her mother. Catherine de Medici, having failed to curb her energetic son-in-law by the usual methods, had resorted to new tactics. The provisions of the Treaty of Bergerac were quietly ignored by Henry III and his aides, and Margot was urged to persuade her husband to adopt a less militant course.

The scheme might have been effective had Henry loved his wife more than principle and power. He was fond of Margot, but knew she was a cold-blooded daughter of a Medici, and paid no attention to her advice. Their relations became increasingly strained when he used revenues from her estates to support his ever-growing army. She complained bitterly and at length, and compounded her error by taking a lover during one of Henry's frequent absences from Bordeaux.

Many of Henry's followers were eager to report Margot's indiscretion to him, but he could not prove the charges against her. She denied any misconduct, and they quarrelled bitterly. Catherine de Medici and Henry III, trying to intervene as mediators, only succeeded in widening the rift.

Henry solved the problem by sending his wife to a remote provincial castle which he owned, and as women's rights were virtually nonexistent, Margot had no choice. She was forced to swallow her pride and retire to the château outside the little village of Usson, taking a large staff of servants into "exile" with her. As she indicates in her *Memoirs*, one of the most candid of seventeenth-century documents, the separation at first did not make her unhappy. She was free to lead her own life; she loved the beautiful countryside of Auvergne; and her only complaint against Henry was that he gave her too small an allowance. It might be noted in passing that, after the separation, Henry and Margot established an unusually friendly relationship and corresponded steadily. The tolerant Henry insisted that the daughter of Valois be treated as a queen, and in later years, after their marriage had been dissolved by the Pope and he remarried, he insisted that she be received with full honors throughout the realm.

Catherine de Medici seized the opportunity to use the separation for political purposes, and the few rights that had been granted to Huguenots were revoked. Henry unhesitatingly declared war against the crown, and won a series of smashing victories that compelled Henry III to sign a new treaty late in 1580.

Both sides spent the next few years increasing their forces, hiring foreign mercenaries, and maneuvering for position. An uneasy balance of power was maintained: Catherine de Medici and her son were far wealthier, but Henry of Navarre was bolder and more imaginative. A fresh crisis erupted in 1584 when Henry III's sickly young brother, François, suddenly died, and Henry of Navarre became first in line for the throne. But, as a result of an extraordinary decree signed by Henry III, he was specifically excluded from the succession, and was denied the right to use the title of dauphin, or crown prince. For a time there was no official heir-designate.

He responded with typical vigor, and the flimsy peace was shattered by what is known as the War of the Three Henrys. *clever*

The League unwisely accepted Henry's challenge to fight in Guienne, and during the next two years he won a series of victories so decisive that relations between Henry III and Henry, Duke de Guise, became strained. The King of Navarre, whose position became stronger with each passing month, now felt sufficiently secure to visit Paris from time to time. His object was to win the support of Henry III for recognition of his claim as heir to the throne, and Catherine de Medici, with her usual cunning, negotiated on behalf of her son. When the Guise faction became increasingly vehement in its disapproval, Catherine solved the problem in typical fashion by arranging the murder of the duke and his brother. The League retaliated by driving Henry III out of Paris, and Catherine was forced to ask her son-in-law for support. His price was recognition of his rights, and he was officially proclaimed heir to the throne. *Silly Good Catherine* *37 yo*

The death of the Queen Mother in January 1589, left Henry of Navarre as the real ruler of the country, and he became King of France in name as well as in fact on August 1, when an assassin plunged a knife into Henry III. *awesome!*

But the struggle against the League continued for several years. Late in 1589 Henry IV defeated the leader of the League and new head of the house of Guise, Charles of Mayenne, at Arques. More and more Frenchmen rallied to the cause of their legitimate monarch, and the League was forced to rely on Spanish and Papal troops. Henry won a series of major victories and suffered only minor reverses during the next three and a half years. Finally, in July 1593, when he became a convert to Catholicism, due in large part to the influence of *41 yo*

Gabrielle d'Estrées, domestic opposition to his cause virtually disappeared.

The League was supported only by foreigners now, and Paris voluntarily opened its gates to Henry. On March 22, 1594, he and Gabrielle made a triumphant entry into the city.

Provinces that had not capitulated to Henry were conquered by force or won in negotiations. Gabrielle, acting on Henry's behalf, used her influence to make peace between the former Protestant King and the Catholic house of Guise, and the struggle with the League became no more — and unfortunately, no less — than a war against Philip II of Spain.

In 1598 the Edict of Nantes was promulgated, with Gabrielle playing a key role in the delicate negotiations between Catholic and Huguenot leaders. With the signing of the Edict, a new era of religious tolerance began, unique in the tortured history of Europe since the start of the Reformation. When a treaty was signed with Spain that same year, a united France was free to work out her destiny in peace at home and abroad.

Henry demonstrated amazing energy and breadth of vision. Corrupt and incompetent officeholders were replaced by able men loyal to the crown. The nation's debts were wiped out, and Sully amassed a huge treasury reserve. Henry encouraged foreign trade, gave generous aid to the farmers, and introduced several industries which have remained important in France to the present day. Among them were tapestry weaving and the manufacture of silk, wool, and glassware.

Cool

A network of canals facilitated commerce, large sums of money were spent on exploration and settlement in the New World, and merchants obtained loans from bankers at relatively low rates of interest. A new navy was built, and the army was completely reorganized, the feudal system being replaced by central authority. Henry was interested in the arts, too, and added new wings to the Louvre and the Tuileries. Both the Palais-Royale and the Hôtel de Ville date from that period.

His foreign policy was deceptively simple: he wanted peace. *again King* But he knew that the Hapsburg kings of Spain and Austria were aggressive and covetous, so he tried to contain their ambitions by a series of alliances without going to war. The Protestant states were eager to become his allies, and he made treaties with England, Holland, Sweden, the Swiss cantons, and the German states. Obviously he needed Catholic support, too, *y u4o4* and he paid a high price for it. In 1600, one year after the death of Gabrielle d'Estrées, he married Marie de Medici, daughter of the Grand Duke of Tuscany. As a consequence, he was able to make favorable treaties of alliance with Tuscany, Venice, and, most important of all, Pope Paul V. Subsequently, Savoy and Lorraine also joined the alliance.

Throughout the better part of the period from 1600 to 1610, Henry devoted most of his time and talents to internal matters, and France became the wealthiest and most powerful nation in Europe. The King never lost his sympathy for the common people, and the lowest of his subjects were free to approach him at any time to discuss their problems. *humble King*

His personal life was drab and unhappy after the death of Gabrielle. Henry's experience with Catherine de Medici caused him to treat his wife gingerly and with respect. He also went to great lengths to prevent her interference in the administration of the realm. His failure was not his fault, for Marie had been born and raised in an atmosphere of intrigue and conspiracy.

The Queen bore him five children, the eldest of whom became Louis XIII, but Henry never ceased to love Gabrielle's two sons and daughter, and they lived with the royal family

good father

where he could keep an affectionate and protecting eye on them.

The last of Henry's mistresses afforded him no happiness beyond occasional carnal pleasure and may have been responsible for his death. Henriette d'Entragues, Marquise de Verneuil, was a cold-blooded woman who became the King's mistress in 1600, about six months after Gabrielle's death in 1599. Subsequently she tried to stave off his marriage to Marie de Medici by claiming he had promised to marry her, and made such a nuisance of herself that he was forced to banish her from his court for a time.

She joined the cabal against the King headed by Marshal Biron, and when the plot was discovered in 1606, she was banished a second time. But in 1608, Henry, who enjoyed her sexual appetite and refused to treat her intellect seriously, took her back into favor.

Late in the following year, contrary to his better judgment, he was forced to declare war against the Hapsburgs. In 1610 while he was working furiously to organize the armies of the allies against the common foe, he was assassinated by a man in the hire of the Spaniards and Austrians. How the assassin managed to get close to the carefully guarded King is a mystery that has never been solved, but there are shreds of evidence suggesting that Henriette d'Entragues, Henry's fifty-sixth mistress, was in the pay of the Spaniards and a party to the conspiracy.

4: RENDEZVOUS AT CHARTRES, 1591

In January 1591, a few weeks after Henry IV paid his celebrated visit to the château at Coeuvres disguised as a woodcutter, his army laid siege to the city of Chartres, which was in the hands of the League. Royal troops occupied the open countryside that surrounded the city, and the King established his headquarters in a small castle outside the nearby village of Bonneval.

A member of his modest entourage at the time of his arrival was Corisande d'Audoins, Countess de Guiche, who had been his principal mistress for approximately two years. Like all of the women in Henry's life, Corisande was beautiful, and possessed the added assets of a fiery disposition and a voluptuous body. But she had never learned that discretion was a prized asset in the mistress of a monarch and talked too much for her own or Henry's good.

Every knight in the royal army knew that the King had grown weary of Corisande's charms, for she freely discussed her situation with anyone who would listen. Officers returning from a day of duty at the trenches being dug around the besieged city were regaled with detailed accounts of what Henry had said to Corisande and what she had replied.

Suddenly, in mid-January, the verbose countess disappeared, vanishing into the murky limbo reserved for the inconsequential mistresses of great men. Officers familiar with the habits of the Béarnais, privately speculated on the identity of Corisande's successor. They were not forced to wait long. Before the month ended, Madame de Sourdis appeared at headquarters with her lovely nieces, Diane and Gabrielle d'Estrées.

Isabelle de Sourdis had valid reasons for joining the royal party, chief among them being the fact that her husband had already attached himself to Henry. De Sourdis had been governor of Chartres under Henry III, whom he had also served as Lieutenant for the Chartrain country. The ambitious de Sourdis couple suffered from an embarrassment peculiar to the civil war, for Isabelle's brother, Georges Babou de la Bourdaisière, was the commandant of the League forces holding the city, and she was undoubtedly anxious to demonstrate her loyalty to the King.

The political situation at Chartres was unusually complex. The citizens defended themselves with extraordinary vigor, and when Henry demanded that they surrender, as he did on an average of twice a week, they replied that they would open their gates to him at once if he would accept conversion to Catholicism, but would resist him forever if he remained a heretic. Henry had good cause to ignore their impassioned speeches, for inside the gates, the Bishop of Chartres, Nicolas de Thou, secretly headed a royalist party which was conspiring to deliver the city to the King.

The odds were overwhelmingly in Henry's favor. His troops had cut off Chartres from all contact with the outside world, and hunger and a shortage of gunpowder eventually would force the proud inhabitants to surrender. Consequently, he was able to devote at least a portion of his time to matters other than the siege, primarily to winning Gabrielle's affection.

Dancing and merry-making enlivened the evenings at the castle of Bonneval, and Henry made no secret of his admiration for Gabrielle, openly paying court to her in the presence of his generals and aides. She made no secret of her feelings, either, and rebuffed him, much to the distress of her aunt.

"The King," Diane writes in her *Memorial*, "showed valor in the siege of Chartres that he conducted by day, and my sister showed equal courage in the siege of Gabrielle that he conducted by night. She spurned his advances gently, but with such frequency that our aunt and uncle feared that their future was ruined."

According to tradition, Gabrielle became the mistress of Henry at Bonneval during the siege, which finally ended on April 19. But there is no solid evidence to substantiate tradition. On the contrary, Gabrielle and Diane returned to Coeuvres as soon as their uncle was restored to his former posts, Governor of Chartres and Lieutenant for the Chartrain country, and Henry did not see her again for the better part of a year, even though he often traveled through Picardy.

Henry, as his conduct in later years demonstrated, was not the sort of man who would drop Gabrielle after making a conquest. There seems to be no question that he completely lost his heart to her at Bonneval. And it seems just as probable that she remained as indifferent to him as she had been when he had visited Coeuvres.

Why, then, did Gabrielle go to Chartres? And why did Antoine d'Estrées, knowing of the King's dishonorable interest in his second daughter, permit her to make the journey?

The first question is easily answered. In Diane's words, "Life at Coeuvres became even more quiet than usual when the armies left the vicinity, and we were overjoyed when our Aunt de Sourdis invited us to accompany her to Bonneval."

So it is clear that escape from boredom was one of Gabrielle's reasons. An even stronger motive was her continuing interest in Bellegarde, and she had no way of knowing that her unfortunate suitor was under royal orders to pay no attention to her. But when Bellegarde remained conspicuously absent from the castle at Bonneval, Gabrielle soon guessed that he had been instructed by his royal master to avoid her. In one of the few communications written in her own hand that has survived the centuries, she says to her father, "I have seen Roger at a distance, but he is afraid to speak to me. I fear that my hopes of becoming the Duchess of Bellegarde will not be realized."

This brief letter is the clue to Antoine d'Estrées' chief reason for allowing Gabrielle to visit a place where she would see Henry. The unhappy father may or may not have known that Bellegarde had already compromised Gabrielle. But he hoped, as did the girl herself, that the young duke would make an honest woman of her. In other words, the marquis took a calculated risk, believing that Henry would lose interest in Gabrielle if Bellegarde married her. He lost his gamble because, like so many others, he underestimated Henry of Navarre's determination.

A minor military incident in the summer of 1591 was long used by those who believed that Henry and Gabrielle had become intimate at Bonneval as "proof" of the theory that Antoine d'Estrées deliberately pushed his daughter into the King's arms in order to win greater power for himself.

Henry, awaiting the arrival of a large corps of German mercenaries and a smaller unit of English allies before attacking the League army commanded by the Duke of Parma, whiled away his time by capturing small towns that continued to oppose him. On July 25 he laid siege to Noyon, which was located near Coeuvres. When the town fell on August 19, Henry promptly added it to the domain administered by

Antoine d'Estrées, who formally accepted the responsibility in a short, stiffly worded communication.

Sully, in his unreliable *Memoirs*, states that the siege "was undertaken by the King at the earnest entreaties of Mademoiselle d'Estrées." Bishop de Thou makes a similar observation in a letter to a fellow cleric, but admits that he is merely guessing.

It is the privilege of the biographer to second-guess the contemporaries of prominent historical persons: it is inconceivable that Henry IV had made a deal with Gabrielle's father. The conduct of the marquis in the months immediately following the fall of Noyon is irrefutable evidence that d'Estrées was making desperate attempts to place his daughter beyond the reach of the lascivious King. And Henry was too astute a judge of human nature to offer a prize as insignificant as Noyon in return for the favors of Gabrielle.

Reconstructing the past, it seems reasonable that, after the surrender of the town, Henry offered its administration to the highest-ranking nobleman in the vicinity. Antoine d'Estrées happened to be that man. Neither the King nor his loyal nobleman was naïve, of course, and both probably recognized the gesture as an indication on Henry's part that he would welcome the assistance of Gabrielle's father in his campaign.

But Noyon was no bribe. That flat statement can be made without fear of contradiction because Gabrielle did not see Henry when he was in the vicinity of Coeuvres. It is not possible to determine whether she was acting on her own initiative or at the instigation of her father, but what is known is that she and Diane traveled to Chartres while the siege of Noyon was in progress. The supposed purpose of their visit was to attend the baptism of Madame de Sourdis' infant son.

It is significant to note that the sisters remained at Chartres until after Noyon had fallen and had been handed to Antoine d'Estrées on a royal platter. Henry left the vicinity of Coeuvres at the end of August, and the following week Gabrielle and Diane returned home.

It is true that Henry spent the better part of the autumn of 1591 in Picardy, but he and Gabrielle did not meet during that time. The King was busy. Fourteen thousand German mercenaries and six thousand English troops had arrived to bolster his forces, and he was preparing for what he hoped would be a decisive encounter with the League army.

The campaign that followed was bitter. Henry laid siege to Rouen, and when the Duke of Parma marched into France from the Low Countries, the King went to meet him, leaving Biron in charge of the siege. The young general bungled, and the siege was lifted. In the meantime, the wily Alexander Farnese, who used all of his cunning to evade the traps set for him by Henry, finally escaped to Paris with most of his troops intact, by building a bridge of boats across the Seine.

The old duke, proud of his exploit, wrote to Henry asking what the King thought of his maneuver. Henry, weary and deeply disappointed after a campaign that had lasted into the early summer of 1592, forgot that he was expected to reply in chivalrous terms and wrote bluntly, "I call it flight."

While he was occupied with the most urgent of military affairs, Gabrielle was forced to endure a severe crisis in her personal life, and the vindictive Sully declares, "Like Alexander Farnese, the fair d'Estrées took refuge in flight."

5: MARRIAGE, 1592

Early in June 1592, Gabrielle d'Estrées was married to Nicolas d'Amerval, Sieur de Liencourt. D'Amerval was a middle-aged widower whose late wife had been a cousin of Antoine d'Estrées. He was the father of two teenage daughters and one of the wealthiest members of the minor nobility in Picardy. His mother controlled the family fortune, and he spent much of his time at her estate near Amiens.

D'Amerval was not an attractive man. Short and plump, with a round face, weak chin, and small eyes, he was diffident in the presence of his superiors. But his neighbors knew him to be greedy and his peasants complained that he usually took more than his fair share of their produce.

Gabrielle had probably known him since childhood, as all of the nobles who lived near Coeuvres and Noyon were acquainted, but she had not thought of him as a husband prior to their betrothal. As François-Annibal says in his *Memoirs*, "When my sister first learned that a marriage contract had been entered into on her behalf by our father with the Sieur de Liencourt, she was stricken dumb, and spoke no word to any person for four days and three nights."

The arrangements for the marriage were made by Antoine d'Estrées during the period when Henry's fortunes were at their lowest ebb. The King was meeting repeated failure in his attempts to smash the forces of the League; many lords who had declared in his favor were quietly leaving his army, returning to their own homes with their knights and men-at-arms. The Béarnais never lost faith in himself or his cause, but laboring day and night to improve his fortunes, he had no time to pay court to a charming young lady.

Antoine d'Estrées saw his opportunity and took advantage of the King's preoccupation… Bellegarde could no longer be regarded as a suitor, Henry was not thinking in terms of an honorable liaison, and the only way to protect Gabrielle's reputation was to see her safely married. Her father lost no time making the arrangements, and d'Amerval was so pleased that he agreed to accept a small dowry.

Bellegarde's *Amours* is the source of several charming fables regarding the romance of Henry and Gabrielle, but none is more fanciful than his account of her marriage to d'Amerval:

"Henry's love for Gabrielle became greater every day. It was a source of grave anxiety to her father, and she herself turned her thoughts to marriage as a release from the tyranny of parental authority.

"A nobleman, who was rich and of good family, but ill endowed as to graces of person and of mind, offered himself for the alliance. Gabrielle, having assured the King that he could rely on her faithfulness, made him swear that on her wedding day he would come and take her away to a place where she need only see her husband when she liked.

"But the day passed, and the King, unable to abandon some important enterprise, failed to put in an appearance. In vain she waited for his arrival, and wept bitter tears when he did not come for her. She believed he had abandoned her to her fate, and was so miserable that those who loved her feared for her sanity and her health.

"Gabrielle swore again and again that she would be revenged on him and never consent to gratify his desires; so that her husband, thinking to establish his authority more firmly in his own house than in the town where he had married her and where the Marquis d'Estrées was governor, took her away.

"But she took with her so many of the ladies of her family, who had been present at her wedding, that he found that it was still impossible for him to have any wishes that were not hers.

"Not long afterwards the King came to the nearest town and sent for the husband, who brought his wife with him, thinking that at any rate he would by so doing gain favor at Court. On leaving the town the King took her, and her sister and her cousin, with him, and went off to attack the town of Chartres.

"The father of Gabrielle was well pleased with what had transpired. He could say to all who dared to lift their voices in criticism of him that he had done his duty before God, and had seen his daughter married, that it was not his fault that Gabrielle had made a secret compact with the King, and that he had been without means to prevent the King from taking her away. He could say also that she had no longer been under his authority, and that her husband, not he, had been responsible for her at the time the King had taken her to Chartres. Only three people in all the world knew of the agreement that had existed from the first in this matter, they being the King, Gabrielle, and the father of Gabrielle."

The facts of history dispute Bellegarde's airy tale. Foremost among his errors is his claim that Antoine d'Estrées had been a *père complaisant*. The marquis arranged the marriage in order to prevent an affair between Gabrielle and Henry, not sponsor it, while trying to protect his own reputation. And when Gabrielle became the King's mistress in spite of her father's efforts, Antoine d'Estrées was so angry that he severed relations with her. He did not pardon her until several years later, when Henry finally decided to marry her. On a number of occasions during the intervening period, Gabrielle temporarily patched up her feud with her father, promising each time that she would have nothing more to do with Henry. Each time, of course, she blithely broke her word.

A paragraph in a letter written by Henry to Gabrielle on June 26, 1593, gives an accurate account of the relationships: "I thought you were at Saint-Denis but I suppose you have been kept away by your father. I am very glad you are again on good terms with him, and you shall reproach me no more for having to suffer his anger on my account."

François-Annibal, writing his *Memoirs* long after Henry's death, is also in a position to speak the truth: "When Gabrielle and the Baron de Benais had been joined in matrimony, our father said in a voice that all who were near him in the church could hear, 'Now she is safe, and Henry will not have her.'"

And Diane declares in her *Memorial*, "After Gabrielle was married and safely lodged in the house of her husband, our father slept soundly once more, and his disposition improved. But all was wasted when she went off to join the King, and our father swore that had he who seduced her been any other than our liege, he would have paid for his transgression with his own blood."

In passing, it might be noted that Bellegarde is confused about details, too. The siege of Chartres had taken place the previous year, and at no time did Gabrielle accompany the King there while the town was being attacked.

As to Gabrielle's relations with Henry immediately prior to her marriage, she did not even see him, and if they exchanged letters, none have survived. It is doubtful that Gabrielle wrote to the King at this time, although he may have sent her a number of letters. It must be remembered that she was not interested in Henry, and had made her indifference clear to him at Bonneval. She remained a notoriously lax correspondent long after she became his mistress, and did not mend her ways until she fell in love with Henry.

It is probable that she was unhappy at having to marry d'Amerval, although the accounts given by her and other witnesses at the time of her divorce should not be accepted literally. There is no reason to believe that sixteenth-century divorce case testimonies hewed closer to the thin line of truth than they do in the marriage termination mills of the twentieth century.

However, it does seem reasonable to believe that Gabrielle was less than pleased with the husband chosen for her. Her beauty had been widely recognized. She had had an affair with a handsome nobleman of high rank. And even though she had rejected Henry's advances, she could take pride in the knowledge that a king had wanted to make her his mistress. A girl who had been pampered and spoiled for years could not have looked forward with pleasure to the prospect of spending the rest of her days with a fat, inarticulate little man whose chief interests in life were his cows, pigs, and chickens. It is doubtful, too, whether she relished the idea of acting the role of stepmother to two girls only a few years her junior. And, never having been burdened with responsibility, the thought of supervising the staff of a large household must have been terrifying.

Regardless of her feelings, she had no choice. Sixteenth-century fathers did not abide by the wishes of their daughters in making marriage contracts. Social custom demanded that Gabrielle obey her father as long as she remained under his roof and that she become subservient to the wishes of her husband from the moment she married him.

The first weeks of Gabrielle's life with d'Amerval must have been painful, aside from her relations, whatever they were, with the man himself. She had not seen her mother for ten years, but could not have been untouched by the scandal that rocked the country when Françoise Babou d'Estrées and her lover, the young Marquis de Tourzel-Alègre, were brutally murdered. Isabelle de Sourdis left Chartres and joined her niece when she heard the news, and the whole family went into semimourning.

Gabrielle's life was further complicated by the sudden reappearance of Henry, who, startled by news of the unexpected marriage, had arrived at Liencourt a few days later, ostensibly to give the bride a princely gift, or to be precise, two gifts. The official letter he wrote, assigning property to her, still exists. It states:

The bestowal of Assy and Saint-Lambert upon Madame Gabrielle d'Estrées. June 10, 1592. Henry, by the grace of God King of France and of Navarre, to the loved and loyal members of our Council.

This is to make known that we wish to render thanks to our loved and loyal Knight of Saint Michael and the Holy Ghost, Captain of fifty men-at-arms, the Sieur d'Estrées, our Lieutenant General in the Ile-de-France, for the great services he has done to our predecessors and to us on various occasions, and desiring, by reason of the services aforesaid, to gratify our dear and well-beloved Dame Gabrielle d'Estrées, his daughter, wife of the loved and loyal nobleman of our chamber, the Sieur de Liencourt, we hereby give and bequeath our estate and manor of Assy in the dependency of our Earldom of Marie, together with the house, woods, meadows, grounds, mills, farms, and the seignorial rights and privileges and all appurtenances such as they are and such as ourselves and our tenants have always enjoyed.

Also we bequeath to the aforesaid Dame Gabrielle d'Estrées our château of Saint-Lambert, with the whole of our ancient demesne and patrimony, to have, to hold, and to possess during her lifetime.

Given at Liencourt this 10th day of June, of the year of grace 1592, and the 4th of our reign.

Henry

Having written the above, the King spent only one night at Liencourt, traveling the following day to Clermont.

Previous estimates must be revised in the light of these gifts. Perhaps Henry was making a generous gesture to one whom he had loved and lost, but the possibility seems remote. A monarch who was noted for his frugality was not the sort of man who would give a pretty stranger two valuable pieces of real estate.

Therefore it seems as though Gabrielle had indeed become his mistress at Bonneval. If so, the affair could have meant little or nothing to her, in view of her subsequent indifference to Henry during the first months she openly lived with him.

It would appear, from the sources previously cited, that Antoine d'Estrées deliberately kept the King uninformed of the marriage of his daughter, and that Henry, when he learned of the event, reacted with typical impulsiveness. He hurried to the manor house of her husband, and there presented her with the properties, each of which would give her an assured, independent income.

M. Desclozeaux, who is strongly prejudiced in Gabrielle's favor, declares in his monograph that Henry could only have given her Assy and Saint-Lambert "as a consolation for the pitiful state to which she had been reduced."

It is difficult to agree with him. D'Amerval was no Adonis, but the least that could be said for him was that he was decent, law-abiding, and very wealthy. Many women, among them several of Gabrielle's relatives, had made worse marriages.

The modern student can do no more than make an educated guess as to what happened, basing their deductions on their knowledge of the principal players' characters. Gabrielle may or may not have slept with Henry at Bonneval; the question is not important for the simple reason that she herself gave it little, if any, significance. Henry learned of her marriage after the event, rode to Liencourt, and made her a gift of two dazzling estates. Why?

The Béarnais was not in the habit of offering consolation prizes to others in games which he himself had lost. His whole life is a constant reiteration of the theme that here was a man who refused to acknowledge defeat. In spite of his best efforts, he had failed to impress Gabrielle, and now found her married. So he forcefully called himself to her attention in a language she understood. She loved clothes, jewels, and luxuries, and the income from Assy and Saint-Lambert would buy her a large number of baubles each year.

Another question also arises: Did Henry sleep with Gabrielle at Liencourt on the night of June 10, before his departure for Clermont the following morning? Something more than reviving scandals almost four hundred years old is involved. The relationship between Gabrielle and her husband could not have been good prior to Henry's arrival at the manor. After his brief visit, it deteriorated rapidly.

Nicolas d'Amerval's contemporaries held him in low esteem, but today it is difficult to feel unsympathetic toward him. If any man ever was in an uncomfortable, if not untenable, position, the Sieur de Liencourt was that man. Even if it is assumed that Gabrielle and Henry had had an affair at Bonneval and that d'Amerval had learned of it, there is nothing to suggest that the unfortunate husband realized he would walk into a royal hornet's nest when he exchanged vows at the altar with Gabrielle.

He must have been surprised, to put it mildly, when he heard Henry pounding on his door a few days after he had, in good faith, taken a bride. He would have been less than human had he not felt hatred for the monarch and his magnificent wedding gifts. But there was literally nothing a nobleman could do to retaliate when the donor was his own king, and especially when the warrior's splendid army of approximately forty thousand men was camped a few miles from his house.

If Henry really did crudely ignore the husband's presence at Liencourt and bed Gabrielle in d'Amerval's own house, the cuckold's rage must have been apoplectic.

Either the gifts alone, or the gifts in combination with personal intimacy between Gabrielle and Henry, caused d'Amerval to keep his distance from his wife. Both later swore they had not slept together during the three months they had spent under the same roof. Even if their assertion is doubted, members of d'Amerval's household, who afterward continued in his employ, declared under oath that to the best of their knowledge the claim was true.

Gabrielle's statement to the court in her divorce proceedings to the effect that her husband was impotent raises another question and will be considered in greater detail later. At this point it is sufficient to cite the court record in order to obtain some idea of the atmosphere in d'Amerval's house during the unhappy three months:

"When interrogated concerning the day of her wedding, the Dame d'Estrées replied that she believed that a blow or some disease had rendered her husband impotent. She also said that she had no quarrel or dispute with the aforesaid Sieur de Liencourt, and as long as they were together they had lived peaceably, and earnestly did she desire that things might have been different."

Gabrielle is thus presented by her lawyer as having been a tranquil, compassionate young woman. But one of her own supporting witnesses at the divorce hearings gives another picture. One Sieur du Fay, an officer in the regiment of Picardy, who had been a page in the household of the Marquis d'Estrées at the time of the wedding, told the court that, prior to the ceremony, he had heard Gabrielle say, "Ah, well, they wish me to marry d'Amerval, and to put me out of the way; I will do it, but it will be against my will."

Ensign du Fay further testified that Gabrielle had spent virtually all of her time weeping during the weeks following the marriage. Madame de Sourdis, Diane, and other relatives of Gabrielle also dutifully told the presiding judge that the bride had wept copiously each day that she spent in her husband's house.

The curious reader, putting together the pieces of the puzzle, can only conclude that if d'Amerval was indeed impotent, it was small wonder.

According to tradition, it was Henry who deliberately chose a venal, obliging husband for Gabrielle in order to release her from the authority of her father. Many members of Henry's own court subscribed to the theory, and Sully dwells on it at length in his *Memoirs*. But subsequent events and common sense indicate that tradition may be mistaken.

Scarcely two years after the marriage, Henry went to great lengths to obtain a divorce for Gabrielle. His political situation at the time was delicate, and he risked offending many of his staunchest supporters in both the Catholic and Huguenot parties; but he took the chance, deliberately using all of the enormous prestige and power of his high office to have Gabrielle set free. He was not yet thinking of marrying her himself, so that could not have been one of his motives. And certainly he, of all men, knew the whispers were far louder when he took a mistress who was married in preference to one who was single.

Gabrielle's relations with her father were strained for a long time when, still married to d'Amerval, she went to live with the King, and Antoine d'Estrées made repeated attempts to reassert his authority over his daughter. He was exerting his legal right, in the absence of any similar action on the part of Gabrielle's husband, and the Church considered his attitude correct. Huguenot leaders agreed with the bishops, and it is no exaggeration to say that, in the furor that arose when Henry and Gabrielle first lived together, the austere elements of both religious groups finally found something on which they could unite.

A transaction conducted by the King two days after his visit to Liencourt often has been cited as proof that d'Amerval accepted a royal bribe in return for his willingness to close his eyes and pretend his wife's affair did not exist. A royal decree, signed by Henry and his Secretary of State for the kingdom of Navarre, one de Loménie, states:

> At Clermont, in Beauvoisis, on the morning of Friday, June 12, 1592, in the King's palace, and in the presence of two royal notaries, Henry IV, King of France and of Navarre, acting more particularly in this place as Comte de Marle, Seigneur de la Fère, gave full power to the nobleman, Philippe de Longueval, Seigneur de Manicamp, Director of His Majesty's affairs in the county of Marle, to sell and to dispose of, entirely and for ever, the estate and manor of Falvy-sur-Somme, with all its appurtenances and dependencies, powers and privileges, with no exception, on behalf of and for the advantage of Messire Nicolas d'Amerval, Seigneur de Liencourt, Knight of Saint Michael and the Holy Ghost, Gentleman of the Chamber, formerly governor of the town

and bailiwick of Chauny, for the sum of 12,000 écus, in discharge of a debt of 8,000 écus advanced to His Majesty by the aforesaid Sieur de Liencourt while he was governor of Chauny, to pay the garrison of that town and for the repairing of the fortifications and keeping them in order for the King's service, as he duly put it before His Majesty, who holds himself content and satisfied therewith.

The remaining sum of 4,000 écus to be delivered into the hands of Master Julien Mallet, Councillor, Treasurer and Receiver-General for His Majesty, for the house of Navarre.

Henry
Countersigned, de Loménie

The evidence that Henry bought off d'Amerval is flimsy. The sum of eight thousand écus would have been a very small payment for the honor of a man whose fortune, combined with that of his mother, was worth several hundred thousand.

Far more important is the fact that the man chosen to represent Henry in the transaction was Philippe de Longueval, a cousin of Gabrielle's on her father's side. De Longueval was a strict moralist who had said publicly, on more than one occasion, that, royalist though he was, Henry's sexual excesses tempted him to join the League. He lived according to his principles, and early in 1594 successfully defied Henry in a startling incident.

The siege of the town of Laon was in progress at the time, and when Henry went there to take charge of the operation, Gabrielle traveled with him. The King, seeking a comfortable château in which to lodge her, had sent word ahead to de Longueval, who owned the largest residence in the neighborhood, saying that Gabrielle would arrive there before sundown. The stern de Longueval read the letter, mounted his horse, and rode off to meet the royal party on the road. Behaving with great firmness and dignity, he announced to

Henry, in the presence of Gabrielle and a large group of officers and ladies, that he would not and could not admit the King's mistress into his house, even though she was his cousin.

It is patent that Philippe de Longueval was not the sort who would lend himself to an underhand transaction.

The payment to d'Amerval was one of many made in a similar manner by Henry, whose finances were at the time in a shambles. It was the custom for his local governors to pay royal debts out of their own pockets and, when a sum large enough to be brought to the King's attention had accumulated, to present him with the bill. There was only one way Henry could pay his debts, and he frequently resorted to it — by selling royal property. Nicolas d'Amerval had been governor of Chauny for two years, and it is not stretching credulity to imagine that, when Henry was a guest in his house on June 10, he seized the opportunity to present his modest account receivable.

It might be observed, too, that the penny-pinching Henry pocketed the 4,000 écus' difference between the sale price of the property and the sum he owed d'Amerval. It is unlikely that this display of parsimony could have accompanied a financial transaction intended to silence the husband of the woman Henry wanted.

Complete records of Henry the Great's expenditures are extant, some in duplicate and some in triplicate, and d'Amerval never received another copper from him. Had the two men made a deal regarding Gabrielle, d'Amerval probably would have received additional payments from time to time. And it is reasonable to assume that he would have made token appearances at court in order to maintain the fiction that he and his wife were still living together in order to relieve Henry of the embarrassment of admitting that Gabrielle was his mistress.

But the King was not easily embarrassed. He had lived with too many other women, some married and some single, to start worrying now about his personal reputation or that of his current lady. He believed it was his right to conscript the manpower of France for his war against the League, and his behavior over a period of a lifetime indicates that he considered the country's attractive women a national asset that he, the incarnate symbol of France, was privileged to utilize as he saw fit.

The Lord of Liencourt was an unfortunate outsider whose wife shunned him and who was specifically excluded from the King's bounty. In 1594, at the time of Gabrielle's divorce, d'Amerval made a pathetic attempt to gain possession of at least a portion of the large fortune that his wife had been given by Henry. His first step was to draw up a new will, in which he wrote, "I give and bequeath to Charlotte and Marie d'Amerval, my two daughters, the whole of my real and personal estate, acquired conjointly with my wife, and I wish there to be included therein all that has been acquired by Dame Gabrielle d'Estrées, my wife, since we have been joined together in marriage."

His attitude reveals a curious state of wishful thinking, as he and Gabrielle had been separated for more than two years when he put his desires on paper. He soon realized that he had no hope of gaining control of her property, however, and dropped the project. Apparently his lawyers convinced him that, although he was entitled under the law to claim Gabrielle's estate, any move in that direction would bring him in conflict with the King. Men far stronger and more courageous than Nicolas d'Amerval shrank from such a confrontation.

As it happens, there were valid reasons for Henry's insistence on his mistress' divorce in 1594, but in order to understand them it is necessary to follow the astonishing changes in the complex relationship of the compulsive monarch and the lazy young beauty from Picardy. Certainly, until Gabrielle walked out of her husband's house in 1592 she was something of a shadow-figure, seen only through the eyes of others.

Perhaps, as some critics have intimated, her character remained unformed until constant association with the Béarnais disciplined her personality. Or it may be, as her enemies charged, that she was so shallow that she had no real character of her own, and that Henry trained her to become the sort of woman he wanted.

Regardless of what caused her growth, the fact remains that she grew, and when she changed, so did France.

6: THE LOVE GAME, 1592–93

Tallemant de Réaux, the popular seventeenth-century French court historian and gossip, states in his *Historiettes* that Gabrielle d'Estrées, accompanied by her Aunt de Sourdis, left Liencourt on September 4, 1592, and joined the King at Chartres the following day. He also states that what impelled her to abandon her husband was an impassioned letter from Henry, begging her to join him before he went off to fight the Duke of Parma, who had gathered together a new army in the Low Countries.

De Réaux is the only writer who assigns a specific date and reason to the event, and although he may be right, he does not quote Henry's letter. The letter itself has also vanished, but the question becomes academic when other authorities state that Henry and Gabrielle were together on the seventh of September. Armand de Chiverny, the King's legal adviser and, incidentally, the long-time lover of Isabelle de Sourdis, writes in his *Memoirs*, "His Majesty celebrated the arrival of Dame Gabrielle d'Estrées by ordering that the sum of 10,000 gold crowns be paid to her forthwith out of the royal treasury, in return for which he pledged himself to reimburse the treasurer out of his own funds, these having been depleted by the purchase of necessaries for the winter campaign to be waged against Alexander Farnese and the hosts of the League."

Diane reveals in her *Memorial* that the desire to see Henry was not uppermost in her sister's mind at the time: "Gabrielle was not happy at Liencourt, but she was surrounded by the comforts so needful to her well being, and was reluctant to leave. Our aunt saw the many advantages that would be derived at court, and earnestly persuaded her to change her mode of living, Gabrielle finally consenting in the hope that the King's passion would cool and that she could resume her liaison with Bellegarde, with whom she had maintained a correspondence in the months she had lived at Liencourt."

Gabrielle, it appears, had inherited the trait so natural to the Babou sisters, that of intrigue in games of love. Henry was not a man she could ignore, but Bellegarde was still her first love. She was foolish, which was the prerogative of an eighteen-year-old girl. Bellegarde, on the other hand, must have been aware of the risks he and Gabrielle were taking, for he not only knew that Henry's temper could be destructive, but he had been warned to keep away from the young lady who had become the King's choice.

Hardheaded Isabelle de Sourdis undoubtedly knew that her niece had not become starry-eyed over the homely monarch, but realized, even if Gabrielle did not, that the King's favorite would enjoy those things that were more important than food or drink to the Babou women — power and money. She must have believed, too, that she could cope with Bellegarde, for she used all of her influence to urge the girl to join Henry. She succeeded.

On September 9, Henry arrived at Noyon, the town in which Gabrielle and d'Amerval had been married and which was under the governorship of Antoine d'Estrées. He stayed there a full week, an unusually long period for him to remain in any one place, and there is unanimous agreement in memoirs and diaries that Gabrielle was with him. The King conducted minor, routine business of state during this week. There is no evidence that matters of importance caused him to linger, so it would seem that he and Gabrielle were enjoying an illicit honeymoon.

Immediately thereafter Henry resumed his peripatetic existence, writing to one of his aides on September 16, "I shall sleep at Compiègne, and tomorrow I shall be at Senlis; the day after tomorrow at Saint-Denis."

Gabrielle accompanied him, and from that time forward adapted her life to his nomadic existence, which must have been a strain on a girl who loved luxury. Chiverny describes the royal way of living in his *Memoirs*, and himself shows more than a trace of bitterness:

"The King would go, according to circumstance, now to Saint-Denis, now to Mantes, now to Chartres, followed by us, the members of his Council, or quite alone, according to the nature of his business. None of us knew at what hour he would decide to leave the abode in which he had made his court for the night. Often we were awakened at dawn by lackeys and hurried into the saddle before we could break our fast with as much as a crust or a beaker of wine; but none dared to complain, for the King thought only of his great task, the unification of his Kingdom under his own hand.

"Having no liking for royal trappings, the King was content to travel as poorly clad as any merchant soldier selling his sword to the highest bidder, and those among us who were not content to live in rags were sore put to replenish their wardrobes. The ladies found it more to their convenience to remain in one place, where we would join them when we could, as they could not travel with their many leather boxes.

"But the King was so enamored of the Dame Gabrielle that he would not have her out of his sight in those days, and she carried little more than the clothes she wore on her back. Like us, she did not raise her voice in complaint, but her silence was not of her own doing. She who was the fount of feminine wisdom sealed the lips of her niece so the King would hear no word of her true feelings."

Obviously, Isabelle de Sourdis had her hands full.

But Gabrielle needed few lessons in the fine art of how to fool a man. Late in September, Henry increased the pace of his preparations for the winter campaign and was forced to leave Gabrielle behind as he rode to the various bivouac areas where his troops were assembling.

She settled down for a short stay at the governor's palace in Chartres with her aunt and uncle, and there received word, on September 27, that Henry had fallen ill. She sat down at once and wrote him an anxious letter in a round, childish hand:

> My King and my beloved:
> I die of fear: reassure me, I beseech you, by telling me how fares the bravest of the brave. I fear his ill must be great, since nothing else would rob me of his company today.
> Give me news, my lord, for you know how the least ill of yours is fatal to me. Although I have twice heard of your condition today, I could not sleep without sending you a thousand "good nights," for I am dowered with no feeble constancy. I am the Princess Constancy and sensible of all that concerns you, and insensible of all else in the world, be it good or bad.
>
> Ever your,
> Gabrielle

The sentiments she expressed were somewhat less than original and infinitely less than true. Henry, whose judgment was usually sound, must have been too ill to think clearly, for the messenger he sent to Chartres the following day was Bellegarde. The handsome young duke dutifully reported on his master's condition, and then remained at Chartres for three additional days and nights in order to give the consolation which only he could offer.

Henry exploded, but not for the last time. In the months that followed he was often consumed by jealousy, irritation, and frequent outbursts of blazing anger. Whenever he and Gabrielle were separated, he wrote her at least once a day, a practice he followed until the end of her life. Those of the late months of 1592 and approximately the first half of 1593 reveal a lover who has forgotten his royal dignity as he repeatedly lists his many grievances against a girl who remained lazy, indifferent to him — and unfaithful.

Strangely, the King made no move to punish Bellegarde, whom he could have banished, imprisoned, or murdered. There were two reasons why Henry chose to tolerate the competition of his rival, and one was his aversion to assassination. His belief in tolerance was a compulsive passion, and never in his busy life was he put more to the test than during the period when Gabrielle blandly distributed her favors without partiality to both men.

Henry's other reason, succinctly stated by Chiverny in his *Memoirs*, significantly reveals much about the character of a great man. "The King was troubled and much vexed by the unfaithfulness of his mistress, and was urged by many of the Council to put her aside or dispose of Feuillemorte. He said he would do neither, having been challenged and thus compelled on his honor to win her affections fairly."

Gabrielle was enjoying the first taste of freedom she had ever known in her young life, and apparently neither knew nor cared that her conduct was shameless. "Our father," François-Annibal writes in his *Memoirs*, "sent my brother and me to Chartres on his behalf, and there we delivered to our sister stern orations and reprimands, but she turned them aside. In truth, she who had been so impassive and solemn was now so gay that we scarcely knew her. In vain we appealed to our aunt, who told us that she had no ability or means in the termination of the close friendship that existed, to the displeasure of the King, between our sister and Saint-Larry."

If Gabrielle would not listen to Isabelle de Sourdis, she was not in a mood to take advice from anyone, and it is obvious that she felt certain of her power over the King. Her relatives were afraid she would push her luck too far, and must have been secretly relieved that Henry was so busily engaged in his military preparations.

The court was established at Saint-Denis in October, November, and December, and Gabrielle traveled there from Chartres whenever Henry could afford to spend a day or two with her. But she drove him to distraction by arriving late and offering no apologies for her tardiness. Then, when they were separated again, she didn't bother to answer most of his letters. Henry was notified whenever Bellegarde rode to Chartres from Saint-Denis, and consequently the King was besieged with problems other than the pending fight with the Duke of Parma.

A letter he wrote to Gabrielle in late November 1592, is as indicative of his anguish and anger as it is of her lack of morality and her indifference:

To the Dame Gabrielle d'Estrées.
There is nothing that confirms me more in my suspicions, or serves more to increase them, than the way in which you conduct yourself toward me. Since it pleases you to command me to banish all suspicion, I will; but you will not take it ill if, in the openness of my heart, I tell you the grounds on which I suspect you, inasmuch as you appear not to have understood certain things that I have laid to your charge, openly enough

as I thought, or so at least I judge by your replies. It was for this reason that yesterday I began my letter with the words: "There are none so deaf as those who will not hear."

In the first place, I assure you, my dear mistress, that the grudge I had against you has left no lingering bitterness in my soul, now that I am more than satisfied with the pains you have taken to set my heart at rest; I only speak to show you what grounds I had for my suspicions.

You are well aware that I was offended at the journey taken by my rival. Your eyes have such power over me that they saved you half my complainings; you satisfied me by the mouth, not from the heart. Had I known then what I have learned since, at Saint-Denis, of that journey, I should not have seen you…

I should have broken with you altogether…

Yet I would rather burn my hand than write this to you, and cut out my tongue than that such words should be spoken.

You know how little you have done since I saw you. Have you banished the cause of our disagreement, as I hoped you would? Which of your promises have you fulfilled? By what faith can you swear to me, you who have broken faith a second time? You complain of my suspicions, yet take no offence at the perfidy and want of faith of others; it is indeed a grave injustice.

You send me word that you will keep the promises that you made me previously. Just as the Old Testament was superseded at the coming of Our Lord, so have your promises been set aside by the letter that you sent to me at Compiègne. *One should speak of doing, not of going to do.*

Make up your mind then, I pray you, mistress, to have but one servant. It lies with you to make me a different man, with you to please me; you do me wrong if you think that anyone in the world could serve you with a greater love than mine. Nor could mortal man be more faithful. If I have ever been unwise and indiscreet, think but of the folly that is committed in the name of jealousy, and do you blame yourself!

Never before has mistress given me cause for jealousy, and never have I known man more discreet than I, myself, have proved to be. Feuillemorte has, out of dread for the Leaguers, made it known that he is not my friend, and that he is not in love.

So much do I long to set eyes on you that I would cut off four years of my life to see you as soon as this letter, which now I bring to an end, kissing your hand a thousand times. And so, alas, you think me unworthy of your picture?

There was no signature, and although the earlier portions were written in Henry's usual fine, even hand, the last two paragraphs appear to have been scrawled in haste. The letter completely covers four pages, and there are neither margins nor blank spaces. There are three erasures, and the words, "at Saint-Denis" are inserted between lines.

This extraordinary communication does not read like a letter written by a great king. It is the tortured outburst of a suffering man. Henry makes his meaning emphatically clear when he indicates that Gabrielle must make up her mind and choose only one lover. He helped her to speed the process by dismissing Bellegarde, for a man who had publicly proclaimed that he was not the King's friend was unworthy of holding the post of grand equerry. Yet Henry took care not to force the duke into making an alliance with the League, and granted him the right of access to the royal court at all times.

The Duke of Parma inadvertently helped the King's cause, too. In early December, as Farnese was leading his army south from Brussels, he died suddenly of a heart attack, and within a day and a half his entire striking force fell apart. The Spanish and Flemish troops retreated to the Low Countries, and Henry, disappointed because he could not come to grips with the enemy, returned to Saint-Denis, arriving there on December 9, 1592.

Either by accident or design, Gabrielle and Madame de Sourdis left Saint-Denis earlier that same day for Chartres, and it is not known whether relations between the King and his mistress were strained. If they were quarreling, however, they made up their differences during the next ten days, for Henry joined Gabrielle at Chartres on December 20, and remained there until the end of February 1593. Henry, of course, was incapable of staying quietly in any one place for a prolonged period, and absented himself from Chartres several times, but Bellegarde remained in the city as an unofficial member of the court.

However, Henry's patience was growing thin, and Bellegarde prudently found matters that would occupy him elsewhere whenever the King reappeared. Gabrielle, too, began to understand that the monarch was in earnest and would not remain tolerant forever. Late in January 1593, Bellegarde's absences from Chartres grew more protracted.

And by mid-February Henry had become sufficiently complacent to send her a letter in which he said, "Only the existence of a rival could change my love."

Their relationship was becoming deeper, and by April 15, Bellegarde had disappeared permanently from Gabrielle's personal life. On that day the King, replying to a letter he had just received from her, stated happily, "Your fair words banish all of my former suspicions, deep as they were!"

Still another change of attitude is indicated in a letter he sent her in the middle of June 1593. In it he declared flatly, "I am certain of your love."

Gabrielle had become an adult under Henry's tutelage, and of her own volition had ended her disgraceful affair with

Bellegarde. "She herself told me," according to Diane's *Memorial*, "that she was shocked when she reflected on her former, depraved conduct. But she silenced me when I spoke of her previous innocence and tried to place full blame on Saint-Larry. She would have none of it, and insisted she herself had been to blame for the deplorable matters about which even the King's friends have taken offense, and which the adherents of the League use to blacken his name.

"It is my own view, having seen my sister for the first time since early winter, that her nature has changed, and our aunt confirms the accuracy of my observation. But our father will not hear her name, and I know that in his own heart he couples my sister with her who met her rightful fate when the knife of an assassin was plunged into her breast."

Diane d'Estrées was right. Gabrielle had fallen in love, not as an adolescent but as a woman, and everyone who saw her commented on the change that had taken place. Even Sully grudgingly acknowledges, in his *Memoirs*, that her attitude was different: "The d'Estrées no longer simpered, cast her eyes at the gentlemen of the court, or laughed too loudly at ribald jokes. Her manner became demure, and she had eyes only for the King. He wanted her thus, and was blind to the many faults that others saw in her." He cannot resist adding, "She was an actress of consummate skills, and took care to keep up the same pose of gentle frailty to the end of her days, thereby assuring that she would not lose the affections of the King."

No whisper of a relationship other than her affair with Henry ever touched Gabrielle's name after April 1593, but her bad habits of living for the day had not yet been altered, much to Henry's despair. He, who had never known the meaning of relaxation, literally worked day and night, and one of the jokes in poor taste that the League circulated intimated that his affairs were lies foisted on an unsuspecting public in order to make him seem like a carefree, very human person. Obviously, the League adherents declared, he had no time to take a woman to bed, for he scarcely paused in his work to relieve himself.

Certainly he was a man of tremendous vitality, making it a practice to appear out of nowhere, surprising subordinates who were taking it easy in the belief that he was miles away. He applied this same principle to his dealings with his enemies, and his troops learned to endure grueling, all-night marches, unknown to the warfare of the period, so he could make an unexpected appearance and confound his foes.

He dictated letters steadily to batteries of secretaries during meals, when his barber shaved him, and, later in his life, as he was being dressed in robes of state. Early each morning, while he sipped a mug of watered wine after arising, aides read incoming correspondence to him. And the members of his Council gave up all hope of leading private lives. They discovered, as did officials of less stature, that they might receive a royal summons at any hour of the day or night, and that when they appeared, Henry wanted to discuss state problems at length.

A story, probably apocryphal, illustrates his maddening punctuality. Henry, Duc de Montmorency, Constable of France and therefore the second most important person in the country, allegedly was due to be received by the King at the Louvre one day in 1595, for a meeting at which the two were planning to discuss the reduction of the provinces still holding out against them. Obviously, this was a matter of the gravest nature.

The duke, whose appointment was scheduled for noon, spent the morning with his staff, preparing documents and maps that would be required at the meeting. Suddenly, at eleven o'clock, he was stunned when an apoplectic Henry stalked into the great hall of the ducal town house, demanding to know why the Constable was late.

Montmorency stammered his apologies, then protested that he had apparently misunderstood the arrangements, thinking the appointment had been scheduled for noon. Henry, so the story goes, roared at him, "Will you never learn that when we are to meet at noon, I expect you promptly at the hour of ten?"

Gabrielle had no concept of the meaning of punctuality, and one day was like another to her. Again and again she agreed to keep a rendezvous with the King, but rarely appeared until several days later, thereby infuriating and baffling him. His letters to her during the spring and summer of 1593 were filled with complaints, but he was so much in love that he repeatedly forgave her, to the surprise of his aides, who had known him to get rid of a mistress for no reason other than sudden displeasure with her hair or gown.

Henry was being led on a not-so-merry chase by his spoiled young mistress, who neither held him in awe nor made any attempt to mend her ways. Even today there is a pathetic note in the correspondence of the infatuated, middle-aged man trying to hold in his hands the quicksilver of youth. Excerpts from several letters he wrote to Gabrielle in April 1593 illustrate his problem.

On the nineteenth, writing from the town of Mantes, he says: "You assure me, by Arsoir, one of my lackeys who returned quite late, that you will not fail to come, as you promised. I waited for you in vain today, and was saddened when you failed to join me in time for dinner. The news he brings me consoles me much, hurried as I am with the work I find here to do; but the bearer of your letter tells me later, by word of mouth, that you do not leave until tomorrow morning. The delay will kill me, for I dread the slowness of your coming. My passion must be my excuse, my sweet angel, for all my fears."

When, on the following day, Gabrielle still did not appear, Henry wrote to her again, in a forgiving, tender mood: "So it will be tomorrow, my dear love, that I shall kiss your fair hands a thousand times. The hour of meeting draws near, and I hold it dearer than my life; yet if you are late by but a single day, I shall not survive."

The hours of the twenty-first passed slowly, with again no sign of Gabrielle. Henry, contrary to his expectation, did not expire, but he did lose patience. That evening, sitting alone in his private chamber, he wrote: "Yesterday I had no news of you; I know not what to think. If you linger out of respect for Easter Day, I must tell you that I hold the day in no such respect. If you absent yourself through mere idleness, you do me wrong. It is now midday, and you have not come. It is far from the time when, by your promises, I was to expect you. *When will you learn to be true to your word?* Not thus do I treat my promises!"

Members of the court were sure the King would soon grow tired of the flighty girl, and Isabelle de Sourdis was afraid that her niece would be dropped from royal favor at any time. Chiverny, her lover and confidant, declares in his *Memoirs*: "The aunt of the King's mistress, the only member of an eccentric family who consistently behaved with sensibility and dignity, was much in dread that the King would dismiss Dame Gabrielle from his court. Dame Isabelle knew that the King would be acting justly, for Dame Gabrielle's tardiness has mocked His Majesty, casting doubt on the institution of the monarchy which he personifies. It was often said among the King's followers that if his mistress showed him no respect, he deserved none from others. We who serve His Majesty believed that Dame Gabrielle would be gone before fruit appeared on the trees."

Chiverny was wrong, and Isabelle de Sourdis' fears proved to be groundless. No one realized that Gabrielle's hold on Henry's affections was so strong that, reversing the custom he had followed since his youth, he would accept Gabrielle's lack of consideration, with only occasional mild flashes of fire.

On June 26, when he was making his temporary headquarters at the town of Dreux, he appears to be the supplicant in a lovers' quarrel when he wrote to her: "I have received the letter that it pleased you to write to me on the twenty-third of this month. I thought you were at Saint-Denis, but you have been kept away at your father's orders… You say that if any of your letters have displeased me, then certainly this one will. But do you forget my resolution 'to make no more complaints?' Nay, I will make another resolve: 'Never again to be angry with you.' The first will keep me from importuning my friends, the second will uphold my spirit."

It was difficult for him to keep his resolution, and in another letter written to her in the same month, he displays his exasperation. "I waited patiently for one whole day without news of you, for in reckoning the time I saw that it must be so. But when on the second day I did not hear, I could only put it down to the sloth of my lackeys, for to put the blame on you, my sweet angel, I cannot. I pray I am correct in my deduction, and that it is they, not you, who must bear the blame. My heart would be filled with sorrow should I find that I must, once again, point a finger of accusation at you."

Even when showing her kindness and giving her gifts which he could ill afford, her tardiness and indifference continued to upset him. On June 23, he wrote: "I have discovered, only an hour ago, a way to complete your plate. See how thoughtful I am for you, while the least thing seems to make you forgetful of me. Had I not sworn to make no more complaints, justly might I cry that you strain my patience to its limit. Do you doubt that blood flows in the veins of a King? Think you that I shed no blood when I am pricked with a sharp needle of disregard? Mend your ways, I beg you, mistress, so we may spend our days together in amity."

Gabrielle's sloth, however, did not lessen the King's regard for her, for, to the astonishment of his subordinates, he opened his purse and showered her with money and gifts, something he had done for no other woman. The carefully kept records of the Kingdom of Navarre reveal that, in 1593 alone, he borrowed fifty thousand écus from the state treasury in order to make her a princely gift of gold.

His generosity continued. In January 1593, she became a royal pensioner, receiving four hundred écus per month for the maintenance of her personal staff and household. On February 1 of the next year he increased the allowance to five hundred and by 1596 the monthly pension had risen to a thousand écus.

Obviously, in the early days of their affair, Gabrielle's tardiness was no bar to royal favor, but it is impossible to guess how long Henry would have been willing to tolerate it, along with her indifference. But his influence and, to a lesser extent, that of his sister, gradually brought about changes so that by July 1593 Gabrielle was a different kind of woman and the King's complaints ceased. From that time forward he uttered no word, either in his letters or in the presence of others, criticizing her.

Love, it appears, was once more the magic potion that worked miracles. Diane, writing in her *Memorial*, says that in August 1593, "My sister told me that she loved the King with her heart and soul, and was so sincere in her protestations of that love that our father forgave her transgressions."

7: THE POWER BEHIND THE THRONE, 1593

Gabrielle d'Estrées did not participate in the affairs of state until she fell in love with Henry IV, some time after July 1593. From September 1592, until then, she had lived with him openly as his mistress, but there is no indication in any memoirs or other documents of the period that she was even cognizant of the world around her. In all probability she had remained a luxury-loving, lazy, and narcissistic adolescent.

From July on, however, she matured rapidly. Henry's cause became her cause, and she plunged unhesitatingly into the rock-strewn rapids of national and international politics. It cannot be claimed, of course, that her motives were unselfish. She would have been less than human had she not thought of becoming Queen of France, in spite of the enormous obstacles that blocked her accession to the throne.

The greatest of these obstacles, as Gabrielle knew, was Henry himself, since it had not crossed his mind to marry her. Far more urgent matters consumed his attention. Paris remained in the hands of the League, as did Rouen, and he had no capital. Philip II of Spain and Pope Clement VIII were sending reinforcements to Mayenne, and the forces of the League appeared in no way weakened by the death of Alexander Farnese, Duke of Parma. There was still a long road to travel before Henry could retire from the battlefield and ponder the question of taking a consort.

But Gabrielle, in spite of the flightiness she had shown, was endowed with the shrewdness of the Babou women and the intellect of her brilliant grandfather, Jean d'Estrées, and she was content to proceed one step at a time. She had heard many members of the court declare that if Henry became a Catholic, every city in France, including Paris and Rouen, would open its gates to him, and the League would be exposed as an instrument of foreign aggressors. Then, it was argued, all patriotic Frenchmen would rally to the cause of the King, and the Spaniards would be expelled from the country, along with the mercenary troops.

Another, and equally formidable obstacle to Gabrielle's becoming Queen was the fact that only the Vatican could untangle the marital snarls that stood in the way of a marriage. An ecclesiastical court headed by a bishop could dissolve Gabrielle's marriage to Nicolas d'Amerval, but Henry, a king who was married to the daughter of a king, was condemned to a lifelong alliance with Margot unless Pope Clement granted him a divorce. Obviously, the Pope would take no action to help a heretic. Henry knew it, as did Margot, and the cloud hovered over their already phlegmatic correspondence, in which both frequently mentioned the desirability of a divorce.

Gabrielle, whose mind was uncluttered by sophisticated notions, thought the perfect solution would be the King's conversion to Catholicism. The matter was enormously intricate, but she thought in simple, direct terms, and this was, in large part, the source of her strength.

The strongest personal influence barring Henry's conversion was the attitude of his sister. Catherine of Navarre was as devout a Protestant as her brother and, having spent most of her life in Navarre, where she had acted as Henry's titular regent since 1585, she cordially detested papists. She and Henry had not met in many years, but early in 1593 she made a journey to France and, falling in love with the country, remained there until the end of her days.

She and Henry met at Tours on February 28, 1593, and a series of festivals, tournaments, and balls were held to celebrate their reunion. Gabrielle was present at the festivities, and, strangely, the strait-laced Catherine took an immediate liking to her brother's mistress. They spent much time together, exchanging miniatures and confidences; later they corresponded regularly and met frequently.

Catherine was a brilliant, highly educated woman, and the fact that she was only moderately attractive made her no less eligible as a potential consort for a king. At one time or another, negotiations were conducted on her behalf with every Protestant monarch in Europe, and Henry maneuvered unceasingly until she finally became the Duchess de Bar.

In 1593 she wanted to marry a distant cousin, the Comte de Soissons, a Catholic whose suit Henry had at one time favored. The King had since changed his mind, however, because of the count's questionable loyalty. Suspecting that Catherine's passion was unabated, Henry issued a decree forbidding the marriage.

Catherine needed a friend at court, and found a willing one in Gabrielle, who promised to use her influence to help Madame. Henry's stubborn refusal to change his mind was irrelevant, and the women became close friends. Gabrielle lost no time in utilizing that friendship to promote the cause of the King's conversion, as a letter she wrote to Catherine on July 1, 1593, indicates:

> Dear and respected Madame:
> Those who call upon His Majesty to accept conversion become more clamorous daily, and press upon him the argument that the war will end if he will but renounce the Huguenot faith. I do not ask that you add your voice to theirs, but the withdrawal of your opposition to such a move would

clear His Majesty's mind and heart. Do you but reflect that he who is your close friend is a son of the Catholic Church, and you will surely know that all such are not Devils with cloven hooves.

It is my honor, Madame, to be your respectful servant,

Gabrielle d'Estrées

Catherine took the hint, and dropped her opposition to Henry's conversion.

But there was no way Gabrielle could cope with the complicated political situation. Soon after the assassination of Henry III, many of his former adherents declared themselves the subjects of Henry of Navarre. The League chose François Cardinal de Bourbon, the King's cousin, as their monarch, but he was guarded by a regiment of Henry's troops at Amiens, so the Duke of Mayenne was elected to govern in his name.

Both sides made strenuous attempts to convoke a meeting of the States-General for the purpose of electing and crowning a king, and for Henry the issue was crucial. Each time the League announced that such a meeting would be held, Henry, backed by his troops, called for a similar session.

It was as obvious to Henry as it was to his enemies that if the League should gain control of the person of the cardinal, elect him at Reims, and crown him in the cathedral there — where French kings were traditionally crowned — the war-weary country would accept their choice.

The cardinal, however, was an amiable man who enjoyed the clerical life at Amiens and was content to remain there. Since he had no desire to sit on the throne, the League had to find someone to take his place. Luckily for Henry, there was no lack of candidates. Philip II claimed the crown for a Spanish princess, the Infanta Isabel, a granddaughter of Henry II, and in order to make France secure for the Hapsburgs, proposed to marry her to Archduke Ernst of Austria, who would sit on the throne with her as co-monarch. The Duke of Savoy put in a claim on his own behalf, and there were several French candidates, too. Some members of the Guise family claimed the crown for the young Duke of Guise; the Duke of Lorraine had no legitimate claim, but nevertheless he threw his plumed hat into the ring, as did the Duke of Nemours, a soldier who had prevented Henry's capture of Paris in 1590. Only Mayenne, the most powerful officer of the League, hesitated to put in his own claim — which would have been as valid as the others; on the contrary he offered to withdraw his opposition to Henry if the Béarnais would accept a number of conditions, among them conversion to Catholicism.

The situation became increasingly serious for Henry in 1592, the year that Gabrielle began to live with him as his mistress. Mayenne invited the deputies to a meeting of the States-General at Reims, but only a limited number of gentlemen were willing to risk their necks by traveling there. He then proposed a meeting at Soissons, but had to abandon that idea for the same reason, since Henry held all of the open country between the two cities.

Mayenne then called for a meeting in Paris, to be held in December, but the death of the Duke of Parma caused a postponement until the end of January 1593. The danger to Henry was tremendous, and he reacted with characteristic vigor, issuing a royal decree in which he threatened not only to execute all who attended such a meeting, but to burn to the ground any city or town in which the League's adherents elected anyone other than himself.

Consequently only the most fanatic of his opponents dared to attend Mayenne's meeting. No nobles were present, no jurists, no princes. Most of the delegates, as might have been expected, were clergymen.

Several days were devoted to formalities, to hearing speeches by a special Papal Legate, the Spanish ambassador, and other foreign dignitaries. A French cardinal named de Pellevé brought cheers from his audience when he announced that the Vatican had sent a gift of six hundred thousand écus to prosecute the war. But there were few such addresses, and when Mayenne arose to speak, his face was so pale that his duchess was afraid he had been taken ill.

Henry was active, as usual, and after upholding his rights in a stirring declaration at Chartres, sent a gentleman of his court, Thomas le Homme, to Paris under a flag of truce.

Mayenne electrified the assemblage when he announced, "I have lately received, at the hands of a herald of the opposing side, a resolution from the princes, prelates, officers of the Crown, and principal Catholic lords, who are as much in the counsel of the King of Navarre as others nearer his person, which expressed the hope that an understanding might be arrived at with a view to the establishment of that state of rest so essential for the preservation of the Catholic religion and the State."

Henry, in other words, was prepared to bargain, and Mayenne indicated his own willingness by asking the delegates to vote on the question of whether a conference should be held with the opposition.

Cardinal de Pellevé reminded those present that the Pope was an active member of the League, and added that if the delegates took his own personal advice, they "would administer the whip to the herald, to teach him to refrain in future from taking upon him such ridiculous business."

After a long but desultory debate, it was voted, almost unanimously, that "no communication whatever be made with the King of Navarre or any heretic; only will we confer with the Catholics who are upholding his cause, for reasons affecting their religion and the State; on no account will we accept any proposal to establish a heretic upon the throne of France."

His peace gesture rejected, Henry counterattacked. Late in April, at the little town of Suresnes, he gathered together all the Catholic lords and high-ranking clergymen loyal to him. There were so many great men present that all châteaus, manor houses, and castles in the surrounding area were commandeered for their use. Here they renewed their pledge of fealty to Henry, and announced that as it was their belief that he would, in due time, become converted to the Catholic faith, there existed no valid reason to refuse him recognition as King of France.

Henry accepted their allegiance, but carefully refrained from making a specific commitment. His Huguenot followers were urging him to hold firm, and every detail, real and imagined, of the St. Bartholomew's Day Massacre was recalled. Old hatreds were revived, the issues became confused, and intelligent men desperately searched for a solution that would satisfy everyone.

The King's enemies were engaged in far worse disputes. Philip II, arrogantly believing that he could dictate to the French members of the League, sent Suarez de Figherra, Duke of Feria, to Paris, and the duke almost brought the roof of the Louvre crashing down on his head when, on May 28, 1593, he proposed that the crown be offered jointly to Archduke Ernst and the Infanta Isabel, whose betrothal had just been announced.

Every man present, aware that Henry IV would be merciless in his treatment of those who accepted the Spanish suggestion, felt compelled to make a long, patriotic statement passionately rejecting the idea. Feria, quickly realizing that the suggestion had not found favor, made several attempts to withdraw it, but the speechmakers were not to be satisfied until they had placed themselves on record. A sea of words swept through the hall, and not until July 10 did the unhappy duke have an opportunity to make another nomination. Knowing little of France and the French, he offered the young Duc de Guise as a candidate, and another uproar greeted him. Whatever slim chances young de Guise might have had, were now completely shattered. The delegates, having tasted freedom, adamantly refused to accept foreign dictation.

The farce in Paris strengthened the hand of Henry, who was using every advantage he could grasp. Barred from Paris by League troops, he traveled incessantly, circling the city as he visited Chartres and Dreux, Mantes and Compiègne and Saint-Denis. He exuded self-confidence, but he knew that his situation was desperate. Although many prominent Catholic nobles and bishops had supported him for four years, he realized that if the League-controlled States-General elected someone else, whom Pope Clement then recognized, it would be virtually impossible for true Catholics to remain loyal to him.

Many lords shared the doubts of Chiverny, who had been one of the first Catholics to join the King after the assassination of Henry III. The Chancellor, the nation's highest-ranking jurist, reveals his confusion in his *Memoirs*: "At the time of my joining Henry IV, I had to contend on the one hand with my feelings of affection and obligation toward the State and the obedience I owed to the King, and on the other with my just fears for His Majesty's success. For nearly the whole of France, with a very powerful army at her command, was against him. His Majesty has since achieved a marvelous military recovery, but his religion still stands against him. Unless he changes it, it is impossible to guarantee him the kingdom."

Some of the more militant Huguenots, of whom d'Aubigné is an almost perfect example, hoped that the King would force the entire country to adopt the Protestant faith. And a handful of extreme Catholics in Henry's camp were convinced that, if the King could be converted, he would banish the Huguenots from the country.

Neither group understood the Béarnais, who believed passionately in religious and personal tolerance. Most of his principal advisers, however, shared his advanced views, and gradually he convinced them that the course he had privately chosen for himself was right. The first step, he said, was to rid France of the Spaniards, and the nobles, watching the spectacle in Paris from a distance, agreed with him. He intended to become master in his own house, Henry told them, and would establish an equal balance between the two great religions, placing himself in the center to prevent excesses on either side.

The nobles concurred, and thought, too, that he was right when he declared that his own faith was not an issue. Unfortunately, as Chiverny and others often reminded him, the people of the great Catholic cities did not agree. For four years they had chanted the same refrain, "Become a convert, and we will open our gates." Those gates remained closed, and time was running out.

Some members of Henry's unpretentious court retired to their homes, discreetly trying to protect themselves in the event that the League's States-General elected a new monarch.

The bishops who had braved excommunication in order to remain loyal to the King were becoming alarmed, and money, which had always been scarce, now became almost nonexistent.

Henry, who had known his own mind since childhood, hesitated for the first time in his life. And at this supremely critical hour, early in the summer of 1593, Gabrielle d'Estrées actively intervened and helped to change the course of history.

Her own position was secure as long as Henry remained on the throne, but no longer. He had given her a title in her own right, and she was known now as the Marquise de Monceaux, with appropriate lands and castles to accompany her new status. Her motives in helping the King to make up his mind were purely feminine and, consequently, completely personal. She loved Henry, and although he didn't yet know it, hoped to marry him. Certainly she knew that if he lost his throne, she would be the first to be swept aside by the League. Therefore her entire future was bound, irrevocably, with his.

Gabrielle's religious convictions could not have been strong, and at no time in her life did she show evidence of great faith. She had been raised in a household in which a few outer forms had taken the place of real piety. The great Jean d'Estrées, her grandfather, had been a Huguenot for years, but had returned to Catholicism shortly before his death. Antoine d'Estrées attended church services in his own house, but never displayed any deep faith. And Gabrielle's younger brother, François-Annibal, promptly resigned his bishopric and became a layman when the death of his brother made him the heir to their father's title and estates.

On the maternal side, there was no evidence of any religious belief of any kind. The Babou sisters earned their notoriety, and Françoise was the most depraved of the lot. Gabrielle followed closely in her mother's footsteps during the period of her simultaneous affairs with Henry and Bellegarde, and although her conduct improved, she displayed no interest in religion. Unlike many great ladies, she kept no personal confessor attached to her suite, and a contemporary wrote that her library contained only one volume on religion, a missal, which she seldom read.

Catholicism, then, was a minor factor in her life, and the charges made against her by some of the more fanatical Huguenots to the effect that she was "conniving with the bishops" are groundless. She reached the conclusion, quietly and privately, that it would be in the King's best interest — and therefore her own — if he changed his religion. It was in that belief that she wrote to his sister.

It is impossible to conclude that she was proselytizing when she tried to persuade Henry to become a convert. Neither at that period nor at any later date was she on friendly terms with any clergyman, and the cardinals, bishops, and Huguenot ministers who were present at the court shunned her with stern impartiality. There is no evidence on record that anyone thanked her for the role she played in Henry's conversion, and the Pope later took brisk measures to prevent her marriage to the King.

But Gabrielle sought neither thanks nor credit. Her influence was great for the fundamental reason that she had no other ax to grind but Henry's, and he knew it.

8: THE CONVERSION, 1593

In the latter part of June and early portion of July 1593, Henry IV spent his days discussing with his Council the pros and cons of becoming a Catholic convert, and every evening, when his day's work was done, he continued to weigh the subject with Gabrielle. The political situation was more delicate than any in which Henry had ever been involved, and the consequences could not be predicted.

If he remained a Huguenot, the chances were great that he would wage a losing fight for his throne. If he changed his faith, there was no sure sign that he would triumph. Certainly he would alienate his Protestant supporters, and there was no guarantee that the Catholics would remain on his side. But neither he nor they had the final voice in the matter. For the first time in Henry's life, his future seemed to depend on the decision of another man.

That man was Clement VIII. A Florentine priest of great piety, he was probably the only man in Europe who worked as hard as Henry the Great. The Pope was a lover of peace, and it is an irony of history that he became embroiled in two of the most ferocious religious battles of the Renaissance, one with Henry and the other with Elizabeth I of England. He was the equal of both his formidable foes, and under his guidance the Church regained much of the strength it had lost during the previous century.

Pope Clement was a wise man, but he had his blind spots, and for a long time Henry of Navarre was the most prominent of them. Clement was unalterably opposed to Henry in 1593 and, with his ally, Philip of Spain, was the principal supporter of the League. He had excommunicated Henry long before the King sought conversion, and added insult to injury by writing an open letter to the people of France, declaring that Henry was not capable of reigning.

So the major question that confronted the King and his advisers was whether the Pope would accept a conversion. Two priests who were members of the clerical faction loyal to the crown had undertaken a supposedly "unofficial" journey to Rome in order to sound out the Holy See, but they returned to France empty-handed. Clement, like Henry, was not a man to reveal his strategy to his opponents.

Henry's conversion would be meaningless if Clement failed to sanction it, in which case the Béarnais would lose both his Catholic and his Huguenot supporters. Logic indicated, therefore, that the final decision was the Pope's.

But Henry, a student of history as well as of human nature, knew that logic had played little part in the Great Schism that had shaken the Church to its roots in the fourteenth and fifteenth centuries. Then the clergy and people of France had demonstrated their hatred of Italian domination when they had pledged their unqualified fealty to the Schismatic popes of Avignon, and Henry was inclined to believe that his subjects were true descendants of those courageous patriots.

The hesitation of Mayenne, the self-justifying speeches of the priests attending the meeting of the States-General in Paris, and the anguish of his own Catholic followers tended to confirm his view that, if he moved with sufficient caution, France would stand behind him, regardless of Clement's reaction.

The Council debated endlessly, but Gabrielle argued that the risk was small. In all other matters Henry's judgment of his people had been remarkably accurate, she told him, and she

112

saw no reason why he should doubt himself now. Wherever he rode, his subjects shouted, "To Mass!" and she was convinced that France would accept the conversion joyfully. As Henry listened to her night after night, gradually his own fears and doubts disappeared.

Sully, who hated the Catholics and was cordially detested in return, pays grudging tribute to the role played by Gabrielle in the King's conversion, declaring in his *Memoirs*, "The Dame Gabrielle d'Estrées, now flaunting the title of Marquise de Monceaux, was able to accomplish what no cardinal, bishop, or prince had been able to do. She, and she alone, was responsible for the King's failure to remain true to the faith for which so many of his friends had suffered and died. She alone flattered and bemused him, until he scarce knew what to think, and when his brain became addled by her seductive temptations, she used her sly wiles to speak of the benefits that he would reap if he became a papist.

"Eve was aided by the Serpent when she persuaded Adam to taste the Forbidden Fruit, but the d'Estrées needed the help of no Serpent. She herself was Evil Incarnate, and well did she do her work."

Unwittingly, Sully pays her a compliment when he adds, "The sycophants who flocked around her spoke in later days of the 'Peace d'Estrées' that followed the King's conversion, but there could have been no peace in the soul of the King, for he had abandoned the faith in which he had been tutored."

D'Aubigné also disapproved of the part played by Gabrielle in Henry's conversion, and absented himself from the court for many months. Until the day of his death he refused to forgive Henry's apostasy, but not even he could hold out against Gabrielle's charm, and in 1595 he made his peace with her. At the time of the conversion, however, he was so angry that he almost lost his reason, and expresses himself on the subject of Gabrielle's influence in no uncertain terms:

"The conversion of the King was an act of treason committed against the people of France, and in that act the Marquise de Monceaux was the accomplice of the King.

"Many were the true believers, old friends, who pleaded earnestly and long, hoping the King would not waver. But the most powerful argument of all was the Marquise de Monceaux. At the beginning of her liaison with the King, the Marquise would have about her none who did not hold communion with the Reformed Church.

"She was for ever praising the trustworthiness of those who did hold it and complaining of the tyranny which the Catholics exercised over the King, and beseeching him to persevere in his religion. But when the hopes of attaining to royalty by marriage were presented to this lady and it was borne in upon her that not all the ministers in the world could dissolve her former marriage, save only the Pope of Rome, then did she entice and cajole him, in the manner of those who, having changed their opinions, boast that they have very carefully sifted their earlier convictions.

"From that time on, with the aid of her great beauty, at all convenient hours of the day and the night, she encouraged him in his leanings toward the change. Had she not been a supplicant on behalf of Rome, the King, who had persevered in his faith in the Reformed Church in spite of obstacles great and small, would not have changed. And by that change, he, who had been marked from birth by the touch of greatness, became as an ordinary man, weak, pitiful and confused. If there be Holy Justice in this world, she whose tongue destroyed a great King will be burned at the stake by the Roman Inquisition, for Surely she is a witch, if such there be."

D'Aubigné's bitter prejudice is understandable, and certainly is an effective reply to those of Henry's biographers who claim he made up his own mind, unaided.

In mid-July a final decision was reached, and Henry began to take instruction in Catholicism from the Archbishop of Bourges, the Grand Almoner of France. The Protestant members of his Council were disappointed, but were forced to admit that, if his gamble proved effective, he would win his greatest victory.

A story has persisted for centuries that the Béarnais was not sincere in his conversion, and that he undertook it solely for political reasons. According to one of the most famous lines ever attributed to him, he supposedly said, "Paris is well worth a Mass." That sentence does not appear in any of his written works, however, and whether he actually made the remark can be debated endlessly.

Of far greater importance is that he tried, to the best of his ability, to lead a good life, and after his conversion followed his new faith to the letter.

Once his decision was made, he acted swiftly, and as he could not be received into the Church at Notre Dame or the cathedral at Reims, he chose Saint-Denis, the church closest to Paris. On July 20, accompanied by Gabrielle, he proceeded to Mantes, where, by arrangement, he met Catherine. Madame was crushed when she heard the news, but carefully refrained from weeping in her brother's presence. Later, when she and Gabrielle were alone, the tears flowed freely. Desolate as she was, she agreed to make no attempt to persuade her brother to change his mind. She did not intend to witness the ceremony, of course, and Gabrielle tactfully remained behind with her when Henry rode to Saint-Denis on July 22.

The following morning the King wrote a letter to his mistress in his own hand: "I arrived early last night, and was importuned by the priests until bedtime. We believe that peace will be concluded this day. As for myself, I am in the hands of the Leaguers. I am to speak with the bishops this morning.

"In addition to the troops I demanded for your escort yesterday, I am sending you fifty trusty arquebuses. The hope that I have of seeing you tomorrow stays my hand from writing more today.

"On Sunday I take the perilous plunge.

"At the moment of writing to you, a hundred troublesome people are hanging round my neck — they make me hate Saint-Denis as much as you hate Mantes. Farewell, my heart; come early tomorrow, I beg."

Henry's comment to the effect that he was about to "take the perilous plunge" has often been cited as proof that he regarded his conversion flippantly. Others consider it certain evidence that he was in earnest. No attempt is made here to evaluate the remark, but there can be no question about the solemnity of the conference that followed the writing of his letter.

Complete and separate accounts of the meeting were kept by a royal secretary and a monsignor on the staff of the Archbishop of Bourges. The two records tally in every respect.

Present were the Archbishop, the Bishops of Chartres, Nantes, Mans, and Perron, and the Bishop Elect of Evreux. All were distinguished theologians who had been chosen with care for the function they were being called upon to perform. It is interesting to observe that in the long session, which lasted from six in the morning until one o'clock in the afternoon, the King, rather than his spiritual peers, led the discussion.

"Must one pray to all the Saints?" Henry asked early in the meeting, and the bishops replied in the affirmative.

He wanted to know, too, whether Auricular Confession was obligatory, and was told that it was.

His most searching questions concerned the authority of the Pope, and the reply was blunt: "He has absolute authority in all matters spiritual, and in regard to temporal matters, can interfere, to the prejudice of kings and kingdoms."

This reply did not satisfy Henry, and he pursued the subject, asking what would happen if he and the Pope should disagree on a temporal matter concerning the welfare of the people of France. The Bishops, all of whom were his supporters, assured him they could not imagine the possibility that such a situation would arise. Henry was content with their answer, and it seems to have been implicitly understood by everyone present that only one man would sit on the throne of France.

When the discussion turned to the Eucharist and the Real Presence, Henry promptly declared, "Here I have no doubts, for I have always believed it."

News of the meeting soon reached Paris, and when large, cheering crowds began to gather in the streets, the officers of the League became alarmed. An exhortation was published, addressed to all French Catholics and signed by several cardinals and bishops. The document stated that Henry's forthcoming conversion was invalid. Ecclesiastics and laymen were forbidden, on pain of excommunication, to attend the ceremony at Saint-Denis or to respond in any way to the King's public appeal, made to all of his subjects, to witness the event.

Parisians ignored the exhortation, and on Sunday, July 25, a huge crowd left the city for Saint-Denis.

Henry had given serious consideration to the question of whether the ceremony should be conducted by Cardinal de Bourbon, and had discussed the matter at length with his cousin. Both had agreed that Rome would be sensitive and the French members of the League touchy. Therefore, they concluded, nothing would be gained by rubbing salt in open wounds. The Archbishop of Bourges, assisted by the others who had taken part in the conference two days earlier, was in charge.

Henry, dressed from neck to toe in white satin, but wearing his familiar plumed, black hat, rode through the streets of Saint-Denis to the church at nine o'clock in the morning, followed by princely relatives, members of the Council, other crown officials, and an impressively large number of high-ranking noblemen. The troops of his personal guard led the procession, and no one lost sight of the significance of the presence of standard-bearers carrying the ensigns and pennants that the King had won in battle.

The streets were strewn with flowers, huge tapestries hung from balconies, and the crowd was so dense that it was difficult for Henry and his party to make their way through it. Again and again the procession halted, and a grinning Henry removed his hat and greeted his subjects. The Parisians responded with the fervent cry, "Long live the King!" and their shouts were a guarantee that he had triumphed over the League.

The Archbishop of Bourges, who stood at the entrance to the church, silenced the crowd and asked, "Who are you?"

Henry replied in a loud voice, "I am the King."

"What would you?"

"I would be received into the pale of the Roman Catholic Apostolic Church." Henry dropped to his knees and took an oath of abjuration. Then, after handing the Archbishop a written copy of the same words, he entered the church. The cheers of the crowd assembled inside were so loud that the voices of the choir could not be heard, and order was restored with difficulty. The oath of abjuration was repeated, the Bishop Elect of Evreux heard the King's confession in a booth behind the altar, and the Bishop of Nantes celebrated High Mass.

Only one woman was present in the church. Gabrielle, dressed in a gown of white satin cut from the same bolt of cloth as the King's doublet, sat alone in a corner, protected from view by brocaded screens. Members of the League later charged that the clergymen had objected to her presence, but that Henry had refused to become a convert unless she was there to witness the event. There is no evidence available to substantiate the Leaguers' charge.

After a Te Deum had been sung and coins thrown to the crowd gathered outside the church, Henry and his suite rode slowly to his lodgings, a château on the far side of the town. Gabrielle, heavily veiled and with a strong escort, followed by a circuitous route.

Great care was taken, up to this point, to make certain that the King's mistress should offend no one. But later, when Henry and his guests dined in the open on the grounds of the château, caution was thrown aside. The people, many thousands of whom had flocked to the scene, were free to gape at the royal party across the moat, and everyone could see that Gabrielle d'Estrées, Marquise de Monceaux, sat at the King's left, the place of honor on his right being occupied by the Archbishop of Bourges, who delivered a sermon at the conclusion of the meal.

That evening Henry and the male members of his party mounted their horses and rode to Montmartre, where once more vast crowds gathered to cheer him. Gabrielle, again wearing her heavy veil, was waiting for Henry when he emerged from the church on the butte, and together they watched a gigantic display of fireworks, which, of course, was plainly visible in Paris, stretching below them. Henry was losing no opportunity to wage psychological warfare against the League.

Paris was delirious with joy, and the troops of the League could not prevent the citizens from lighting huge bonfires in every part of the city. Mayenne and the Spaniards were astonished when the women of Paris, who knew every tidbit of gossip, gathered in groups and shouted, "Long live Gabrielle!"

In the last attempt to stem the tide of popular opinion, which was turning so rapidly in Henry's favor, the League decided on desperate measures. Rather than attack the Béarnais directly, it was decided to concentrate on Gabrielle, and a monk named Guarinus, who was a celebrated preacher, was given the task of excoriating her.

He preached several sermons of vehement abuse, but the crowds hissed him. Later, when they began to pelt him with garbage, the officials of the League realized they had made a mistake and Guarinus was silenced. After that, a number of delegates to the States-General, knowing that Paris would inevitably fall to the King, secretly left the city and sought interviews with Gabrielle, hoping she might intercede on their behalf with Henry.

She received everyone from the enemy camp who approached her, and in each instance Henry was happy to accept the oath of fealty from a former foe.

The King sent letters to the parliaments of every province in the country, announcing his conversion and asking support. And before the end of July he sent a mission to Rome to lay the groundwork for an official conciliation with Pope Clement. Mayenne, seeing the large, clear handwriting on the wall, ignored the protests of the Spaniards and the Papal Legate and signed a three-months truce with the King. Less than three weeks later Mayenne decided he needed more of a breathing space, and proposed that the armistice be extended until the end of the year. Henry, with everything to gain and little to lose, graciously agreed. For all practical purposes, the States-General assembled by the League was no more.

One immediate, major task remained to be performed after the conversion. The Huguenot leaders who had stood behind Henry for so many years were angry and fearful, and it was necessary to mollify and reassure them. Henry summoned each of his old friends to a private conference, and kept no record of what was said. Apparently he promised his Protestant nobles that, although he himself was now a Catholic, he would continue to fight zealously for their rights.

Either Henry or Gabrielle conceived the idea that each royal interview should be followed by a less formal meeting with the King's mistress, and Sully leaves, in his *Memoirs*, a biased account of these sessions:

"Each of us who had sworn to uphold the King of Navarre, a faithful member of the Reformed Church, was now required to visit the salon of the d'Estrées, mistress of the Catholic King of France. She played her role with pretty gestures, sweet exclamations, and fervent protestations that all would be as it had been in former years.

"Having nowhere else to turn, the great gentlemen believed her, pitifully hanging upon her words and accepting her promises. I, alone of all that number, saw through her pretenses, but knowing she would report me unfavorably to the King if I permitted her to see that I knew she was lying, pretended to accept at face value her false words."

The old man writing that account apparently forgot the Edict of Nantes, which guaranteed the Huguenots virtually all they had been struggling to obtain since the beginning of the Reformation. Sully's angry denunciations to the contrary, Gabrielle d'Estrées kept her promises, and so did Henry IV. In fact, Sully's memory was so poor he failed to remember that he himself was one of the Protestant nobles who worked with Gabrielle in helping to reconcile the two factions during the months prior to the promulgation of the Edict.

In any event, Gabrielle achieved a minor miracle in 1593. She, who more than any other person had been responsible for the King's apostasy, was able to win the trust of leading Huguenots less than one month later. It seems reasonable to assume that a keen mind was developing behind the façade of a lovely face.

9: PARIS IN THE SPRINGTIME, 1594

The truce between Henry and Mayenne ended at midnight on December 31, 1593, and one minute later a large, well-equipped royal army began to surround the city and lay siege to it. On January 1, the town of Meux fell into the King's hands, and Paris was cut off from all of its suburbs. The fall of the capital was expected at any time, and as Gabrielle wanted to be present for the great event, she elected to live in the field, with the army.

No act that she had performed up to that time better demonstrated the change that had taken place in her character. She who had loved luxury and had refused to travel when the sun was not shining now deliberately and of her own free will lodged in a draughty tent pegged on the heights of Montmartre. The mid-winter weather was bitterly cold, snow fell daily, and the roof of the tent sagged. But Gabrielle made no complaint.

"I accompanied our father on a visit to my sister, at Twelfth Night," Diane writes in her *Memorial*, "and we found her in the best of spirits, even though she lacked every convenience and comfort which formerly she had held dear. She spent her days in the company of knights wounded in the siege, and her nights were devoted to the King, she insuring that he lacked neither good food nor pleasant conversation."

Gabrielle's good cheer paid handsome dividends. As previously noted, her allowance was increased on February 1, and on that same date the royal household of Navarre relinquished overlordship of a large estate, the manor of Vandeuil, to Messire d'Escoubleau de Sourdis, the Bishop of

Maillezai, who was the eldest son of Isabelle de Sourdis. Two days later the Bishop announced that he had acquired the property, which was worth the huge sum of fifty thousand gold crowns, on behalf of his cousin, Gabrielle.

That was only the beginning; as Henry's fortunes improved, he deluged his mistress with gifts. A combination of love, sin, and royal luck made her wealthy in 1594.

Two months after she had been given Vandeuil, the King ordered the Treasurer-General of France, in a commission dated April 8, to give and grant to Gabrielle "all and sundry of the moneys due to His Majesty and proceeding from the special taxes levied upon the country and duchy of Normandy, by his lieutenants-general and others, up to and including the year 1593, for ammunition, forage, rations, provisions, gun horses, soldiers' pay, impositions on goods and merchandise, and in general on all accounts, of what nature soever, excepting only the general taxes of the realm."

The French were as reluctant to pay their taxes in the sixteenth century as most people are in the twentieth, and in November of the same year Henry sent a letter to the magistrates-in-ordinary of the Court of Accounts at Rouen, ordering them "to collect the said taxes, as His Majesty had commissioned and deputed them."

On April 18, 1594, Gabrielle received the sum of 21,033 francs, which had been collected from newly appointed officeholders, who followed the feudal tradition of making small gifts to the sovereign upon receiving their commissions. And four days later Henry officially granted her an additional 2,200 francs "to be derived from the sums brought in by the sale and additional costs of lawsuits in the duchy of Normandy, cognizable in the Parliament of Rouen."

On April 30, the King gave her an unspecified sum "paid to his lawyers out of the revenue of bonded salt, all except 10,000 francs, which His Majesty gave to the Comte de Thorigny."

On August 31, she received the most dazzling gift to date, "all and sundry of the moneys arising from the sales, amended and supplemented, heretofore effected, of all the wastelands and other demesnes of the duchy of Alençon and earldom of Evreux, belonging to Monsieur, the King's brother, lately deceased."

That Henry's younger brother, who had spent most of his life in Navarre, had died and thus given the King the right to dispose of his property, was an accident of fate. But the other gifts were concrete signs that Henry was faring better in the world. Paris, of course, was the key to his success.

As the siege of the capital continued, its citizens were becoming more vehemently royalist, and Henry, always sensitive to the feelings of his subjects, deliberately refrained from shelling the city, which he could have captured far more quickly had he used his artillery. The people were grateful to him, and Louis, Comte de Belin, the Governor, secretly opened negotiations with the enemy, hoping to deliver Paris to Henry intact.

Mayenne became suspicious of the Governor and replaced him with Charles de Cossé, Comte de Brissac. The choice was one of the most inept blunders ever made by Mayenne in a career that had never been noted for its brilliance. De Brissac for years had played a double game, secretly supporting Henry while maintaining his place in the upper echelons of the League.

His appointment, late in February, soon showed astonishing results. Gates were left unguarded, soldiers frequently were absent from their posts, and citizens often wandered out of the city to fraternize with the enemy. Mayenne knew when he had been beaten, and on March 6 he and his family left Paris under a flag of truce. The duke, a portly man who was too heavy to ride a horse, sat weeping in his carriage, declaring he would never see Paris again.

The fall of the capital to the royalists was no longer in doubt, but Henry was impelled by strictly personal considerations to obtain its capitulation at the earliest possible date. Gabrielle was pregnant, and although she endured the hardships of makeshift camp life with fortitude, refusing to return to the home of her father or to the palace of her aunt and uncle at Chartres, Henry was afraid her health might be impaired if she continued to live in a tent.

"My mistress," he told his Constable and Biron, "is not a gypsy, and it grieves me that she will not change her mode of living until Paris is mine."

Negotiations with key League nobles were intensified, and on March 15 a promise was obtained from Hector, Marquis de Villars, to deliver Rouen to the King. (This is the first appearance of the name of Villars in the annals of the Bourbon family, but not the last. The marquis eventually became one of Henry's closest associates, a member of his Council, and a field commander of his army. And the association continued for generations: Claude Louis Hector, Prince de Martignes and Duc de Villars, grandson of the marquis, who was one of the greatest generals in French history, was the "strong man" who implemented the grandiose policies of Henry's self-aggrandizing grandson, Louis XIV.)

De Brissac, aided by the Provost of Paris, a member of the minor nobility named Le Huillier, secretly worked out the details for the delivery of Paris to Henry, in spite of the presence of a large Spanish garrison in the city. Royalist troops and regiments of Frenchmen ostensibly loyal to the League gathered on both sides of the Porte Neuve on the night of March 21, and at five o'clock in the morning all was ready. The gates were opened, and the King rode into his capital, refusing the protection of any troops except a small honor guard of arquebuses. "The crown and the people," he declared, "are indivisible."

News of his arrival spread so rapidly that de Brissac must have anticipated the event by stationing heralds in various parts of the city. Deliriously happy citizens poured into the streets by the thousands to welcome the King, and a huge crowd accompanied him to Notre Dame, where he heard the Te Deum sung.

His aides were busy, too. The Constable surrounded the Spanish garrison, which surrendered, and was ordered to leave instantly. Cannon and scaling ladders, catapults and battering rams were delivered to the royalists, but the ten thousand foreigners were permitted to keep their small arms. Henry joined his Constable, and they sat side by side on their horses, watching the minions of Philip II march out of the city, their pennants dipping in salute.

De Brissac was wasting no time, either, and as soon as the last company of Spaniards had withdrawn, a delegation of former League officers escorted the King from the Porte Saint-Denis to the Louvre. There, standing on the parade ground in front of the palace, he took the salute from the French regiments that had abandoned the League, and promptly incorporated them into his own army. The Comte de Brissac was rewarded on the spot with the gold baton of a Marshal of France.

That night Gabrielle slept in her father's town house, the Hôtel d'Estrées, and the King slept at the Louvre. Only the

Bastille continued to hold out, but the recalcitrant Leaguers who had barricaded themselves in the old fortress, realizing their cause was hopeless, surrendered on March 27. Before sundown that day, Henry ordered the Lily flag hoisted over the Louvre, thus notifying his enemies that his occupation of Paris was complete.

When, forty-eight hours later, Villars opened the gates of Rouen to the royalists, the two most important cities in France were Henry's. Underscoring the importance of these developments, on March 30, the Parliament of Paris issued a formal declaration, posting printed copies in every quarter of the city:

> The Court revokes and declares null and void all that has been done, ordered, and decreed by the so-called deputies of the assembly held in the town of the realm, considering them as no more than the deeds of private individuals, chosen for the most part by the factious spirits of the kingdom, the friends of Spain, having no legal right whatever; and it forbids the aforesaid so-called deputies to assume any authority or meeting in this town or elsewhere, under the penalty of being looked upon as destroyers of the peace and guilty of high treason, and charges those of the aforesaid so-called deputies who are yet at this present in the town of Paris to retire each to his own house, there to take the oath of allegiance before a judge duly appointed for the purpose by His Catholic and Apostolic Majesty, Henry of France and of Navarre, and dwell in obedience to the King.

Meanwhile, Henry and the members of his Council were busily debating at the Louvre. Some members were urging the King to make his formal entry into Paris, a gesture that was considered essential. He, however, believed that the time was ripe to strike new blows against his disorganized foes, and in the face of heavy opposition, decided that formalities could wait. The weather was turning warmer, the ground was drying, and conditions were perfect for operations in the field. Senior officers took command of various columns — de Brissac being given one of them — and the royalist corps marched off to invest a number of towns still held by the League. Henry, incapable of standing aside idly while others did his work for him, undertook the siege of Laon.

Gabrielle insisted on accompanying him, even though her pregnancy was far advanced.

"Our Aunt de Sourdis," Diane writes in her *Memorial*, "was much concerned over the welfare of my sister, and earnestly persuaded her, abetted by the pleas of the King, to end her confinement in Paris. But my sister was firm in her declarations that her place was at the side of the King, and none could dissuade her from riding with him to Laon, our Aunt de Sourdis accompanying her thither."

Gabrielle was not play-acting for Henry's benefit. She had become the liaison with Leaguers who were anxious to obtain royal pardons, Huguenots again were demonstrating their trust in her, and she believed the services she was rendering her lover could be performed by no one else. She was not disturbed by her pregnancy, and unlike most great ladies of her day, did not retire to her couch.

"The d'Estrées," Sully sourly declares in his *Memoirs*, "thought of herself as a minister of state, and acted with as much authority as though she held the King's commission and seal. She seemed little concerned about the forthcoming event of motherhood, and the anxiety of the King was far greater than her own, she making light of discomfort, so great was her love of power."

The château of Laon was located some distance from the town, and Gabrielle, preferring to remain closer to Henry, took up residence in the small village of Coney, just outside the walls of Laon. There, as she held conferences and awaited the birth of her child, she could hear the roar of cannon, the rattle of arquebus fire, and the screams of the dying and wounded.

Bellegarde, who had been restored to royal favor after Henry had become confident that his mistress was no longer afflicted with a roving eye, gives a somewhat stunned appraisal of her situation at Coney, writing in his *Amours*, "Gabrielle, who carried in her belly the first child of the head of the house of Bourbon, lived at Coney in circumstances as mean as those of the wife of a fishmonger or stonemason. The house was small, furnished only with those essentials necessary to all persons for daily existence, and was so cramped that only her aunt and two serving-women could reside there with her. The house contained but a single chimney, one side opening on the chamber where the food was prepared, the other on the private chamber of Gabrielle. Never had one of her station dwelt in circumstances so humble."

On the morning of June 7, 1594, two royal surgeons, three midwives, and Isabelle de Sourdis milled around in the crowded bedroom while Henry, temporarily leaving the siege in Biron's hands, paced up and down outside the house like any ordinary father-to-be. Shortly before noon Gabrielle gave birth to a son, and the elated King immediately named the infant Caesar. It might be mentioned in passing that his choice of names was indicative of his opinion regarding his own status and that of his family, their second son being called Alexander.

The troops were given kegs of spirits, military operations were suspended for the day, and the cannon fired a salute of one hundred and one salvos, as though the baby was legitimate and heir to the throne.

Two weeks later the pleasure of Gabrielle was marred by the death of François-Louis, the elder of her brothers, who was killed before the walls of Laon at the age of nineteen. François-Annibal, who recently had been appointed Bishop of Noyon by Henry, quickly filed with the King papers of resignation from the clergy and, assuming the title of marquis, began his long and distinguished career.

The death of François-Louis was the only misfortune that spoiled the happiness of Gabrielle in the golden summer of 1594. The arrival of her son was a lucky event, according to her fortune-tellers, Diane reported in her *Memorial*. The soothsayers happened to be right.

Biron captured two large convoys carrying provisions to Laon, and the town surrendered on July 21. Poitiers, Concarneau, and Quimper fell in quick succession. Provence was delivered from the yoke of the Spaniards; Henry's ally, Elizabeth of England, sent him troops to help him hold Bretagne, and the Dutch also dispatched a strong contingent for the same purpose.

On August 12, Henry signed a treaty with one of the most capable of his foes, Louis, Marshal de Balagny and Prince de Cambrai, who later became his supporter and, afterwards, the husband of Diane d'Estrées. Towns were now surrendering rapidly, and on a single day, August 18, the King accepted the pennants of Beauvais, Doullens, Péronne, and Saint-Malo.

The time had arrived for the formal entry into Paris, and Gabrielle was sufficiently recovered to take part in the triumphal ceremony. Never had she stood higher in the King's favor, and Henry, who believed and lived according to the principle that time was precious, spent a portion of every morning and afternoon making gurgling, paternal noises at his first-born son.

On Tuesday, September 13, Henry and Gabrielle arrived in Paris, traveling incognito, and the King carefully supervised the preparations for the mammoth celebration. For reasons that remain obscure, the King and his mistress suddenly became sensitive to "public opinion," and Gabrielle spent the night at the Hôtel d'Estrées while Henry, who could not appear at the Louvre incognito, went to the house of a nobleman named Dumortier. They had planned to remain in the city for two nights, but on the morning following their arrival, Henry became concerned about the health and welfare of Caesar, who was lodged at a royal dwelling in nearby Saint-Germain-en-Laye. The officials in charge of the preparations made hasty reports to the monarch, and Caesar's parents returned to the side of the baby shortly before noon.

At seven o'clock on the evening of September 15, the royal party arrived in Paris for the triumphal entry. Eight regiments of troops, four commanded by the Constable and four by Biron, marched in the parade. Every nobleman of consequence in the kingdom was in attendance, and the entire Council of France had assembled for the occasion, as well as the Council of Navarre.

Four cardinals, one of them Cardinal de Bourbon, and a score of bishops were waiting at Notre Dame. Every man, woman, and child in Paris who was able to walk was in the streets, and Henry, aware of the value of a spectacle, had provided the citizens with thousands of torches, which burned brightly. Tapestries and flowers decorated balconies, streamers fluttered everywhere, increasing the danger that a fire might sweep the city, and music was provided by military bands and church choirs.

Members of the diplomatic corps, escorted by de Brissac, were first in the line of march, and went straight to the Ile de la Cité, where they awaited the King in front of the cathedral.

The Constable's regiments, two of cavalry and two of infantry, preceded the dignitaries. This was a wise precaution, as the troops could clear the path for the great ladies and gentlemen, who otherwise might have been trampled by the enthusiastic crowds.

Gabrielle, making her first public appearance as a member of the royal suite, held the place of honor, and actually preceded the King in the procession. It was the only occasion in the entire reign of Henry IV that anyone, male or female, took precedence over him.

She was carried in a litter, and the crowd went wild. She was dressed in a gown of pale green velvet that was noticed by no one, for her jewels were the most magnificent Paris had ever seen. Henry, the most miserly monarch in Christendom, had opened his purse and emptied it for her; no contemporary was able to guess the value of the gems she wore. Thousands of pearls were sewn onto her costume, and she wore a tiara, necklace, and earrings of diamonds so glittering that their beauty became legendary. For the next century it was said that their brilliance made the torches look dim.

Over her shoulders was thrown an unadorned cape of black satin, which at first glance appears to be a strange addition to her costume. But Henry was demonstrating, once again, that he knew what he was doing. He himself, riding a white stallion directly behind her litter, was dressed from head to toe in unornamented black. It would seem that he wanted to call attention to her rather than to himself, although he was shrewd enough to realize that the people would applaud his understated garb.

M. Desclozeaux sums up the King's probable motive in his monograph when he declares, "It seems that from this moment Henry wished Gabrielle to take part in his triumph and to be associated with him in his royalty."

It was of significance, too, that Gabrielle accompanied the King to Notre Dame and sat beside him in the royal pew during the service. She had taken her place as his consort for the whole world to see, and was no longer forced to hide behind screens. The clergymen, who had been so sensitive to her proximity at Saint-Denis, now accepted her new public role without a murmur, and from that time forward she lived in the glare of royal publicity.

Obviously, Henry was responsible for her emergence from the shadows, the birth of Caesar, it seems, having changed his attitude on the question of public recognition of his mistress. His new course required courage, as his dispute with the Vatican was no nearer a solution, but the King apparently was unconcerned. Most of France was now under his rule, and Gabrielle was closer to him than any other living person.

10: THE DIVORCE, 1594

The birth of Caesar altered the relationship of Gabrielle and Henry in other ways, too, and the King's reasons for using his prestige and power to obtain a divorce for his mistress at last become clear. The child had no family name and, under the law, should have been acknowledged as the son of Nicolas d'Amerval. Neither the first citizen of France nor the child's mother had the right to retain possession of the infant's person, and had d'Amerval elected to demand custody of the boy, Henry could not have prevented any court in the realm from granting the Sieur de Liencourt's claim.

The King was anxious to acknowledge the paternity of his son, whose resemblance to him was distinct, but d'Amerval stood in his path, and any property given to the baby automatically would be assigned to Gabrielle's legal husband as custodian. There were other pressing considerations. Gabrielle herself had become a major landowner, and the fact that d'Amerval had made no move to get his hands on her property did not necessarily mean he would remain quiet forever.

Obviously, something had to be done, but Henry had not yet made up his own mind to marry his mistress. Marriage was one of the strongest weapons in a monarch's diplomatic arsenal, and even though Margot was the uncrowned Queen of France, Henry's envoys to Rome had given him to understand that Pope Clement might grant him a divorce if, thereafter, he contracted an alliance satisfactory to the Vatican. So, no matter how much Gabrielle might dream of becoming Henry's wife, the realities of power politics forced the Béarnais to consider other possibilities.

On July 2, 1594, a scant three and a half weeks after Caesar's birth, the King summoned Chiverny and discussed the situation at length with his chief legal adviser who, as Isabelle de Sourdis' lover, was for all practical purposes a member of the family. "His Majesty told me repeatedly," Chiverny writes in his *Memoirs*, "of his earnest desire to bestow every honor at his disposal on his son, and he requested that I find some means of creating the infant legitimate in the eyes of the law.

"We who were members of His Majesty's Council knew that no marriage could be contemplated by him with the mother of Caesar, many kings and potentates having pressed claims on behalf of their daughters, nieces, and other near relatives. I had anticipated such an interview with His Majesty, and informed him forthwith that he need not marry the mother of Caesar in order that the princeling should be recognized as the legitimate offspring of royalty. There was precedent which would enable His Majesty, under letters patent in the form of a decree, to declare the said child his lawful issue."

When Henry realized that a stroke of the pen would make Caesar legitimate, provided that Nicolas d'Amerval were no longer in a position to make a claim, he took immediate action, and attorneys started preparing Gabrielle's divorce suit.

The first hurdle to be overcome was the ticklish question of where the case should be heard. Gabrielle and the Sieur de Liencourt had been married at Noyon, and custom decreed that they should apply to the ecclesiastical authorities of that diocese for a dissolution of the marriage. But François-Annibal d'Estrées' nomination as Bishop of Noyon had been forwarded to Rome for approval, and even though the young man had subsequently resigned from the clergy, Henry had not yet sent the resignation on to the Pope.

Chiverny, ever conscious of Clement's opposition to the King, thought it less than tactful to notify the Vatican that a young man bearing the name of d'Estrées had chosen to reject a life in the Church. The Chancellor recommended that Henry hold François-Annibal's resignation in private and that, for the time being, Gabrielle's brother should continue to exercise the functions of Bishop Elect.

That matter having been settled, it became impossible for Gabrielle to file her suit in Noyon, as Henry's foes would raise a storm, and even his friends might gag at such an abuse of power. The King was afraid d'Amerval might oppose the divorce action, and as it would be senseless to give him grounds for such a stand, Noyon definitely was ruled out.

The prelates of the church in Amiens, on the other hand, previously supporters of the League, were now anxious to win Henry's favor. The King decided to give them their chance, and on August 27, 1594, Gabrielle addressed a formal supplication to the bishop of that diocese:

"Dame Gabrielle d'Estrées, supported by her aunts and sisters and other relations, puts it before you that, as she was only eighteen years of age at the time of her marriage, she must have been unduly compelled by her father and other male relations to marry Messire Nicolas d'Amerval, Sieur de Liencourt, to whom she has been wedded for the space of two years or thereabouts, in compliance with the marriage laws."

She claimed that her husband was impotent, and, adding that she had taken her aunts, sisters, and other relations into her confidence, declared that they had advised her "to appeal to you, as to an ordinary judge, for means of an escape from so unfortunate a position."

The appeal ended on a firm note: "In consideration of which, my Lord Bishop, may it please you to grant the supplicant authority to summon her husband into your presence, to the end that they both may come before you, that the facts aforementioned and others, may be verified for a separation, and that the aforesaid marriage be declared null and void."

The document bore the signatures of Gabrielle, of the inevitable Isabelle Babou de Sourdis, and of Anne de Maridor, wife of Jean-Antoine de Longueval, Seigneur de Barancourt, Gabrielle's uncle by marriage. The paper was presented by a young attorney of considerable promise, Paul Accard, who had recently "resigned" as a member of Chiverny's staff. A few weeks after the end of the trial, late in December, Accard was knighted and given a higher place in Chiverny's office.

The magistrate of Amiens, François Roze, acting in the name of the bishop, signed a summons requesting d'Amerval to reply to the petition, but for unknown reasons nothing happened for more than a month. Finally, on September 30, Abbé Adrien Vérité, Prebendary Canon of the church of Amiens, signed an order commanding d'Amerval to appear before him on October 6. The Canon further requested neighboring ecclesiastical judges to allow the proceedings to go forward, if necessary, through the territories of their jurisdiction.

Although the wheels seemed to have been spinning more forcefully, d'Amerval was not at home, and the summons was received by his brother. October 6 came, and the Sieur de Liencourt did not appear. The court adjourned for four days awaiting him, but he apparently had vanished. On October 13, Accard appeared before the jurists to declare that d'Amerval was actually in Amiens and request that a new summons be issued.

As a matter of fact, d'Amerval was making no secret of his whereabouts: he and his daughters were spending the autumn and winter at the château of his mother, Dame Adrienne Cauchon de Maupas, just outside the city. Inasmuch as Henry and Gabrielle were anxious to bring the case to a successful conclusion as rapidly as possible, the many delays are inexplicable. Father Christophe Fillet, an Amiens priest, finally delivered the new summons to d'Amerval on December 8, and the Sieur de Liencourt replied, "I will satisfy them and go myself to the place whither I am called, or will send someone thither in my stead."

It can only be assumed that other, more pressing matters occupied Henry's attention until December. No attempt was made to hold d'Amerval in contempt of court for his failure to respond earlier, and no reason was given, either then or subsequently, for the many weeks of inactivity.

Now, however, the wheels did turn. Gabrielle arrived in Amiens on December 15, and after duly appearing in person before François Roze, the magistrate, she took up residence in a house that Accard had rented for the purpose. According to custom, the attorney resided there, too.

On the same day, one Pierre Roche appeared before the court, announcing that he was an attorney and was appearing on behalf of d'Amerval. Accard immediately protested that the issue was a personal one and that d'Amerval would have to appear himself. The following morning he again went to the magistrate and injected an important new element into the case. D'Amerval's first wife, Anne Gouffier, had been Antoine d'Estrées' cousin, and Accard emphasized that Church law specifically prohibited a widower from marrying a relative of his previous spouse.

In midmorning on December 16, His Catholic and Apostolic Majesty, Henry, King of France and of Navarre, arrived in Amiens. The announced purpose of his visit was to accept the capitulation of several nearby towns, all of which happened to have been in his hands for periods ranging from six months to three years. He took up official residence at a château outside the city, but he never set foot in the place. Instead he went straight to the house that Accard had rented, and where Gabrielle was waiting for him.

The "coincidence" of the King's arrival at a time when the divorce case was being heard fooled no one. Certainly Nicolas d'Amerval could not have believed that Henry had come to Amiens for any purpose other than that of using his mere presence to influence the court.

D'Amerval's position was unenviable. Regardless of whether the charge that he was impotent was true, a matter that will be discussed subsequently in greater detail, he was undoubtedly suffering from the airing of the question. But he could not evade it, nor could he hide behind a lawyer. The maximum penalty for contempt of court was a life sentence in a dungeon, and if the Sieur de Liencourt failed to go before the magistrate, he had good cause to believe that, at Henry's urging, the court would send him to prison.

Cornered, d'Amerval could fight back only in secret. Within hours of Henry's arrival, the Sieur made out a new will, in which he left Gabrielle's property — over which he would have no control once the divorce became final — to his daughters. Then, in a pathetic attempt to clear his name with future generations, he added a final paragraph:

"And because that, to obey the King and in fear of my life, I am about to consent to the dissolution of my marriage with the Dame d'Estrées, in accordance with the petition lodged with the magistrate at Amiens, I declare and protest before God that if the dissolution be ordered and brought to pass, it will be done by force, against my will, and only out of respect for the

King, seeing that the assertion, confession, and declaration that I am impotent and incapable is untrue. In witness whereof I have signed this my testament and this declaration, which I have written by my own hand, and which I intend, hereafter, to be used by myself and by my children to nullify what shall have been done and ordered by the said magistrate to my harm, which testament and declaration I have wished to be kept secret, and to this end, have folded and closed the sheet of paper on which it is written, and sealed it with my seal, on which are imprinted my arms."

Two notaries witnessed his signature on an accompanying declaration stating that the attached sheet contained his will and testament. Then, having made his feeble attempt to protect what remained of his good name, d'Amerval appeared the same day before the magistrate and formally appointed Pierre Roche his attorney.

No man could have protested more vehemently against the pending dissolution of his marriage, but it is difficult to understand why the Sieur de Liencourt should have wanted to remain married to a woman who was the mistress of the King and the mother of the King's child. The paragraph leaving Gabrielle's property to his daughters affords a clue to d'Amerval's thinking; perhaps he was making a last, hopeless effort to obtain financial compensation for the many humiliations he had been made to suffer.

Whatever his reasons, he publicly reversed himself, and in the days that followed repeatedly told the court he was willing to end the marriage. He openly admitted to the magistrate that he was impotent, and freely made the same confession to the physicians who were ordered by the court to examine him. According to his own words in his will, he was prepared to make any admission because he was afraid he would lose his life if he opposed the King.

There is no evidence to indicate that Henry threatened him with death or other punishment, either directly or indirectly, if he fought for his rights. In fact, the King's conversations with Chiverny indicate that Henry believed the Sieur de Liencourt would put up a battle. As has previously been noted, Henry was opposed to the principle of assassination and murder, and never resorted to either. His policy toward those members of the League who surrendered to him or were captured by his forces was lenient, and he made every attempt to win their support.

Only in the case of Marshal de Biron did he display a different attitude. In 1606, when it became clear that Biron was the key figure in a Spanish-financed conspiracy against the crown, a formal trial was held, and every attempt was made throughout to give the Marshal the benefit of the doubt. The case against him was clear-cut, however, and as he was guilty of high treason, he was executed. He holds the unhappy distinction of being the only man whose death warrant Henry signed.

So, it would seem, d'Amerval's fears were groundless, and sprang from his own imagination. Nevertheless, even though the danger that frightened him was nonexistent, he cannot be blamed for feeling as he did. Even the most tenderhearted of monarchs possesses enormous powers, and Henry's sieges had given him an awesome reputation. D'Amerval, quite simply, was taking no more risks than necessary.

The morning of December 17 was devoted to legal formalities, in which the two principals, who came face to face for the first time since September 9, 1592, when Gabrielle had joined Henry at Noyon, admitted the jurisdiction of the court to try the case. At three o'clock that afternoon, Accard presented Gabrielle's petition, and Roche countered with d'Amerval's replies. Records of the trial reveal there were six major points:

• Gabrielle declared that she had married the Sieur de Liencourt about two years previously, "being unduly constrained thereto by her father, and other relations, who had greatly importuned her. She had never frequented his society nor borne him any friendship in consequence of a report having come to her ears concerning his health and indisposition." Roche replied that his client had no knowledge of the attitude taken toward the marriage by Gabrielle's father.

• "To prove that the report concerning his indisposition was true," Gabrielle claimed "that never from the day of their marriage had she known the said d'Amerval intimately." To this, the Sieur de Liencourt's attorney replied "that that which was contained therein had not come to his knowledge."

• Accard told the court, "From the time they were married, they had not known each other intimately, although they had lived together for some time." D'Amerval "confessed that that was true." The court immediately noted that there was a discrepancy between this acknowledgment and his denial of knowledge of the preceding point.

• Gabrielle's attorney declared "that, since her marriage, it had come to the knowledge of the petitioner that the said d'Amerval had had some secret malady since the decease of the late Madame Anne Gouffier, his first wife, and that this was the reason of his impotence." D'Amerval "confessed that that also which was contained therein was true."

• This charge, although neither side realized it at the time, was critically important. Accard said, "The deceased wife of the said Sieur de Liencourt was cousin to Sieur d'Estrées, father of the petitioner, of which fact the relations of the two parties took neither heed nor thought, but which was well known to the said Sieur d'Amerval, his mother, and others of his relations, and was a reason sufficient in itself for declaring the said marriage null and void and contracted against the holy laws and canons of the Roman Catholic Apostolic Church." D'Amerval "said also that he agreed with the contents of the said clause."

• Gabrielle's attorney further declared "that all of the foregoing statements were true, as the said Sieur d'Amerval knew full well, and that he had acknowledged and confessed them to several people and affirmed them to be true, to the said Dame d'Estrées." To this Roche said, on behalf of his client, "that, in respect of the sixth clause, he equally agreed with its contents and confessed them to be true."

D'Amerval, who was thoroughly confused after his blundering attempt to deny the second charge, was questioned at length by the court, and admitted all six charges. Gabrielle was questioned at the same session, and substantially repeated what her attorney had said. Both parties were asked if they were acting in collusion, and both firmly denied they had either spoken to each other or been in touch through third parties.

In the days that followed, Accard bore down heavily on the charge that d'Amerval was impotent. Magistrate Roze seemed far more interested in the family ties between Antoine d'Estrées and the Sieur de Liencourt's first wife, but most of Accard's witnesses talked about the husband's alleged infirmity, and others discussed Gabrielle's reluctance to marry him. Accard, in spite of his brilliance, seemed unable to realize he could win his case on technical grounds and that the court, aware of the fact that the whole country was watching, would hesitate before granting a divorce on the questionable issue of d'Amerval's alleged impotence.

On December 22, Gabrielle was called a second time. The magistrate asked her whether, in view of her husband's supposed infirmity, she would consent to live under the same roof with him as sister and brother. She replied, firmly, that she would not. Magistrate Roze inquired whether she had known of his impotence before marrying him, and again she replied in the negative, adding that at no time since the marriage had she consented to lie with d'Amerval. She told the court where she had been married, but could not recall the name of the priest who had performed the ceremony.

In all, she could have spent no more than fifteen minutes being interrogated, and then went back to the house where Henry was waiting for her.

Magistrate Roze took command of the proceedings, and the next two days were devoted to testimony by witnesses who swore to the family ties between Antoine d'Estrées and Anne Gouffier. Accard understood at last that here was a clear-cut issue, one on which the court could not be criticized, and he bent all his efforts on substantiating the testimony, producing genealogical charts and other documents for the edification of the magistrate.

Meanwhile d'Amerval was being subjected to fresh humiliations. Two physicians, Jehan Juvenis and one Lebouef, both of whom bore the title Physicians in Waiting to the King, interrogated the husband at his mother's château. He told them he had suffered a fall from his horse that had produced grave consequences, and the doctors reported back to the court, in a long, learned paper written in Latin, agreeing that he was impotent.

All France was laughing at d'Amerval, and Parisians were singing a ribald song about the trial:

A mare there was,
As lovely as she was frisky,
Who learned to her great dismay
That the married state was risky.
A stallion she married,
Only to find
He was a gelding, and harried.
Still wanting a fling,
To another she turned,
One who among stallions was king.

Chiverny, who arrived at Amiens on December 23 accompanied by Isabelle de Sourdis, duly reported to the King, and declares in his *Memoirs* that Henry was disturbed when he heard the song. Having himself used the weapon of satire to dull the effectiveness of the League's assembly in Paris, he was conscious of the potential impact of ridicule. His own public image was being harmed, and he decided the time had come to bring the trial to an end.

Final testimony was taken the following day, December 24, and the court adjourned, announcing it would render its verdict in due course.

Henry knew delays would be dangerous, and Chiverny admits in his *Memoirs* that he communicated the King's fears to Magistrate Roze. The court then had second thoughts on the matter, and the decision was prepared, signed, and deposited in the office of the Bishop of Amiens that same afternoon. It was not read to the attorneys until January 7, a week-long celebration of Christmas making this particular delay inevitable.

Gabrielle and Henry spent Christmas Day at Amiens, as the court session of the previous afternoon had detained them until sundown. The outcome of the trial could not have been in doubt, however, for a few days after they returned to Paris on December 27, a significant change took place in their living arrangements.

For the first time since Henry had occupied his capital, Gabrielle moved into the Louvre. A suite of rooms on the second floor, which stood near the King's own private chambers, had been prepared for her. Caesar and his nursemaids occupied still another suite directly across the corridor.

From that time forward, Gabrielle lived at the Louvre whenever Henry was in residence there. But she was sensitive to possible criticism, and François-Annibal remarks in his *Memoirs*, "My sister took a solemn vow upon the occasion of the commencement of her dwelling at the palace that only when the King was present would she consent to sleep there. It was her declared aim, at all other times and upon all other such occasions when he should be absent from Paris, to make her home in the city at the house of our father. Many persons were present at the time she made her declaration, which was received with broad smiles of skepticism, it being believed that she had no intention of keeping her word of honor. The vow was kept with solemnity, however, until the last months of her life, when changed circumstances enabled her better to withstand the shafts of malice aimed at her by her enemies."

A curious custom practiced by the ecclesiastical courts of France in the sixteenth and seventeenth centuries caused Nicolas d'Amerval to suffer great — and needless — embarrassment for the rest of his life. It also cast a shadow on Henry's reputation.

According to this judicial procedure, only the principals in a case, or their attorneys, heard the judgment of a court read aloud, and the reasons for a magistrate's decision were not made public.

François Roze dissolved the marriage of Gabrielle and the Sieur de Liencourt on the ground that the marriage had been illegal from the beginning because of the kinship of Antoine d'Estrées and Anne Gouffier. The magistrate added that he believed himself incompetent to judge whether d'Amerval was impotent.

The public, knowing nothing of the technical grounds, naturally assumed that a venal magistrate who wished to curry favor with the King and his mistress had pronounced d'Amerval impotent. The French people were amused, and the story spread abroad that d'Amerval was the father of eight children. By the time the tale crossed the English Channel, the number of his alleged offspring had increased to fourteen.

That was the origin of a legend that has refused to die, and as recently as three quarters of a century ago, Henry was criticized by French biographers for taking unfair advantage of a man who was not in a position to strike back. The charge is just, of course, as Henry and Gabrielle expended every effort to convince the court that d'Amerval was indeed impotent. Magistrate Roze, aware that posterity would render its own verdict, took care to find a less flimsy basis for his judgment.

Nicolas d'Amerval seriously considered the idea of appealing the case to Pope Clement, but was dissuaded, either by his own friends or by those of Gabrielle and Henry. He was in a position to cause the King great damage, and the farsighted Henry must have known it, so it is possible that one of the King's men in Amiens dropped a hint to the unhappy d'Amerval. Certainly a word or two would have sufficed, as the man lived in dread of his monarch's displeasure.

A few weeks later he found a suitable method of obtaining revenge, one that was both totally safe and that proclaimed the story of his impotence a lie to the entire world. He took a third wife, marrying a girl whose family name was d'Autun. She bore him no children, so there was no absolute proof that the claim made at the trial had been false, but he and his bride lived together happily, and virtually no one in the kingdom had believed Gabrielle's accusation anyway.

The divorce, mismanaged from the start, remained a serious blot on the reputations of the King and his mistress. Henry's enemies were given fresh ammunition to use against him, the Vatican was in a stronger position, and the Spaniards were encouraged. Philip II announced at Madrid that he intended to raise a new army to relieve France from tyranny, and the prospect of new international troubles loomed ahead.

But the crude display of royal power caused no domestic difficulties in France. The towns of Orleans and Meaux opened their gates to the King's forces before the beginning of the New Year, and Henry's power was so formidable now that not even his closest associates dared to criticize the unsavory divorce action.

Montmorency, writing a long letter to a cousin in Languedoc on December 29, 1594, said: "The Council held its first meeting today since the return of His Majesty to the capital. Henry, usually the most amiable of men, from the start revealed a rare distemper, which I can but attribute to his apprehension that his recent presence at Amiens and the conduct of the Marquise de Monceaux at the trial lately concluded there would be held up to scorn. I wisely held a tight rein on my tongue, the others behaving in a like manner, but there was no greater pleasure in His Majesty's attitude. At supper the Marquise displayed her usual charm, and smiled at all who were present."

Gabrielle had every reason in the world to smile. Long inured to gossip, she had taken an important stride toward her goal, and although it was still too early to be measured by the court jeweler for the coronet of a queen, she had reason to hope that her dream might come true.

It is odd that Montmorency made no mention in his letter of an incident that shocked Paris on the evening of Gabrielle's and Henry's return. Immediately after arriving in the city, the King and his mistress went either to the Hôtel d'Estrées or another mansion that stood nearby, the Hôtel du Bouchage, both of which are mentioned in contemporary accounts.

Henry, still dressed in his traveling clothes, was greeted by a group of some thirty or forty nobles assembled in Gabrielle's drawing room. He had no opportunity to remove his cloak, heavy boots, and spurs, but went through the ritual of embracing the gentlemen who approached him, among them the Prince de Conti, the Comte de Soissons, and the Comte de Saint-Paul.

Two young lords, members of the distinguished families of Montigny and Ragny, came up to him and each dropped to one knee. As Henry leaned forward to raise them up, a youth less than twenty years old and of very short stature, leaped forward and struck the King with a knife.

Had Henry not bent down at that instant, the blow might have killed him. Fortunately, he sustained only a slight cut on the right side of his upper lip.

Many of the gentlemen who witnessed the attack later wrote accounts of the incident, and without exception they reported that Gabrielle screamed and, unmindful of danger, raced to her lover's side.

The would-be assassin was seized, and identified himself as one Jean Chastel, the son of a clothier and a student at a Jesuit college. An investigation was conducted by a royal commission, to which Henry wisely appointed only Catholics, and another Jesuit student, named Guignard, was found also to be a fanatic who wanted to murder the King.

Guignard foolishly had committed his views to paper, and no other evidence was needed to condemn either youth. Henry chose to believe that, at the instigation of the League, the entire Jesuit order in France was engaged in treasonable activity against him, but it cannot be determined whether his view was true or merely a convenient excuse to be rid of a hardheaded, defiant group of priests.

In any event, justice was swift. Jean Chastel was publicly hanged in the Place de Gréve on January 7, 1595, and when he was pronounced dead, his body was burned. Guignard suffered the same fate two days later, and the following week the Parliament of Paris issued a decree, which Henry countersigned, banishing the Jesuits from the kingdom. The chances of making peace with Pope Clement appeared more remote than ever.

Gabrielle's favorite fortune-teller of the moment, a "Madame Cozzini," who numbered the Countess de Brissac and other ladies of high station among her clients, told the King's mistress that as the attempted assassination had taken place in her presence and in her quarters, the year to come would be filled with sorrow. But the Marquise de Monceaux, freed at last from the legal bonds of an unwanted marriage, refused to believe the prophetess of gloom.

No matter what the omens indicated, she was convinced that at last she would come into her own great glory, and she was absolutely right.

11: THE LADY AND THE POPE, 1595

Gabrielle d'Estrées became a divorcée on the same day that Jean Chastel was executed. The royal court must have had advance word of the former, for it occupied the first place on the daily list of events, the equivalent of a court calendar, drawn up by Henry's secretaries. The hanging of the would-be assassin was not mentioned.

From that day forward, Gabrielle never again was called the Dame d'Estrées or Madame de Liencourt. Madame the Marquise de Monceaux came into her own immediately. On January 8, Henry announced the appointment of a miniature court to attend his mistress, assigning to her four ladies-in-waiting, a grand equerry, two assistant equerries, and two gentlemen-at-arms. An executive decree issued the same day and bearing the King's signature ordered that all foreign ambassadors be presented to Madame, and required all French lords, clerics, and magistrates visiting the court to pay their compliments to her after being received by Henry himself.

She was being accorded the honors due a queen, but as a marriage ceremony binding the pair was conspicuously lacking, Henry invented a new title for his love. She was called by the somewhat impressive and indubitably startling name, "Titulary Mistress of His Majesty, the King of France."

The Béarnais then turned his attention to his son, and issued formal letters patent which made Caesar legitimate under the law of the realm. Such pronouncements usually bore only one date, that of the month in which they were drawn, in this instance, January 1595. As the grounds on which this manifesto was based were less than solid, on February 3 Henry took the added precaution of having the document registered with his Keeper of the Archives. The Parliament of Paris voted unanimously to accept it without changing a comma. Henry was leaving no loopholes. The work was so thorough that Caesar's legitimacy was never questioned in the course of his long life, either in the reign of his half-brother, Louis XIII, or that of his nephew, Louis XIV.

Henry read aloud the solemn document, written in his own hand, which opened with the statement that the kingdom was almost irretrievably ruined at the beginning of his reign. "It has been seen," he continued, "that we have succored it and, by the grace of God, restored it to its ancient strength and dignity, nor have we spared in the task either our labor, our blood, or our life."

Having reminded his readers that his sacrifices entitled him to make an other than orthodox legal decision regarding his son, he expressed the hope that his courage and his strength might be inherited by those who came after him. Then, without further preamble, he established his point:

"Since God has not yet seen fit to grant us any children in lawful wedlock, the Queen, our wife for ten and more years, now being separated from us, it is our desire that, until He grant us children who may legitimately succeed to this our Crown, we seek to beget elsewhere, in worthy and honorable manner, such children as may serve the Crown faithfully, as others of like nature have been seen to serve it and to render it great and notable service.

"And having come to recognize the many graces and perfections, of mind no less than of body, that are to be found in the person of our dear and well loved Gabrielle, Marquise de Monceaux, we have for several years sought her out for this reason, as being the subject most worthy of our love.

"We have considered ourselves entitled to do this with fewer scruples and less burden on our conscience in that we know that the marriage she had contracted with the Sieur de Liencourt is null and void, as is proved by their separation and the dissolution of the said marriage, which has followed in due course.

"And inasmuch as the said lady, after a lengthy courtship and the exercise of as much of our authority as we thought fit to employ, condescended to obey us and comply.

"A son was born, who up to the present has borne the name of Caesar Monsieur. His remarkable talents have decided us, acknowledging and confessing him to be our natural son, to accord him our royal letters and render him legitimate. We accord to him these letters, inasmuch as the stigma that it attached to the birth of our son excludes him from all hopes of succeeding to this our Crown and all depending thereon, and also to our kingdom of Navarre and all our other property and the revenues of our other property. His state would be but a poor one, were it not for this, his legitimation, whereby he is rendered capable of receiving all the gifts and benefits which may be conferred on him both by us and by others."

In this carefully worded document, Henry has not only declared Caesar legitimate and officially removed the cloud of sin hanging over Gabrielle, but has made it clear that Caesar cannot succeed him as King. Regardless of Gabrielle's daydreams and the machinations of her not-so-gray eminence, Isabelle de Sourdis, it is obvious that Henry was not then thinking of marrying his mistress.

Nevertheless, Gabrielle's position was vastly improved, and Caesar could be granted titles, honors, and property in his own name by his doting father. François-Annibal quietly remarks in his *Memoirs*, "Our father's reconciliation with my sister was now complete."

Henry's position in his struggle against the League had improved, too, and at last he felt free to strike simultaneously on both the military and diplomatic fronts. He took charge of the former himself and, now that Gabrielle's status had been clarified, turned over to her the delicate negotiations with the Vatican. It is a remarkable tribute to his faith in the skill of his mistress that he should grant to her, of all people, the responsibility for dealing with Pope Clement. In his own opinion, at any rate, his letters patent had cleansed her; she was no longer a fallen woman, and consequently could speak on his behalf to the highest authority in the Church.

The war with Spain had dragged on for five weary years without a declaration of hostilities on either side, but Henry was determined to emphasize to the world that Philip, not Clement, was his real enemy. Therefore he issued a formal declaration of war against Spain in February. A few weeks later he sent a warning to the Duke of Lorraine, stating bluntly that he would consider any further cooperation between Lorraine and Spain as an unfriendly act. Then, after notifying the citizens of the border town of Besançon — and through them any other communities still in League hands — that Philip was using the excuse of religion to hide his territorial ambitions, the King joined the army in the field. He and Biron were reunited in Bourgogne, and their campaign was so effective that, in June, they won a major victory at Fontaine-Française, forcing the Spaniards to flee for their lives.

Gabrielle made several journeys to visit Henry during the winter and spring, but spent the better part of her time in Paris, corresponding with the special envoys she had sent, in Henry's name, to Rome.

Previously she had acted as a personal intermediary between individuals wanting to be reconciled with the crown and Henry, a post that had required relatively little intelligence, as she already had the sympathetic ear of her lover. But Clement was a Pope, and was following Church policies established by Sixtus V at the time Henry had come to the throne. A much more difficult task of diplomacy was at hand.

Sixtus had been one of the founders of the reconstituted League, and for a time had been one of its most enthusiastic supporters. But two of Henry's allies, Venice and Tuscany, who had feared Spain, had pleaded his cause. "The League cannot exist by itself," the Venetians had declared in a communication to the Vatican. "It must marry itself to Spain, and it will ask you to pay the dowry."

Sixtus had decided to become neutral in the struggle, and according to a rumor which has neither been verified nor effectively denied, the Spanish ambassador had quarreled violently with the Pope, threatening to dethrone him. Sixtus had died a few days later, on August 27, 1590, and it was commonly believed that he had been poisoned on the instructions of Philip, who, in 1584, had disposed of the Prince of Orange by the same convenient means.

Urban VII, who died two weeks after his elevation, and Gregory XIV, who expired ten months later, were Popes who owed their position to the influence of Spain in the College of Cardinals, and both paid their debt by holding firm in their opposition to Henry. Clement VIII had been supported by the Spanish faction, too, and had accepted without question the policy of waging war against the heretic King of France.

The conversion of Henry had removed one barrier to a reconciliation between the Church and France, but the act making Caesar legitimate had raised another. Members of the

French clerical hierarchy could not issue a formal document condoning Gabrielle's improved relationship with the King, but, as sixteenth-century morals were fluid and kings were granted standards more elastic than those of lesser beings, the cardinals and bishops pointed no fingers at Henry's mistress.

Clement was a hardheaded realist, too, and no matter how much he might deplore Gabrielle's position on moral grounds, he was a statesman who courageously faced facts. Most members of the French clergy and virtually all of the nation's Catholic laymen had accepted Henry as their King. The support of the League was costing the Vatican vast sums of money needed for other projects, and Clement began to have second thoughts.

Such was the situation late in 1594 when Arnaud d'Ossat, Bishop of Rennes, who later was awarded the red hat of a cardinal, arrived in Rome at the head of a French delegation that sought to persuade the Pope to change his policy. Clement hesitated, but continued to support the League with funds and troops while he mulled the problem.

Gabrielle opened her campaign in late January 1595, sending Bishop d'Ossat copies of the decree naming her the King's Titulary Mistress and the letters patent that declared Caesar legitimate. The Bishop promptly sought an audience with the Pontiff and gave him the documents, writing to Gabrielle that he felt encouraged.

She replied at once, suggesting that she open a direct correspondence with Clement. Bishop d'Ossat sounded out the Vatican, but was told that the Holy Father felt he could not engage in an exchange of letters with her. The Bishop's delicate reply said, "It is the opinion of His Holiness that his position makes it necessary for him to communicate only with members of the Spiritual Hierarchy or temporal Heads of State."

That, it appeared, was the end of Gabrielle's attempt to intervene on her lover's behalf, but the same courier who brought her the Bishop's letter brought also a private note from him. This document has been lost, and its precise contents are unknown, but it is mentioned by Montmorency and de Brissac in their letters, is railed against at length by Sully in his *Memoirs*, and there is little reason to doubt that it existed.

In it, the energetic Bishop of Rennes apparently said something to the effect that he would be pleased if Gabrielle wrote her thoughts to him, and that he had made private arrangements to show any such documents to Pope Clement.

Gabrielle must have received some such communication, for she wrote two long letters to the Bishop, one dated March 19 and the other March 30, 1595. There is nothing in either to suggest the dictation or advice of clergymen, members of the Council, or the King himself. They are simple letters that appear to have been written by Gabrielle, unassisted, but it would be naïve to suppose that documents of such importance would have been sent if Henry, his principal secular aides, and at least one or two French cardinals had not gone over the contents with care.

"I know nothing of the struggle between the Powers that divides the World and causes so much suffering," she says in the first. "I have seen war, as Your Grace knows, and am familiar with its horrors. I write as a woman, as one who loves with all her heart one who is a faithful and devoted son of the Church. I shared his travail when, pulled now one way and now the other by followers who sought to impose upon him their own convictions, he struggled with his own conscience and made his decision to find peace for his soul in the arms of the One Church.

"I myself, having been born and raised in the Faith, having from the time of my birth acknowledged the authority of the Holy Father, rejoiced in that decision. What small part I may have played in helping His Majesty was not of my own doing, but was guided by Forces far stronger than my feeble powers.

"My position is not that of an ordinary woman, though ordinary I be, save that I enjoy the confidence of him who is King of France. His son is my son, and together we must strive to make for him, and for others, a community in France, as in all other lands, safe from the ravages of war.

"That safety lies in the One Church, and I do know that His Majesty wants with all of his heart to effect an understanding between himself and the Holy Father, for only in such an understanding can true, lasting peace be achieved."

The second letter was sent long before she could have received a reply or known whether Pope Clement had been influenced by her plea. It was, therefore, a postscript in which she presumably intended to express new thoughts relating to the same subject. Instead she made the same points a second time, often using identical language. But her final paragraph is new, and indicates either that Gabrielle was a sincere, honest woman or a glib politician striving to strike the right note:

"I pray that His Holiness will open his ears when Your Grace goes before him, and that France will soon be accepted within the Church, a prayer in which all women in this realm do most fervently join."

Her appeal was feminine and direct; it was also shrewd. Certainly Gabrielle could not have worded her second letter carelessly when she asked the Pope to readmit France to the Church. She knew, as did everyone else who had been even remotely concerned over Henry's dispute with Rome, that France itself was, both now and previously, a predominantly

Catholic land. A number of bishops had suffered automatic excommunication when they had taken up the King's cause and, more recently, several cardinals had been similarly punished.

But the Vatican had made no attempt to enforce its edict, both sides tacitly understanding that the cardinals and bishops would continue to perform the functions and exercise the authority of their offices until such time as the quarrel was resolved. It was also true that laymen had run the risk of being excommunicated when they had given their support to the King, but the Church wisely had refrained from carrying out its threat and thereby creating a nation of Huguenots.

The issue was a personal one between Henry and the Holy See, not a theological dispute between a nation and the Church. But Gabrielle cunningly shifted the base of argument, and in so doing subtly served notice on Rome that if Henry were kept outside the pale, the Church might be the one to lose.

Her threat was not an idle one. On the far side of a narrow strip of water dividing her from France stood England, which had been removed from the Church by Henry VIII, whose daughter now sat on the throne, making it difficult for Catholics to practice their faith openly. Pope Clement knew that Henry of France and Navarre was a man of great courage and strength, and of proven ability to lead his people. If he could persuade them that the Pope was being partial to Spain at the expense of France, they might be persuaded to follow Henry anywhere. Vatican memories were long, and no one had forgotten the Schism that had led to the establishment of a separate French Church. The danger was even greater now that Protestantism had gained a hold in France, and there was no guarantee that the King, if provoked, might not leave Catholicism and once again embrace his former faith.

To Clement and the cardinals of the Curia, already grappling with the problem, Gabrielle's letter must have given further cause for brow-wrinkling. Bishop d'Ossat and the members of his delegation, who had been devoting every effort to obtain recognition for Henry, could not have been blind to the hint, either.

Few heads of the Church have made public the reasons for their major decisions of policy, and Pope Clement VIII was particularly close-mouthed, listening silently to the advice of subordinates, then retiring to the privacy of his own apartment and making up his own mind. Therefore the precise effect of Gabrielle's letters on him cannot be gauged, but it seems unlikely that the event which followed close on the heels of her communications was coincidental.

For whatever his reasons, Pope Clement wrote to all of the religious houses and orders in France, directing them to pray to God for the prosperity, health, and well-being of Henry IV. His letters were dated April 15, 16, and 17.

The heads of monasteries and convents immediately forwarded the good news to Henry, who jubilantly sent his Chief Almoner, Georges du Perron, Bishop Elect of Evreux, to beg for absolution on his behalf. Bishop du Perron stopped at Florence en route to Rome, and delivered a letter to the Grand Duke of Tuscany, in which Henry extended the hand of friendship and offered an alliance. Tuscany had wanted such a treaty for a long time, and the offer was not only accepted, but word was immediately sent to the Tuscan cardinals, who left the Spaniards and joined the pro-French camp. Princes of the Church in other Italian states, which usually followed the lead of Tuscany, did the same, and the time was ripe for the acceptance of Henry's conversion. A consistory of cardinals was held in May at Monte-Cavallo, and it was subsequently announced that Henry had been admitted into the Church.

The formal ceremony was held beneath the porch of St. Peter's in September, with Bishops d'Ossat and du Perron representing their King. At the end of the ceremony, which was witnessed by French prelates of every rank, the members of the French community went to the Church of Saint-Louis-des-Français and sang the Te Deum. And that night the whole city of Rome joined in a mammoth celebration.

Henry was occupied with the siege of the town of La Fère when word was brought to him by a Florentine gentleman who had been an official at the court of Henry III. The ebullient Colonel Alexandre d'Elbenne rode into the King's camp, shouting the news from his saddle. And the King, standing outside his tent with his Constable, was silent for a moment, then smiled and said, "Gabrielle has succeeded where others failed."

French Catholics gave her credit for winning a victory; the more rigid Huguenots, like d'Aubigné, became louder and more bitter in their denunciations of the woman who had achieved a reconciliation between their King and the Roman Catholic Church. Vatican payments to the League treasury had been halted in the spring, and Papal regiments, which had not taken part in any of the recent battles, were called home.

The League had been dealt its heaviest blow, and those French towns which continued to hold out against the crown were virtually isolated. They no longer had any reason to oppose Henry, and, rather than place themselves at the mercy of Philip II, who had no reason to protect their interests, they sued for peace.

For all practical purposes the civil war was coming to an end. And Gabrielle d'Estrées, victory-flushed, plunged furiously into a new round of diplomatic activities.

12: THE LADY DIPLOMAT, 1595–96

Gabrielle stood so high in Henry's favor after his admission to the Church that he gave her what was tantamount to a blank commission to negotiate on his behalf. The results were mixed; she achieved one victory of consequence but in another encounter did far more harm than good. Her enemies never failed to remember the latter occasion, of course, and Sully in his *Memoirs* fires some of his heaviest rounds at her because of what he calls, "the notorious alliance of the house d'Estrées and the upstart house of Balagny."

The head of the house of Balagny was, as already noted, devoted to the cause of the King, and Gabrielle had played an active role in that conversion, which had taken place in 1593. Balagny, known to many of his contemporaries as "the bastard of Montluc," was an opportunist, an adventurer, and a former bishop who had left the Church when he found more verdant pastures in the temporal world. He married a woman as brilliant, courageous, and greedy as himself, Renée de Clermont d'Amboise, and together they made a formidable team.

Balagny had been a lifelong friend of Antoine d'Estrées, who was about ten years his elder, and often had visited the château at Coeuvres, where he had watched Gabrielle and Diane growing up. He had always been fond of both girls, and they had returned his affections, neither of them realizing how closely their destinies were to be linked.

In 1593, Balagny had been the League's Governor of Cambrai, and had taken advantage of the turbulent conditions to make himself the independent sovereign of the town, with the self-granted title of Prince. He was in a splendid position, and knew it: Cambrai was one of the wealthiest towns in France, and was of enormous strategic importance to Henry, who could threaten Reims if he occupied it. Balagny was determined to make him pay a heavy price for the privilege.

He found his opportunity in the autumn of 1593, when Henry came to Normandy, accompanied by Gabrielle, and made his headquarters at Dieppe, where an incident worthy of inclusion in the most romantic of novels occurred. A beautiful, veiled lady, richly gowned and wearing a fur-trimmed cloak, arrived in the town and requested a private audience with Gabrielle. She was refused, but when she sent in her name on a slip of paper, Gabrielle immediately retired with her secretive guest, Renée de Balagny.

The Governor's wife had come to treat with Henry, and wisely made Gabrielle her confederate. Madame de Balagny offered Cambrai to the King on stiff terms: her husband would hold Cambrai in fealty to Henry, in return for being made a full-fledged Prince as well as a Marshal of France, along with a payment of one hundred and forty thousand écus. The sweetener in the pot was still another offer: Gabrielle was pregnant with Caesar at the time, and Balagny proposed to give her Cambrai as a hereditary property for her children, if Henry approved.

Isabelle de Sourdis was in favor of the arrangement, but there is no evidence to suggest, as was later angrily charged by the people of Cambrai, that Gabrielle actively considered the idea of becoming an independent sovereign.

In any event, Gabrielle went to Henry with Balagny's basic offer, urging him to accept it, and the King agreed to the terms. Thanks at least in part to the royal mistress, Balagny became a wealthy Prince and a Marshal. There is no information available on the question of whether Gabrielle mentioned the possibility of acquiring Cambrai for herself and making it the capital of a sovereign state. If she did, nothing ever came of the idea.

The ties that bound Balagny and Gabrielle were strengthened, and the Marshal made a magnificent gesture the following June, when Caesar was born during the siege of Laon. Balagny sent Henry, of his own volition, five hundred cavalrymen, three thousand foot soldiers, and a supply of ammunition that filled three hundred carts. These, he declared in an accompanying letter, were his gift to celebrate the birth of a son to his old friend and royal master. Quite naturally, Henry and Gabrielle were deeply grateful to him.

In 1595 a corps of Spaniards, moving swiftly in a surprise attack mounted in the Low Countries, laid siege to Cambrai. The inhabitants smuggled a delegation out of the town, and these citizens hurried to the King to tell him of their plight. They also informed him that Balagny was a cruel tyrant and a greedy administrator who extorted money from everyone who owned property. Madame, they said, was almost as voracious as her husband, and they begged to be relieved from rule by a despot.

Henry praised their loyalty to France, and suggested they return to their fellow townsmen with word that the King would follow in the immediate future with his army. He also promised he would put their internal affairs in order. His answer seemed evasive to them, and they said that they could not defend the town successfully unless they were assured that Balagny would be replaced.

At this point Gabrielle intervened on behalf of her old friend, praising him extravagantly and insisting that he be retained. The King yielded to her, and the deputies from Cambrai withdrew in anger.

Henry immediately organized a military relief column, but was himself delayed, and the siege was relieved by a corps of Burgundians, who discovered that the people of Cambrai had delivered their town to the Spaniards. Only the inner defense bastion, the medieval citadel, was still in French hands, and there Balagny, his wife, and two regiments of troops still loyal to Henry had barricaded themselves. On the very day that the town was relieved, the occupants of the citadel had been forced to surrender to the Spaniards because they had no more food, and, when the Spaniards and townspeople appeared to take her to prison, Madame de Balagny had suddenly died. It was commonly believed at the time that her death had been caused by what was universally described as a paroxysm of grief; modern medicine would probably diagnose her fatal ailment as a heart attack.

Henry, who had been marching toward Cambrai at the time of the capitulation, calmly took charge. He had no desire to become embroiled in a dispute with his mistress, but it was obvious that her advice had been bad and he took quiet steps to correct the situation. Balagny remained the nominal governor of the town, but was promoted to the royal Council, where his energies could be put to better use under the King's eyes. No reprisals were taken against the inhabitants, and the tolerant Henry granted them the privilege of electing their own "deputy to the governor," who actually became the crown lieutenant.

Gabrielle's interference had caused considerable damage, but she neither lost Henry's confidence nor her influence with him. Her error in judgment was no worse than errors made by others to whom the King had delegated power, and Henry still

167

relied on her. The affair at Cambrai had been unpleasant, but in the long run nothing had been lost.

Balagny suffered no loss of prestige, either. He had become a member in good standing of the King's inner circle, and if he could no longer extort money from the citizens of Cambrai, he must have consoled himself with the thought that his field of potential operations had been enlarged. It must have been a shock to discover that the members of the Council were scrupulously honest and that, although men like Chiverny promoted their own interests, any official who tried to line his pockets at the expense of the Crown or the people was dismissed and sent into exile.

Under the circumstances, he did what he could to bolster his position. A scant four months after his wife's death, he remarried. His bride was Diane d'Estrées, and the wedding was a magnificent affair.

The ceremony was held at Notre Dame, with Gabrielle acting as her beloved sister's only attendant and the King standing up with the groom. Balagny was now a member in good standing of the semiroyal family, and remained influential until the end of Henry's reign. It is significant to note, however, that he made his headquarters in Paris, rarely returned to Cambrai, and never interfered in the administration of the town. When Henry was burned, he took care never to put his hand in the same fire again.

Gabrielle's second venture into domestic politics was a complete success, and it, too, had its roots in events that had taken place in 1593. In April of that year the princesses of Lorraine, the ladies of the house of Guise, had deemed it wise to make their peace with the King, and had applied for passports to live in that portion of the realm which he had conquered.

Catherine of Clèves, widow of the assassinated Duke and mother of the young Duke, was one of the most celebrated ladies of her time. She had been a great beauty in her youth, and had retained a slender figure by refusing to eat the nine-course banquets that were served nightly to members of the higher nobility. She was witty and wise, but as the views of her contemporaries cannot be substantiated by anything she wrote, their opinions must be accepted or rejected on hearsay.

Her daughter, Louise, was the girl whom Henry had seriously considered marrying a short time before he had fallen in love with Gabrielle. Nineteen years old in 1593, she offers a serene, narcissistic portrait of herself in the *Adventures*, writing, "Daphnis displayed so many beauties and graces that there were none who saw her but thought that love was making use of her to wound hearts and make conquests."

Even the crusty Sully unbent sufficiently in his *Memoirs* to pay tribute to her, and must have been sincere, as he despised all Catholic ladies. He puts his description in the mouth of Henry, claiming that the King said of her that "she has a gentle and pleasant disposition, and a lively manner, and is above all of good family, tall and beautiful, and has the look of a woman who would bear fine children."

Mother and daughter received permission to visit Mantes in April 1593, and Louise writes in the *Adventures* that she and her mother were curious to meet Gabrielle. The feeling, she later discovered, was mutual. The ladies were escorted to the court by Saint-Larry, Duc de Bellegarde, and as it was common knowledge that he had been Gabrielle's lover, both Catherine and her daughter were amused. They were astonished when they discovered that Gabrielle enjoyed the situation, too, smiling broadly when Bellegarde presented the ladies to Henry, then to her.

The flustered young Duke, trying desperately to win the good graces of his monarch, openly paid court to Louise, and even flirted with her mother, making such a ludicrous spectacle of himself that Gabrielle and Louise begged to be excused after trying in vain to stifle their laughter behind handkerchiefs.

The house that was being used as the royal dwelling was small, and the two girls found themselves in the same room. There they laughed until they wept; then, still giggling, they found they liked each other, and began to exchange feminine confidences. "Daphnis and Gabrielle learned," Louise writes in her *Adventures*, "that they shared the same desire, the achievement of a rapport between the royal house of Bourbon and the royal house of Guise. There existed between them, instantly, that rare sense of communion that can arise between two ladies of beauty and grace; albeit neither spoke a word, it was understood betwixt them that they needs must work together in the attempt to achieve their great goal."

This unusual and unexpected alliance became a firm bond, which was cemented on March 22, 1594, at the time of Henry's entry into Paris. Catherine de Guise and her daughter were living in their town house at the time, and there Henry, accompanied by Gabrielle, called on them. "The gentlemen who were in the confidence of the King made every effort to persuade him to send Daphnis and her mother to Lorraine," Louise writes, "but Henry the King gave greater weight to the sage counsel of his beloved Gabrielle, and acting upon her advice, graciously came to the Hôtel de Guise, where he was feted warmly, being offered cakes of sweetened rye flour and a cup of wine made from the white grapes of Lorraine. He drank sparingly, and Gabrielle, who was as abstemious as were her hostesses, drank not at all."

The campaign conducted by the Guise ladies was eminently successful. Gabrielle became their champion, and made so much progress that in November 1594, the King received the schoolboy Duc de Guise in a formal audience. In a gesture that seemed impulsive, but undoubtedly had been carefully planned by the monarch who left nothing to chance, the boy was given the most important government post then open, the governorship of Provence. It was immaterial that he was too young to take an active part in the affairs of state and that Henry cautiously assigned two deputies who wielded the power. The King had made a generous gesture of reconciliation.

But the major feud between the Crown and the house of Guise had not yet been resolved, for Catherine, her son, and her daughter stood on the periphery rather than at the center of the vortex. Catherine's brother-in-law, Mayenne, was the important member of the family, the others being only pawns.

Gabrielle started to work in earnest, attempting to soften Henry, and the de Guise ladies exerted their considerable charms on Mayenne. The obstacles that stood in the way of a treaty were many and complicated on both sides.

The widow of Henry III, Dowager Queen Louise, herself related to the rulers of Lorraine, protested vehemently at the prospect of a pardon being granted to Mayenne, the man whom she considered responsible for the murder of her husband. Henry tried on three occasions to reason with her, according to the *Adventures* of Louise de Guise, but accomplished nothing. Then the task was given to Gabrielle, with whom the widowed Queen had become friendly. Unfortunately, there is no record of their conversations, nor any indication of how often they may have met. The only authority on the subject is Louise de Guise, and her knowledge of Gabrielle's activities was limited.

"Queen Louise refusing to set foot in the Louvre," she writes, "Gabrielle met her at a quiet place in the country, and there convinced her that the interests of France required the making of peace between those who had shed so much blood."

Whatever Gabrielle's tactics, they succeeded; the Dowager Queen finally withdrew her opposition on the condition that she herself would never be required to receive Mayenne, either in public or private audience.

The situation in the opposing camp was even more delicate. Mayenne was considered a criminal by Henry, and was subject to the death penalty if captured. Several of his supporters, all of them high-ranking nobles, were under similar indictments, and the code of honor made it impossible for him to desert them. The disintegration of the League made his position unenviable by 1595, but he still possessed considerable strength.

He retained a firm grip on Lorraine, he was still enormously wealthy, and his nuisance value was great. If he chose to ally himself once again with Philip of Spain, the war might be prolonged. So he was willing to make his peace with Henry only at a high price. Catherine and Louise de Guise persuaded him that it was in his best interests to treat with Henry, but the official negotiators appointed by both sides spent the first months of 1595 haggling over details, demanding that the honor of their respective houses be recognized, and indulging in rounds of endless recriminations.

Louise de Guise relates how the conflict was resolved. Henry appointed Gabrielle to deal directly with the recalcitrant Duke, and a private meeting was held in a château outside Chaumont, near the French-Lorraine border, in October 1595. There can be no greater sign of the King's confidence in his mistress for

Gabrielle's interference had just produced the unfortunate situation at Cambrai.

She met Mayenne and they spent two days ironing out the major points of difference. Then she, her ladies, and the small military escort that had been provided for her returned to Paris, and the official negotiators again took charge. The talks proceeded so smoothly that Henry, who was directing the siege of La Fère, announced that he was taking a holiday in the form of a hunting expedition. Riding off to the forest of Coney in late November 1595, he went to Follembray, where a lodge had been built by Francis I, and there, in the presence of the negotiators of both sides, declared that he was willing to accept the terms arranged by Gabrielle and Mayenne, to which the representatives had added the finishing touches.

The terms were so favorable to Mayenne that many royalists later grumbled about them, but the King knew that peace with his principal domestic adversary was worth every concession made, especially as some of them were meaningless. The Duke, it was agreed, would receive the vast sum of three hundred and fifty thousand écus; the royal treasury was still suffering embarrassment, and Mayenne actually received only half of that amount. The governorship of the Ile-de-France was given temporarily to the Duke's son, but again the gesture was more significant than the deed, as Henry had no intention of handing the inner core of his realm to an untrustworthy supporter, and himself continued to supervise the administration of it.

Mayenne still controlled a large body of troops, which he claimed would take time to disband, so Henry made him Governor of three castles, those at Soissons, Châlons-sur-Saône, and Dreux, for a period of six years. Once again, the King anticipated his former enemy, for, later, when Mayenne's regiments marched into the strongholds, they were met by still larger bodies of royalist troops, who immediately began to convert them to Henry's cause.

The most important concession granted by the King was a complete amnesty for Mayenne and his principal followers. The edict of reconciliation solemnly stated that the Duke and his lieutenants had opposed the murder of prisoners, but had been unable to restrain their subordinates, who had disobeyed their express orders.

In return, Mayenne and his aides swore they would take the medieval oath of fealty to Henry, that they and their sons and grandsons would be his faithful subjects, and that under no circumstances would they take up arms against him. The Duke also declared that all decisions, judgments, and sentences issued by him as head of the League were null and void.

When the terms of the agreement became known, shortly before Christmas, there was a storm of protest. D'Aubigné, writing a typically scornful letter to his brother, says that "if the King persists in his determination to sign this mad agreement, half of Paris will become converted to the cause of the Reformed Church in a single night."

He exaggerated, of course, but the opposition was greater than Henry had ever encountered. Not until April 9, 1596, more than two months after the principals had met and formally signed the document of reconciliation, did the Parliament of Paris finally ratify it, and even then it acted only after Henry had written two sharply worded orders demanding that the Parliament act without delay.

No secret was made of the part that Gabrielle had played in the negotiations, and for the first time since Henry had taken Paris, the people of the capital turned against her. A large crowd gathered outside the Hôtel d'Estrées on the night of December 23, shouting, "To the gallows with the traitress!"

Troops were called out, and the mob was dispersed. Apparently no one realized that, as Henry was in residence at the Louvre, Gabrielle was spending the night in her apartment there.

This unpleasant scene was the only demonstration conducted against Gabrielle. The King quickly regained control of his subjects by appearing in public with Gabrielle on a number of occasions between Christmas and the New Year, and making several short speeches, in which he reminded the citizens that they, like Mayenne, had been his enemies for years. "If I punish one man for treason," he asked, "must I not punish all?"

The people stared reflectively at the gallows which had been erected in public squares throughout the city, rubbed their throats, and quietly returned to their homes.

They might have been harder to handle had they known that the treaty negotiated by Gabrielle and Mayenne contained a secret clause. In it Mayenne promised that if Gabrielle and the King should marry at some future time, he, the members of his family, and all of his friends would declare themselves in favor of her children and support them in their claims to the throne, to the exclusion of all other princes of the blood.

This agreement is the first specific indication that Gabrielle herself had set her heart on attaining the throne. Isabelle de Sourdis, who accompanied her niece everywhere except the bedchamber that Gabrielle shared with the King, had done her work thoroughly.

On the first day of 1596, Mayenne wrote to Henry, asking for a personal interview. The communication was received two days later, and it was decided that, as Gabrielle had been responsible for the reconciliation, she deserved the honor of presenting the humbled prince to his monarch. Therefore it was decreed that the ceremony would take place at Monceaux on January 31.

Gabrielle had become an experienced diplomat, and took great care to make certain that her guest of honor would not be humiliated. She and Diane arrived at Monceaux on January 30, accompanied by a small army of cooks, serving maids, waiters, and valets. The company also contained scores of musicians, minstrels, and comedians, who were lodged with the residents of the town, with strict orders not to come to the château until summoned.

"My sister and I," Diane writes in her *Memorial*, "labored without surcease through the night, halting only when the arrival of dawn and our own exhaustion compelled us to take to our couches."

They were awake again a few hours later, as Henry, the members of his Council, and other dignitaries arrived in midmorning. Gabrielle was too busy to spend any time with her lover, and Henry, like all men who watch in helpless bewilderment when preparations are being made for a party, became angry. "Twice he summoned my sister to his side," Diane says, "and twice she sent word of refusal, thereby arousing his wrath."

Promptly at noon the Duke of Mayenne appeared, modestly escorted by six noblemen. In honor of the occasion the plump former head of the League was mounted, and disaster was narrowly averted when he could not dismount. Gabrielle, who waited at the entrance to the château, quickly sent three men-at-arms to lift him to the ground, where he recovered his breath and his dignity.

He walked up the steps, where Gabrielle greeted him graciously in the presence of a large company of nobles, officers, and clergymen. Then, taking his hand, she led him into a chamber that had been set up as a throne room. Henry was waiting there, and Mayenne silently bowed low three times. As the Duke completed his third bow, he tried to kneel, but the King, obviously sensing catastrophe, came toward him, holding out both hands and smiling broadly. "Is it really you, Cousin," Henry asked, "or do I look upon a dream?"

Mayenne, in no mood for joviality, begged his monarch to believe that the concessions he had signed were engraved on his heart. Henry stepped closer to him and said something in a tone so low that no one else could hear him. Mayenne nodded, the King took his arm, and they retired to the small library of the château. No record of their talk has survived; apparently neither revealed to others what they had each said.

They emerged in good humor, so it seemed that they had reached an understanding. The members of the Council expressed their hope that the Duke would use his influence to persuade the towns still holding out against the crown to surrender. Gabrielle, who had been waiting with the ladies and gentlemen of the court, herself offered them cups of bittersweet mead on a silver platter. Mayenne drained his cup, but Henry took only a few sips and made a wry face.

Gabrielle presented the members of the court to the Duke, a procedure that lasted for some time and made Henry nervous, for he finally interrupted and suggested that he and Mayenne stroll in the garden and enjoy the view of the valley of the Marne. The two men went out into the handsomely trimmed park of the property that had once belonged to Catherine de Medici, the rest of the company following.

Henry, in the forefront, could not resist the temptation to walk rapidly, leading the stout Mayenne up and down hilly paths. At last the panting Duke was forced to halt, and Henry took pity on him, saying, "Take my hand, Cousin. You shall be put to no further trouble on my account."

Then they repaired to a nearby pavilion, and Mayenne was mollified when he saw that the refreshments Gabrielle had provided included several pitchers of his favorite wine. Two small cannon boomed, and the entertainers appeared, dressed as shepherds and shepherdesses. Songs were sung in honor of the reconciled heroes, after which Gabrielle announced that dinner was served.

The tables were laid out in the open, for, in spite of the season, the weather was sunny and mild. The King and Gabrielle sat at a separate table, the Duke and Diane at another nearby. Eleven courses were served, the diners gorging themselves for more than three hours.

At the conclusion of the meal, Henry rose and offered a toast, in which everyone joined: "To the lasting friendship of myself, the King, with my Cousin of Mayenne. To the eternal peace of my kingdom, its glory, and its happiness."

The guests then witnessed an allegorical play written in honor of the occasion by a poet named Sigongne; afterward waiters circulated with plates of supper and all watched fireworks. Henry, who rarely made more than a token appearance at parties, remained until midnight. When he yawned, everyone withdrew, and the most festive celebration of Henry's reign came to an end.

The following day the King returned to his army, still occupied with the siege of La Fère, and Mayenne went to one of his estates to recuperate. Gabrielle and Diane hurried to Paris, where preparations were being made for the wedding of the season, that of Diane and Marshal de Balagny.

Henry rode to Paris for a single day to attend the ceremony and, accompanied by his mistress and his sister, the reception at the Hôtel d'Estrées. "His Majesty," François-Annibal declares in his *Memoirs*, "was in rare good humor, the proximity of my sister relieving him of fatigue. He paid me the high compliment of asking me to accompany him to La Fère, toward which place we rode before the sun set that same day, the King confiding to me that when the town capitulated, it was his intent to appoint me its Governor."

Three days after the wedding, Gabrielle and Princess Catherine set out for the lodge at Follembray, a short distance from La Fère and the King.

An enumeration of Gabrielle's triumphs in such a short span of time indicates how firmly entrenched she had become. She had been the King's hostess at the most important social event of his reign, he had interrupted a siege to attend her sister's wedding, and had gone out of his way to honor her brother. When she and the King's sister rode to Follembray in the same coach, foreign ambassadors sent reports to their capitals saying it was useless to suggest that Henry marry one or another of the various candidates whose names had been proposed to him.

Gabrielle was riding high, in spite of the dire predictions of the fortune-teller, and would soar higher still.

13: KEEPER OF THE KEYS, 1596

All French officials, including members of the Council, acted in the King's name and were dependent on him for their authority. Henry needed to consult no one before making an appointment, and could dismiss any subordinate at will. In a sense, he was omnipotent, but custom had placed limits on his powers. A Council member or cabinet officer held his post until such time as he aroused the King's displeasure, and even then he was not dismissed until the action was discussed at a Council meeting, often in his presence.

In theory, it was his right to reply to the charges made against him, and, again in theory, his colleagues were privileged to support him. In practice, of course, no officer of the crown wanted to be struck by a bolt of royal lightning, and the Council was invariably in unanimous agreement when Henry decided that one of his advisers no longer served a useful purpose.

The authority of the King's principal aides was vaguely defined, but any man who carried a small bunch of golden keys on a chain around his neck found that lesser officials, regardless of whether they were his direct subordinates, were anxious to obey any order he chose to give. Just as the Council members had no desire to incur the King's displeasure, those on lower rungs of the ladder took care not to offend those who were known as Keepers of the Keys.

Gabrielle undoubtedly was aware of these refinements and distinctions, but herself stood outside the pale. She had become one of the most important of France's diplomats, receiving instructions and performing missions at Henry's direct command, yet she held no post in the government and was not entitled to attend Council meetings. Her absence from these sessions might be ascribed to the fact that she was a woman, but other women had been members. Diane de Poitiers, the mistress of Francis I, had been active in the Council, and Catherine de Medici, frequently brushing aside all pretense, had taken the place at the head of the table and had not even bothered to defer to the opinions of her sons.

It is possible that Gabrielle was aware of these precedents; if not, Isabelle de Sourdis could not have failed to be conscious of them. Strictly speaking, Gabrielle did not qualify as a member of the Council, as she held no official government position. She was a marquise, to be sure, and the day was coming when she would be made a countess, then a duchess, but there were many other women whose place in the nobility was higher. And her position of Titulary Mistress of France, though imposing, did not entitle her to a seat at the table where the nation's policies were made.

No one knows whether she broached the idea of being made a Keeper of the Keys to Henry, or whether the thought was his. It may be that the insatiably greedy Isabelle whispered in her niece's ear. On the other hand, Henry had seen for himself that his mistress was capable of performing difficult diplomatic tasks, and it could be that he wanted her to join in the deliberations of the high and mighty. The origination of the plan to make Gabrielle a member of the Council remains a secret locked behind the closed door of the royal bedchamber.

In any event, early in 1596 Henry began to take steps to put the idea into operation. The first step was contained in letters patent which the King wrote in December 1595, and which were duly registered in the archives on January 28, 1596.

He opened his declaration by unnecessarily reminding his Council that he had acknowledged the paternity of Caesar and had rendered his son legitimate. He then continued, "We desired that in all acts and privileges, whether in court or without, he should be held, thought and considered to be legitimate and capable of receiving any gifts and bequests made in his name, and likewise able to hold such charges, powers, dignities, and offices as may be assigned to him, and as he may be decorated withal, either by us or the kings who succeed us.

"And we have thought that one of the chief evidences of this legitimation will be to render the said Caesar able and qualified to enter upon the succession of our dear and well-loved Dame Gabrielle d'Estrées, Marquise de Monceaux, his mother, which however cannot be unless the said Marquise de Monceaux, of her own free will, gives her consent to the said legitimation, the which we hereby do incite her to do.

"We have desired to give and bequeath to her every honorable mark and all the privileges and emoluments which it is customary to give to mothers, and thus to please her insofar as in us lies. For these reasons, and at the advice of the princes, lords, and other great and worthy persons of our Council, we declare, desire, and ordain that our said dear and well-loved Gabrielle, Marquise de Monceaux, from this time forth, have and enjoy all rights and privileges of guardianship, and likewise all gifts and other benefits and emoluments proceeding from us and the kings our successors, and also that all acquests of the said Caesar be ruled and administered during the minority of the said Caesar by and under the authority of the said Dame Gabrielle.

"It is also our wish that the said Gabrielle, Marquise de Monceaux, inherit entirely from the said Caesar in the event of his decease without children begotten by him in honorable wedlock."

In this remarkable declaration, which gave Gabrielle the guardianship of her son's person and property, as well as the right to succeed to all his possessions, Henry blithely shattered all legal and social precedent. Even the most respectable of sixteenth-century women enjoyed few legal rights, and those of unwed mothers were nonexistent. The courts consistently refused to recognize the legal bonds between a mother and bastard offspring, and no woman ever received rights to administer the property of her children. Even queens had been forced to rely on charity when their husbands and sons had died, and some of the most powerful nobles in France owed their wealth to the fact that they were the guardians of property owned by nephews.

Chiverny, who guided the letters patent through the legal maze, says in his *Memoirs* that he expected no opposition to the revolutionary decree, and the Parliament of Paris obliged him by accepting the declaration on March 19, 1596, without a dissenting vote. The Chamber of Accounts, a branch of the royal treasury which theoretically had the right to exercise a power of veto, also accepted the document without a murmur on August 9, 1596.

Meanwhile, Gabrielle took action through an attorney, Pierre Beauxamis, to complete the arrangement, and on February 16, 1596, sent notification to the Parliament that she accepted without reservation the instructions and injunctions of the King. Contrary to all custom and previous law, she and Caesar could now inherit from each other, and such care had been taken in drawing up the documents that, after Gabrielle's death, her father failed in his legal attempt to gain control of a portion of her property.

Soon after the publication of the royal decree, Gabrielle began to call herself Comtesse de Coney, using the name of the town in which Caesar had been born. A document written on April 2, 1596, and bearing Gabrielle's signature, states, "We, Gabrielle d'Estrées, Dame, Comtesse de Coney and Marquise de Monceaux, acknowledge that we have received from Monsieur François Hotman, King's Councillor and treasurer of the royal treasury, the sum of 500 écus in ready money, granted to us in payment of a like sum which had been advanced by us at His Majesty's command for certain affairs connected with his service of which he wishes no mention to be made, etc., and in witness whereof we give our signature."

Nothing is known of the private mission which required Gabrielle to spend money on the King's behalf, so speculation on the subject is useless. Of far greater importance is her bland assumption of the title, Comtesse de Coney. It is the only time she used the title, and Henry's well-preserved letters patent contain no document issuing an order granting this rank.

In fact, Henry could not have made her Countess of Coney without creating an uproar that would have caused endless difficulties, as Coney was within the domain of the Duchess of Angoulême, and not even the King had the right to assign the title to his mistress. If Henry granted Gabrielle the authority to call herself Comtesse de Coney, he immediately changed his mind; if she took the title herself, without consulting him, which is dubious, he persuaded her to abandon it, as she was upsetting the entire social order.

Not until September 1596, did she have the legal right to be called Marquise de Monceaux, although she had been using the title for a long time. Catherine de Medici, for whom the château of Monceaux had been built, owed enormous debts at the time of her death, and her desperate creditors, trying without success to get money during a civil war, finally banded together under the leadership of an able attorney, Pierre Cadet, who began to sell her properties as fast as Henry captured them and surrounding territories from the League.

At the time royal troops entered Paris and restored even greater stability to the country's finances, Cadet and his colleagues gratefully offered Henry the use of Monceaux until such time as it was auctioned to the highest bidder. Henry accepted, and when he "gave" the property to Gabrielle, it must have been his intention to buy it for her. She did not acquire legal possession, however, until March 25, 1596, notwithstanding the fact that Mayenne had been entertained there two months previously.

A royal equerry named du Tillet offered the sum of thirty-nine thousand écus for the land, manor, and appurtenances, and to the surprise of no one, was revealed as the agent for Gabrielle. The house and grounds now belonged to her, but her use of the title of Marquise was a courtesy granted her by diplomats, nobles, and members of the court out of respect — and, possibly, fear.

If the busy Henry thought he had actually granted Gabrielle the title, he was mistaken, and Isabelle de Sourdis remained close at hand to remind her niece of the oversight. Finally, in September 1596, Henry issued the necessary letters patent while visiting Lyons, and sealed the document "with a great green seal."

At last Gabrielle was a real marquise, and the way was open to give Caesar a duchy, make his mother its administrator, and thus give Gabrielle a seemingly valid reason for becoming a member of the Council. It was no secret at court that the King planned to make his son Duc de Vendôme, and the correspondence of many notables contains references to the pending event. But there were complications that compelled Henry to wait. He had pawned many of his properties in the duchy in order to finance his war against the League, and as it was pointless to grant the child an empty title, Henry began the painstaking task of redeeming manor houses and farm lands, forests, and even towns.

There were so many barriers to Gabrielle's entry into the Council that Henry took the matter into his own hands, and, in July 1596, gave her a set of the golden keys, offering no explanation to anyone. His sense of the dramatic undimmed, he chose an important occasion to reveal her new status.

Alexander Cardinal de Medici, who later became Pope Leo XI, was sent to France by Pope Clement as a special legate, and he was a man eminently qualified to perform a delicate mission. The Cardinal, a member of the Curia, was a cousin of the Grand Duke of Tuscany and one of a very few high-ranking prelates favoring the cause of France who had managed to retain the confidence of Philip II. It was his task to act as an intermediary and try to work out peace terms with Savoy and Spain. It might be noted that he succeeded brilliantly in the first instance, and inevitably failed in the second.

A large royal party, which included Mayenne, traveled to the border of Savoy to greet the Cardinal and escort him to Paris. Gabrielle rode in a carriage at the King's side, and at the very moment that Cardinal de Medici and his entourage crossed the frontier, she removed a scarf from her throat, allowing everyone present to see the golden keys of a Councillor hanging from her neck on a chain. She continued to wear them on the triumphal journey to Paris, and the residents of the capital saw them when she took part in the ceremonial procession that marked the Cardinal's entry into the city.

The records do not indicate whether she attended Council meetings that summer, but it is significant that another woman was added to the group at the same time — Princess Catherine also received a set of keys. Henry wisely avoided possible criticism by deliberately creating two new places rather than making just one for his mistress.

By the autumn of 1596, Gabrielle and Catherine were attending Council meetings regularly, and in October of that year both traveled to Rouen, the capital of the province of Normandy, on official business. Henry's financial problems continued to plague him, and although the income of the royal treasury had increased appreciably, expenses soared still higher. Acting on the advice of Sully, he decided to call an "assembly of notables" to deal with the matter.

It was his original intention to hold the meeting at Compiègne, but the loyalty of the Normans was still shaky, so the King decided to dazzle them with an opulent display far greater than any he had ever made in Paris. Commands were sent to nobles and officials to attend their monarch in Rouen, and Claude Groulart, President of the Parliament of Normandy, started to prepare for the invasion.

Gabrielle, now officially the Marquise de Monceaux, was the first person of importance to arrive in the city. Her carriage entered the gates at noon on October 10, and Groulart escorted her to the Abbot's Palace of Saint-Ouen, an elegant building that had been erected earlier in the century. Gabrielle left her carriage to ride through the streets on horseback, and Groulart commented to her, as he later did in his *Correspondence*, on his surprise at her lack of jewelry — the golden keys of a Councillor were her only ornamentation.

The ride on horseback must have caused her some physical discomfort, as she was well advanced in pregnancy.

Henry, for reasons unexplained, did not accompany her on the journey from Paris. He did not arrive, in fact, until six days later, when he rode into the city with an escort of princes and great lords, marshals and crown officials, provincial governors and bishops. Triumphal arches had been erected in the King's honor, and all along the route he saw allegorical statues and obelisks. The weather was brisk and some of the gentlemen were lightly clad, but everyone paused to watch a mock naval engagement in the Seine, and the Kling seemed to enjoy the fight between galleys and heavily armored round-boats.

Groulart made a speech of welcome, and other members of the Norman Parliament had intended to speak, too, but Henry cut the ceremonies short by hurrying to the Abbot's Palace, which, by no coincidence, became his headquarters. He remained in Rouen until mid-February, in part because Gabrielle had given birth to a daughter in November and consequently could not travel much earlier.

The long visit taxed the facilities of Rouen to the utmost. Foreign ambassadors, cardinals, and other high-ranking dignitaries came to the city, which was the temporary capital of France, and as many of the nobles had traveled with their own entourages, housing was at a premium. The wealthiest were forced to content themselves with humble lodgings, and the stalls of the old market were often empty. The whole area was ransacked for food, and the thrifty Norman farmers doubled and trebled their prices.

But Gabrielle kept a close watch on the expenses incurred by the royal household, and Diane, who sometimes went to the Abbot's Palace with her husband for dinner, says in her *Memorial*, "My sister was vexed when the keepers of shops demanded exorbitant fees for simple produce; the King being fond of eggs, veal, and the roe of herring, these items were kept in supply at the Palace, my sister insuring that the larders were filled. She made bitter complaint to M. de Montpensier, the Governor of Rouen, and after that time paid a lower fee for food and produce. Marshal de Balagny observed with much bitterness that the King, who could afford the costs of food better than others, was escaping more lightly, and felt certain our purse would be empty if the meeting of the assembly continued into the spring."

Rouen was poorly lighted, and when several eminent gentlemen were robbed one evening early in their stay, the Governor ordered long candles placed in lanterns and hung on posts at all crossroads. Then, with the local constabulary augmented by a battalion of Montmorency's light infantry, the streets became safe at night.

When Madame, the King's sister, arrived in the city, her golden keys of a Councillor hanging from her neck, the Chief Justice of Rouen, twelve members of the Norman Parliament, and the entire city board of aldermen went to meet her. Their attention flattered Catherine, but she quickly discovered they were indulging in no mere ceremony. Official after official begged her to issue a dispensation that would permit the shops to remain open on the Sabbath. As she was a Protestant, it was assumed that her attitude would be lenient.

But Catherine merely promised to refer the question to her brother. The matter was discussed at a Council meeting, and Henry, who had far more important problems on his mind, deferred to the opinion of the two ladies present. Gabrielle and Catherine had not only agreed that the shops should close on the Sabbath, but issued an announcement in the King's name, requesting that the price of bread be lowered two coppers per pound.

On the afternoon of Monday, November 4, 1596, the members of the assembly gathered in the great hall of the Abbot's Palace to hear an address by the King, a talk that may be the most famous of all his speeches, and is certainly the bluntest. There were no ladies in the audience, and only two were in the great hall. Gabrielle and Catherine sat hidden behind an arras at one side of the dais on which the King's throne was mounted. They were not permitted to speak on this occasion. Henry had made a great concession when he had admitted his mistress and his sister to the Council, but even he did not care to flout convention by letting them take places in the assembly. Perhaps they consoled themselves by jangling their golden keys as he spoke.

It had been the custom for French kings to deliver lengthy harangues, and the gentlemen settled back in their chairs for a long afternoon, but Henry's talk may well have been the shortest speech ever delivered by a monarch to lords who had traveled from every part of the country to hear him:

"Had it been my desire to win the title of orator, I should have learned some fine speech and delivered it to you with becoming gravity. But, gentlemen, my desires urge me to aim at far more glorious titles, and they are those of liberator and savior of the realm. You know well, to your cost, as I to mine, that when God called me to this throne I found France not only almost ruined but almost entirely lost to the French.

"By the mercy of God, by the prayers and good counsel of my servants, by the sword of my brave and generous nobility, all of whom I consider worthy of our finest title, that of gentleman, and by my own labor and toil, I have saved it from ruin. And, my dear people, you who stood by me at the beginning, I desire that now you should share with me this glory. I have not called you, as my predecessors used, to inform you of my wishes, but I have assembled you for the purpose of receiving your counsel and following it.

"I have called you, in short, with the idea of placing myself under your protection, an idea not often entertained by kings, by graybeards, or by conquerors. But the great love I bear my subjects and my heartfelt desire to add the two glorious titles of liberator and savior to that of King make everything seem easy and consistent with honor.

"My Chancellor will acquaint you further of my wishes."

The gentlemen stood, and while they applauded heartily, the King joined his mistress and sister. There, according to one of the most celebrated anecdotes of his reign, he asked Gabrielle her opinion of the speech.

She replied she had never heard better, but had been surprised at what he had said about putting himself under protection.

"*Ventre-Saint-gris!*" Henry exclaimed. "I meant it, but I keep my sword buckled to my side all the same."

The following morning the Council met, and Henry learned that his audience had thought his manner too much that of the soldier. He smiled and said that as the time had not yet come to lay down arms, he was a soldier, and would remain one as long as necessary.

That meeting of the Council was the last that Gabrielle attended in the month of November, for six days later she gave birth to a daughter. A large number of royal physicians and ladies were present to assist in the delivery; Henry, infinitely more relaxed than he had been two and a half years earlier, when Caesar had been born, was attending a meeting of financial advisers. He was informed of the happy event by Diane d'Estrées de Balagny, the only person with sufficient courage to interrupt the gentlemen conversing behind closed doors, or so she claims in her *Memorial*.

It was the custom for babies to be named by their fathers, but Henry granted the right to the mother of the infant, and Gabrielle returned the compliment by calling her daughter Catherine Henriette, after the two members of the truly legitimate house of Bourbon.

The christening took place on November 17, the King choosing the date because it was both his birthday and the anniversary of his most celebrated victory, the Battle of Ivry. The ceremony, which is described in detail by every literate man and woman of the period in letters and memoirs, was celebrated with as much pomp as that of a princess of the line.

Four canopies of silk adorned the old Cathedral of Rouen, and the church was filled with the great of the land. Trumpets heralded the approach of the King, who was preceded by the royal pages, all of them sons of the highest-ranking nobles, and a squad of King's guards. Henry, in uniform, and Gabrielle, in a velvet gown of dark red, which came to be known as "d'Estrées red," and was suspiciously close to the royal purple, appeared at the rear of the church. Between them, and clasping a hand of each, was Caesar, who, in a miniature version of his father's uniform, was making his first public appearance. The trio walked to the front pew, followed by a squad of Swiss mercenary troops.

Again the trumpets sounded, then violins were heard, and François, Prince de Conti, appeared, carrying the tiny star of the occasion. The other participants were of the highest station, too. Florent Cardinal de Gondi performed the ceremony, and the godmothers were Madame de Guise, acting on behalf of Princess Catherine, whose religion prevented her from being present, and the Duchess de Nevers. Montmorency, the Constable of France, was the godfather.

After the ceremony, the "royal family" paused on the steps of the cathedral to acknowledge the cheers of the townspeople, and Gabrielle, dropping her role of great lady, cradled her baby in her arms. Henry delighted the throng by taking the infant and holding her high in the air for everyone to see. A salute of twenty-one guns was fired, and the roar of the cannon, combined with the rarefied atmosphere of the heights over Henry's head, caused Catherine Henriette to protest. The King hastily gave the child to Gabrielle, who soothed her frightened daughter, and the dignity of the crown having been protected, the family rode to the Palace at the head of a glittering procession.

Two days later Gabrielle resumed her seat in the Council for deliberations of a serious nature. Spanish troops had moved down the seacoast from their colonial base in the Low Countries, and had occupied a number of towns, among them Calais. Elizabeth of England had sent a special ambassador to the christening, and shortly after the ceremony the envoy proposed a new treaty of alliance between Britain and France.

Elizabeth was willing to show her good faith by sending fresh troops to help her fellow monarch, and thoughtfully suggested that she could relieve Henry of at least a portion of his military burden by taking Calais for him.

Montmorency was the one Councillor who expressed himself freely on any subject raised at these meetings, but he was en route to Paris to act as the King's deputy in several matters of importance. Henry was the only speaker at the session. Presumably Gabrielle and Catherine felt they had nothing of value to contribute.

France, the King said, was pleased at the offer of a new treaty, and he intended to accept it. He would take Elizabeth's regiments, too, and would place them under the over-all command of Biron, whose troops outnumbered the British four to one. However, he said, he would decline with thanks the Queen's generosity regarding Calais.

Obviously no explanations were necessary. In the past the English had occupied Calais for long periods, and every Frenchman knew that if they established themselves there again, nothing short of a major war would dislodge them.

No other Council meetings were held that month. Henry relaxed by going out on several hunting trips, and Gabrielle, when she was not receiving notables, devoted herself to her children and to supervising the management of a household that, according to Diane's *Memorial*, supported eighty-three ladies and gentlemen, seventeen crown officials permanently attached to the King, and more than two hundred servants.

The proud parents of Catherine Henriette found a new way to amuse themselves on the cold winter evenings. It was the custom at the time for small children, even newborn infants, to be betrothed to the offspring of other members of the nobility. It was an effective method of cementing friendships and shoring up personal political alliances, and not even the King was able to resist the temptation to play the game.

Montmorency, the second most powerful man in the kingdom, was the father of a son born earlier in the same year. Apparently Henry had spoken to the Duke about arranging a marriage, for he wrote to his good friend on November 15, "I am well and so are my mistress and little Mademoiselle de Montmorency. The beauty of the child almost surpasses that of her mother, and when she kneels before the altar to repeat the marriage vows, she will be the loveliest of brides."

In another letter, written on November 20, he enlarged on the theme: "My friend, I am very well, thanks be to God. So is Caesar, and so is little Mademoiselle de Montmorency, for whom I have been offered a husband of good house and very rich, but I have sworn that she shall be Dame de Montmorency et de Chantilly.

"The wishes of my mistress echo mine, and she is prepared to take an oath that she will be satisfied with no lesser alliance than one with your house. If the knife of an assassin should cut me down before Almighty God is ready to receive me, a possibility that is ever-present in these times when enemies lurk behind every door, the Marquise de Monceaux swears that she will let no untoward fate prevent the joining in matrimony of your son and my well-loved daughter.

"I trust, my friend, that it may be so, and I give you a good night."

The assembly debated endlessly on ways and means of raising funds, short of increasing the taxes they themselves paid, and Gabrielle and Henry were kept busy with other projects. In spite of the raw, cold weather, they liked Rouen so much that they seriously thought of building themselves a château there, but nothing came of the project.

Gabrielle accomplished more as a matchmaker than as a supervising architect. A marriage was arranged between one of her younger sisters, Julienne-Hippolyte, and a young man of enormous wealth and impeccable family, Georges de Villars Brancas, Chevalier d'Oyse. The wedding was held on January 7, and the celebrations, which included a banquet at the Palace, lasted for two days and two nights.

Gabrielle presided over the festivities, with the King constantly at her side. He could deny her nothing, and at her instigation presented the bridegroom with a handsome wedding gift, the post of Lieutenant General of Normandy. "Our aunt," Diane declares in her *Memorial*, "was diligent in persuading my sister to urge this appointment upon the King, and overcame her natural reluctance to beg favors for her near relations."

It was assumed, of course, that the idea had been Gabrielle's, and those who were jealous of her influence complained in private of her insatiable greed. Diane's comment is the only evidence suggesting that Isabelle de Sourdis was playing her familiar role of puppet master, and the modern student cannot make a fair evaluation based on the few scraps of opinion that are available. Perhaps it is sufficient to observe that, in one way or another, the members of Gabrielle's family were not made to suffer because of her intimacy with the King.

She and her children did not go empty-handed during the long sojourn at Rouen, either. An inventory of gifts received, written in her own hand, suggests the tremendous power she wielded at the court:

> A large diamond and sapphire bauble, very fine, mounted in gold, sent to me by the Queen of England.
>
> A set of twenty-four goblets of chased silver, sent to Caesar by the Duc de Medici. I to have use of them until he establishes his own household.
>
> Six bolts of the cloth-of-kings, presented to Catherine Henriette by the aldermen of Rouen, each bolt most pleasing to the eye, each of a different hue.
>
> An emerald neck-pin, very fine, presented to me by President Groulart.
>
> A smaller pin, of similar design and cut, presented to Catherine Henriette by President Groulart.
>
> A jar of oil, used for the making of the essence of scent, rare and costly, presented to me by Madame de Guise.

> Two stags, killed by M. de Brissac while hunting with the
> King, presented to me by M. de Brissac.

Gabrielle failed to overwhelm the people of Normandy, however. The citizens of this region, perhaps the most conservative of French provinces in the matter of morals, did not approve of her relationship with Henry. M. Desclozeaux comments in his monograph, that the public rendering of so much honor to a mistress wounded their sense of propriety, and seemed to them to set a bad example. Certainly the members of the clergy attached to the cathedral did not join in the rush to present her with gifts, and M. Desclozeaux writes that their records contain the dry statement, "It is to be noted that neither bread nor wine were administered to Madame la Marquise de Monceaux, His Majesty's great friend, for certain reasons alleged at the time, but at the present concealed."

Gabrielle was riding on the crest of a wave, no matter what certain people thought of her, but life was not one long celebration, as she learned in the following year when she faced her most severe test.

14: THE CRUCIBLE, 1597

The festivities that had been the only positive achievement of the assembly of notables held in Rouen continued unabated when Gabrielle, Henry, and their children returned to Paris in the middle of February 1597. The King was behaving frivolously for the first time in his life, and Gabrielle, always anxious to please him, fell in with his mood.

It was the custom for Parisian merchants to hold a fair immediately prior to Lent, and on Shrove Tuesday the Béarnais and his mistress rode to the stalls and tents that had been erected in a field on the bank of the Seine. Every move made by the pair was duly recorded by other members of the large party, who are in agreement on major details. They add up to the fact that even though Henry was enjoying himself, his basic nature had not changed.

Gabrielle paused to admire a carved ring in a booth operated by a Portuguese jeweler, and tried it on her finger. Henry asked if she wanted it, and she replied that she would be pleased to own it if it were not too expensive. The jeweler said the price was eight hundred écus. It may be that he increased the charge because he thought the King could afford to pay heavily, but Henry professed to be shocked and haggled at length with the man. The jeweler reluctantly reduced the price by fifty écus, but said he could not afford to go lower. Henry made every attempt to persuade him, Gabrielle remaining silent during the discussion, and when Henry found that the jeweler would not budge, he thriftily refused to purchase the ring.

Instead, at another stall, he spent five écus on a little silver sugarplum box, engraved with the twelve signs of the zodiac.

He announced he had bought it for Caesar, and handing it to an equerry for safekeeping, wandered through the fair grounds with Gabrielle on his arm. They paused frequently to admire various objects, and often they made offers for one item or another, but the merchants consistently demanded higher prices than they were willing to pay, and in the end they returned to their coach with only the sugarplum box to show for their outing. It is scarcely necessary to add that the merchants were bitterly disappointed.

On the day before the start of Lent, the people of the capital dressed in masks and costumes, and countless parties were held, some in the streets, some in private homes. Henry and Gabrielle entered into the spirit of the occasion, and after presiding at a mock ceremony of nobles dressed as wizards, started out on a tour of Paris. They themselves were masked, and wore wizards' costumes. They joined in street celebrations, where the citizens recognized and embraced them, much to the alarm of the King's guards, who tried to protect the monarch from possible assassination.

The night was long, and Henry and Gabrielle made the most of it. At some parties they were not recognized, but their hosts must have been dull and unobserving, as a vast crowd had gathered and followed the pair everywhere. Henry defied prudes by escorting his mistress to the house of the notorious banker, Zamet, and there they supped on chicken and baked olives, stuffed oysters and chilled wine. Then, continuing their peregrinations, they went into every quarter of the city and did not return to the Louvre until eight o'clock in the morning.

"His Majesty was lively of countenance and manner, as was my sister," Diane writes in her *Memorial*, "but fatigue and a lack of sleep had exhausted all others."

On March 5, the infant son of the Constable was baptized at Notre Dame. Cardinal de Medici, the papal legate, performed the ceremony, and Henry stood as the godfather of the child who would, if he had his way, become the husband of Catherine Henriette. Gabrielle sat in the royal pew, wearing a gown of green velvet, with a hat and cloak of a lighter shade of green. A splendid feast was held at the Louvre after the ceremony, followed by a concert, a ballet, and a masque.

Henry and Gabrielle, both still in a holiday mood, entertained the company by pretending to argue, the King maintaining that she should have worn fifteen diamonds in her hair, while Gabrielle insisted that it would have been vulgar to ornament herself with more than twelve.

On Wednesday, March 12, Princess Catherine invited Henry and Gabrielle to attend a ballet at her official residence, the Tuileries. At the conclusion of the ballet the musicians struck up another tune, and Henry led Gabrielle onto the floor. They circled the room twice, as the rest of the company watched, but Gabrielle whispered to her lover, and Henry gestured rather sharply. The ladies and gentlemen took the hint, and soon the dance floor was crowded.

The party was interrupted when a courier arrived, his boots and cloak covered with a heavy coating of dust. The man dropped to one knee, and the musicians, sensing a crisis, stopped playing as the King broke the seal and ripped open the message. The scene that followed is one of the most famous incidents in Henry's reign.

Spain, he announced to the shocked company, had launched a surprise attack on Amiens.

Gabrielle alone grasped immediately the terrible significance of this, and she burst into tears.

"It is a blow direct from Heaven," Henry said. "The poor people, by refusing a little garrison I was willing to allow them, have ruined themselves."

He paused for a moment, and only the sound of Gabrielle's sobs broke the silence. Then, in a loud voice heard throughout the huge chamber, Henry said:

"I have played the King of France long enough! It is time I returned to the King of Navarre!"

No one moved, and no one dared to speak.

Henry turned to the weeping Gabrielle, saying, "Mistress, we must put off our finery. I must mount my horse and ride off to wage another war!"

They returned at once to the Louvre and all the gentlemen who held the King's commission hurried away, too. Henry spent the night rallying his troops and shortly before dawn rode north toward Amiens and the Spanish force that had invaded France from the Spaniards' province of Belgium. He headed six regiments of horse and three of infantry, with the Constable as second in-command.

Only Gabrielle realized that the King's situation was truly desperate. He had been hiding his disappointment over the failure of the meeting at Rouen, allowing himself to forget his troubles in a round of parties, but now it was necessary to face the bald truth that the royal treasury was virtually empty.

Gabrielle's response to the crisis was magnificent, as her contemporaries and later historians agree. She went to her strongboxes, one in the Louvre and the other in the Hôtel d'Estrées, and emptied them, giving Henry every penny of ready cash that she possessed, a total of fifty thousand écus. For a time, at least, these funds would pay the wages of the troops and would enable the quartermasters to buy provisions and ammunition.

But that was only the beginning of her night's work. While Henry organized his troops for the long march, Gabrielle returned to her carriage and, still dressed in the gown she had worn to the ballet, visited the town houses of the greatest nobles, asking for contributions to what was literally a war chest, a leather traveling box that sat on the floor of the carriage.

No two estimates of the amount collected by Gabrielle are the same. Diane writes that she obtained two hundred and fifty thousand écus, which is probably an exaggeration, and Sully, in his *Memoirs*, says "the total was less than fifty thousand." The true figure probably lies somewhere between.

In any event, Gabrielle was not satisfied, and went off to the house of Zamet, carrying most of her jewelry with her. The banker was sleeping when she arrived, but became wide awake when he learned her mission, and loaned her one hundred and ten thousand écus, keeping her jewels as security. She knew, as did Zamet, that they were worth several times that amount, but Gabrielle took what she could get. It might be noted that the gems were not redeemed until the early part of the summer, after Sully had introduced a new, centralized system of taxation that refilled the treasury with gold.

In a few hours Gabrielle had raised a substantial fortune, but apparently it did not occur to her that her task was finished. She returned to the Louvre, where an officer of the royal household guard stood sentry duty over the money while she hurried into the palace, kissed her sleeping children, and, not bothering to change her clothes, raced back to the carriage and actually rode out of Paris with the army's vanguard.

She literally started toward Amiens one hour before the King marched out of Paris at the head of the main body of troops. They traveled separately all day, and Henry was astonished to find her waiting for him that night, when he reached the fortress at Beauvais. From that time forward they were united at the front. But they could not have seen much of each other, for Henry was frantically organizing and directing the entire war effort.

Gabrielle was content, however. According to the Constable, who saw her every day, "The Marquise patiently spent what little time the King could spare at the side of His Majesty, sharing his enthusiasm and zeal for the trials that awaited all of us."

Gabrielle's conduct in an hour of national and personal crisis was as astonishing as it was courageous. She stripped herself of money and valuables because Henry needed funds to prosecute the unexpected war, and clearly gave no thought to her own financial security. There was a strong possibility that the King might be killed in battle, in which case she and her children would be robbed of their protector. There was also a chance that France might be defeated, thus making it impossible for Henry to repay the écus she had given him or to redeem her jewelry. Neither possibility alarmed her.

Her decision to accompany him, which was also her own, was equally remarkable. She, who had once loved comfort above all else, could have remained in Paris with her children, and certainly no one would have criticized her. The wives and mistresses of the marshals and generals stayed in their luxurious town houses and suffered no personal discomforts, but Gabrielle deliberately elected to risk the unpleasantness of traveling with an army, the hardships of life in the field, and the hazards of war because she wanted to be near Henry.

Not even Sully could find fault with her behavior, and d'Aubigné, who had consistently damned her since Henry's conversion to Catholicism, changed his tune and again became her champion. She had more than met the supreme test of loyalty.

In order to understand her unselfishness, it is necessary to realize the importance of the news that the courier had brought to the Tuileries. An attack on Amiens was no minor raid, like the temporary capture of Calais by a corps from the Low Countries. Neither France nor Spain had struck a major blow since the Vatican had received Henry into the Church, but the fall of the most important city on the French side of the border could mean only that Philip was launching a campaign intended to destroy his adversary. If Amiens was not retaken, Spanish armies would be in a position to fan out across southern France and capture the whole of the Languedoc country and its capital, Bordeaux. If that happened, Lyons would be endangered, and enemy columns might march all the way to Orleans — and Paris.

Therefore it was essential that Henry repel the invaders, no matter how high the cost. He was in an excellent diplomatic position, as he could claim in all honesty that Philip had been the aggressor, but he knew that no matter how much the world might sympathize, no one would come to his rescue. He alone could rally France at home and in battle, and if he failed in either task he would lose his crown as well as his country.

The King was enraged, as were the people of France, when they learned the details of the attack on Amiens. The Spaniards had used a version of the Trojan horse technique, sending soldiers disguised as civilians into the city on a Sunday morning when most of the inhabitants were in church. The gates had been opened, hundreds of Spanish cavalrymen had ridden through them, and only a few French noblemen and members of their households had been able to put up a feeble resistance. In all, no more than twenty or thirty shots had been fired.

As he marched south, Henry posted guards in every major town, and although he needed troops, willingly left two companies of Swiss mercenaries in Lyons, whose citizens repaid him by raising a regiment of cavalry and another of infantry, both joining him less than one month later. The King thrived in an atmosphere of crisis, making speeches at every stop on the march, dictating to secretaries while in the saddle, working late at night drawing up instructions to the Constable and orders to the Council of civilians in Paris. He laid out the strategy for a diversionary campaign against the Low Countries, cajoling, begging, and threatening northern nobles until they assembled an army and marched. At the same time he supervised the purchase of provisions, and no detail of his own campaign escaped his attention.

There must have been moments when Gabrielle wondered whether she would have been wiser to stay at home.

Marshal Biron and a corps of professional soldiers joined the royal army at Montdidier on March 18, and a few days later the investment of Amiens was begun. The King himself led a surprise attack against the enemy, but was halted at the walls of the city and forced to retire. The troops started the weary task of digging trenches around the city, engineers went to work on catapults, and cavalry patrols roamed through the countryside, searching for convoys carrying supplies to the Spaniards.

A tent was erected for Gabrielle adjacent to the royal pavilion, but she still saw little of Henry. He expected reinforcements, but they did not arrive; he awaited shipments of money, but received only excuses; and nobles who had promised to join him did not appear. He redoubled his efforts, spending his days in the field and his nights writing letters. Gabrielle saw him only when he sat down to snatch a hasty meal.

A new querulous note crept into his correspondence, and he complained that his followers were paying only lip service to his cause. Through the difficult years he had always proved himself staunch in adversity, and no matter how great the odds against him, had never whined. His sudden depression bewildered his generals, and Gabrielle must have known that something was wrong.

On the last day of March, he sent a bitter letter to the Council in Paris, saying, "All France ought to run to help me. For my own part I willingly put my life at the disposal of the public safety, so dear is it to me, and I assure you that could I recover this loss to France at the price of it, I would hold it well spent and could think to find no more honorable tomb."

Gabrielle had never known him in such a mood, and must have been perplexed and lonely. She could confide in no one, and there were no members of her own sex to whom she could talk, for, aside from some camp followers, she was the only woman with the army. She had not made the long journey nor suffered hardships and inconveniences in vain, however, for she soon realized that Henry needed her.

On April 1, the King wrote again to the Council, declaring, "My mistress believes I am not well."

The next day he was convinced that her diagnosis was right, and in a letter to a friend said, "I am not well in my person, and am assailed by so many needs and difficulties that I know no longer to what saint to make my vows, in order to find my way out of my unfortunate position."

Four days later his health had grown worse, and in a confidential communication to one of his civilian Councillors, he wrote, "My mistress attends me day and night, and is ever at my side. The state of my health compels me to retire for a few days to Beauvais, where I am going to diet myself; for I have reason to fear that I am going to be attacked with gravel, from which I hoped I was in no danger. M. de la Rivière has promised to cure me of this ill. My state is worse than that of the King of Navarre, for now I am helped by no one, my mistress excepted."

The Constable remained before Amiens with the army, Biron acting as his deputy, and Henry retired to Beauvais with Gabrielle and three physicians. The "attack of gravel" did not develop, but the King could neither sleep nor rouse himself. Modern physicians probably would have diagnosed his ailment as exhaustion. Certainly he had forgotten that he could no longer expend energy with reckless abandon, but he was incapable of changing his lifelong habits.

Several more regiments were needed to augment the army, and as it seemed likely that the siege would be long, money to pay military wages and buy provisions would be required before summer. The King took stock of the miserable situation, and coming to the conclusion that he alone could shake the country out of its lethargy, pulled himself out of his sickbed and returned to Paris on April 13.

That evening the magistrates of the capital were called to the Louvre, and Henry, looking pale and tired, addressed them briefly: "Gentlemen, it is not care of my health alone that has recalled me from the frontier, but that I may also call upon each one of you to think of the straits we are in, knowing that no one could better or more forcibly put the evil before you and obtain the remedy. You, in your goodness, last year succored the poor, the infirm, and the suffering of your town. I come to ask for alms for those whom I have left at the frontier. You have helped those who were in the streets, or in houses seated by the fireside. I ask for alms for those who are on active service, and who are serving day and night risking their lives so that you may live in peace."

That night he collapsed. The people of Paris were alarmed, but the royal physicians announced that his condition was not serious. Gabrielle refused to leave his side, and a small bed was carried into the King's chamber for her and placed at the foot of the canopied four-poster.

Henry's appeal had been touching, and presumably the magistrates tried to raise money, but met with indifference. Spring had come to Paris, and the war seemed very far away. Some announced that they had already made contributions to Gabrielle, and could not afford to give more. The prospects of the besiegers at Amiens looked increasingly bleak.

The King's physicians kept Henry in bed, and Montmorency returned to Paris to take charge of affairs of state, Biron assuming command of the army. Henry would have held Council meetings in his bedroom, but Gabrielle firmly refused to allow him more than a handful of visitors. Princess Catherine saw him daily, the Constable was free to come and go as he pleased, and a few others were admitted, but the time-honored custom of filling a patient's room with friends was proscribed. Gabrielle showed more common sense in this than the doctors, who had tried to enlist Diane's help on the grounds that Gabrielle was interfering with their regimen.

In spite of Gabrielle's best efforts, too many people had access to Henry at the Louvre, and his response to treatment was slow. Late in April, Gabrielle insisted that he be moved to the royal château at nearby Saint-Germain. She and the children accompanied him, and Montmorency issued a blunt order stating that His Majesty would receive no one except those whom he expressly commanded to come to him.

Gabrielle continued to nurse her lover, and his health at last improved. By mid-May he was walking in the gardens with her and spending an hour or two each morning romping with Caesar. Notices were posted in every quarter of Paris, signed by three royal physicians, saying that the King had made a miraculous recovery.

Henry remained at the château until the end of May. His enforced rest had given him an opportunity to reflect on the ills of the nation, and among those summoned to Saint-Germain was Sully, at that time still the Baron de Rosny. The two men spent an afternoon and evening in conference, the meeting broken only by an hour at dinner with Gabrielle.

Sully, in his *Memoirs*, claims full credit for the new financial policy that grew out of that meeting, of course. Unfortunately, Henry made neither public pronouncements nor private declarations on the subject, so it is impossible to determine whether he or the man who was rapidly becoming his principal financial adviser was responsible for a revolutionary method of obtaining funds.

All the nobles owned property, and a decree signed by the King ordered them to pay a tax on the land they held. The Church per se was exempted from the demand, but a separate letter was circulated by the cardinals and bishops, asking all priests to contribute to the war chest.

The nobles protested in vain, for squads of troops accompanied the tax collectors, and gold began to pour into the treasury. It was plain that Henry meant business, and not even the greatest lord wanted to risk being tried on a charge of treason. Perhaps Henry had planned the new step many months earlier, and had invited the members of the nobility to take part in the assembly of notables at Rouen in order to prepare them for his unprecedented action. Whatever his strategy, it was effective, and his power was so great that not even princes or dukes dared to defy him.

Henry, thinking he had at last solved the problem of a lack of funds that had embarrassed him for so many years, was so anxious to return to Amiens that he rode there with a small escort of cavalry. Gabrielle followed by easier stages.

The siege was in the doldrums when the King arrived, but he injected new vigor into the troops. Two French regiments, aided by a smaller body of English infantry, presently took the village of Cocoment, a key bastion outside the city. Hopes in the camp were high, but fell again when a promised delivery of funds did not arrive. It appeared that the King's optimism had been premature, and on June 21, he returned to Paris to lend the authority of his person to the tax-collecting drive.

Nobles who had found it inconvenient to pay the government suddenly found the funds, and Henry rode back to Amiens, arriving at his bivouac on the last day of the month. Assaults against the city having failed, he stepped up the work of digging attack trenches. The soldiers hated the tedious labor on the trenches, which were moved forward inch by inch, but the newly affluent King offered them six sous for each six feet dug, and the spades flew.

The new tax system produced unexpected complications. The Protestant nobles, who had quietly accepted Henry's conversion to Catholicism, banded together and said that if they were forced to pay money out of their own pockets to support the crown, it was their right to be granted full religious freedom, equal to that of the Catholics, in return. The issue was so complicated that Henry was forced to procrastinate, and promised he would devote all of his energies to the matter at a more suitable time. He realized, obviously, that the siege could not be protracted indefinitely, and he tightened the noose that was strangling Amiens.

The first sign that his new tactics were successful came on July 17, when the Spaniards poured out of the city and fought a desperate hand-to-hand battle in an attempt to drive off the besiegers. French losses that day numbered more than five hundred killed; no figures were given on the number wounded or on Spanish losses. That was the first of a number of similar sorties, and Henry, concerned about Gabrielle's safety, begged her to return to Paris.

She refused. "The Marquise de Monceaux, my mistress," Henry wrote to his Constable, who was remaining in Paris to supervise the tax collections, "displays a loyalty to my person that causes grave concern in me for her safety. Only yesterday the enemy advance-guard rode out of Amiens, and so sharp was their attack that I myself was compelled to enter the fray against them. With two hundred horse and one hundred and fifty carabines I have defeated them, with the loss of no more than two horse soldiers.

"Last evening I found three bullet holes burned into the fabric of my mistress' tent, and begged her to go to her house in Paris, where her life would not be endangered, but she laughed and was deaf to my pleas, saying that the heat of Paris was more than she could bear. I asked if she would not be happy at Monceaux, where all things are pleasing, and she replied that only in my presence is she pleased. I entertain no fears for myself, but daily tremble for her."

Henry had every reason to be afraid. The stakes at Amiens were so high that Philip sent four fresh regiments and a huge supply train to relieve the plight of his garrison. The commander of the column played a trick that should not have fooled as experienced a soldier as Biron, who had charge of the eastern approaches. Feinting in strength, the Spaniards drew Biron's troops out of position, then made a wild and successful dash into the city.

The French countered by summoning reserves from the north. Again the tempo of the campaign quickened. The Spaniards made daily cavalry charges, the heavy guns of both sides fired from dawn until dusk, and Henry grimly worked to close every avenue of escape still open to the enemy, knowing that until victory was won, nothing could be done to alleviate the plight of the citizens of Amiens, who were prisoners behind their own walls.

Certainly the danger to Gabrielle was real. The Grand Master of French Artillery, whose tent was located only a short distance from hers, lost his life one morning as he was emerging from his pavilion, a heated cannonball shearing off his head. Casualties mounted steadily, and no part of the campsite was really safe. Yet Gabrielle would not withdraw, and insisted that her tent remain next to that of the King.

There were few conveniences, sanitation facilities were crude, and day-to-day living was brutal. All meals were cooked in the open by an orderly who served Henry and his mistress, whose diet consisted mainly of roasted meat, stale bread that had been carried great distances, and warm wine or beer. On the rare occasions when men could be spared to bring water so Gabrielle could bathe, a special pavilion had to be erected to insure privacy for her, and the water was heated in kettles, which were carried to a clay-lined pit that served as her tub. Like the men, she washed in cold water every morning.

"Gabrielle suffered many tortures before Amiens," writes Louise de Guise in her *Adventures*. The two women corresponded, so it would appear that Louise was not relying on her author's imagination when she told her friend's story.

"The last of her cosmetic unguents were exhausted on the ninth day of July, and she received no new supply until late in August, when a packet was forwarded to her in a military train.

"Having been horrified when a poor wretch, a foot soldier, spoiled a gown he had been ordered to cleanse, it being ragged from neck to hem, she undertook to wash her own clothes; but soap being in short supply, she was compelled to pound her garments with rocks, after the manner of the meanest of peasants. Nor could she escape from drudgery by the reading of romances, there being no oil, all illumination being provided by candles of the poorest quality."

No motive other than love could have inspired Gabrielle's stubborn refusal to retire to Paris or Monceaux. She resumed her old habit of visiting the sick and wounded every day, and undoubtedly sat down alone to her meat and bread many evenings. Henry often held staff conferences around a night campfire, and frequently dictated letters to his secretaries until dawn.

Mayenne demonstrated his loyalty to the crown by joining the besiegers late in July, and it was the corpulent Duke who later saved Gabrielle's life, thus repaying the debt he owed her for arranging his truce with the King.

The frightening incident occurred on September 15, when Henry, following the suggestion of his physicians, was relaxing on a one-day hunting trip. The Austrian Hapsburgs came to Philip's aid by secretly sending a heavily armed corps to Amiens. About an hour after Henry had ridden off into the forests, a heavy artillery barrage rained down on the headquarters sector of his camp. Cavalry patrols soon brought word that twenty thousand men, their guns at the head of their column, were marching toward them, following the course of the Somme River.

The unexpected appearance of the Austrians confused the French, and two companies of recruits fled in disorder. Gabrielle, according to a number of virtually identical accounts, maintained a monumental calm worthy of Henry himself. Ignoring the artillery fire that fell around her, she stood outside her tent, urging the French troops to resist.

The Austrians pushed forward rapidly when they met only scattered resistance, and Mayenne acted with dispatch to counter the grave threat. Rallying several regiments of veterans, he placed himself at their head and, hurrying forward to the trenches, opened a sharp defensive fire, holding firm while Gabrielle cheered her defenders. He was soon joined by Biron's corps, and a major battle developed.

Henry had heard the cannon fire and turned back before hard-riding couriers reached his side. His first act, when he reached the scene, was to order Gabrielle removed to the rear. He took command of his forces, realigning them; the battle raged all day and far into the night, with the issue often in doubt. By midnight the Austrian offensive was blunted, and three hours later Henry launched such a vigorous counterattack that the shattered enemy withdrew, carrying out its retreat in an eerie silence.

The following day it was estimated that the Austrian vanguard had penetrated to within five hundred paces of the spot where Gabrielle had been standing, exhorting the French.

Philip of Spain may have been a tyrant, but he was intelligent enough to know when he was beaten. When messengers brought word of the Austrian defeat to Madrid, he sent orders to the commander at Amiens to surrender the garrison. The gates of the city were thrown open on September 25. Henry graciously allowed the Spaniards to keep their sidearms and personal baggage, and, at his instructions, the officer who had been in charge of the Spanish defense, Hernando Teillo de Porto Carego, who had been killed a few days before the end of the siege, was buried in the Cathedral of Amiens.

The Spaniards withdrew, marching in single file past Henry, his generals, and staff officers, all of whom were heavily armed. There was no victory celebration in the French camp, as everyone was too weary, but even the most ignorant, illiterate foot soldier knew that Philip had lost his greatest gamble. There would be real peace now between France and Spain, and in time a firm treaty would be signed.

Gabrielle, returning to Paris with the King, did not travel empty-handed. His love for her was greater than ever, and with good reason, for she had demonstrated a devotion to his person and cause that no one else could equal. She had sacrificed her fortune, placed her jewels in jeopardy, collected money for him, nursed him when he had been ill, and had shared the dangers of the siege with him. He repaid her royally.

When he had returned to Amiens at the end of June from his fund-raising trip to Paris, Henry surprised Gabrielle by giving her a chest studded with gold nails. In it were fifty thousand écus, the sum she had given him, and all of her jewels, which he had redeemed from Zamet. There was a scroll in the box, too, stating that he had purchased some important properties on her behalf from the debt-ridden Duchess de Guise — the large manor of Beaufort, the smaller manor of Largicourt, and the barony of Jaucourt, all of which had belonged, at one time, to the noble house of Clèves and previously to the ancient house of Foix. The thrifty Henry had obtained them at the bargain price of forty thousand écus.

The gift was indeed princely, but an even greater surprise awaited Gabrielle. On the morning of July 6, Henry interrupted his siege efforts long enough to hand her another document, and she discovered he had issued letters patent raising these properties to a dukedom for her and, after her, for Caesar.

The order began by extolling the virtue which Caesar, in his father's considered opinion, had shown from birth. The education he had already received, together with his natural endowments, had produced remarkable results, Henry believed. Caesar, he declared, was still too young to sustain a title of honor, "but having considered that there is no one nearer to him than the Marquise de Monceaux, his mother, that all she has of riches and titles will revert to those of her blood, and that she is in herself worthy of every honor, worthy, too, by reason of the family from which she springs, a family which first gave a marshal to France as long ago as two hundred years.

"Not to go too far back, we call to mind that her grandfather served under four kings, in all the wars and all the battles of his time, and always received some special notice for his bravery. His son, too, father of the said lady, who was reared in the house of the late King Francis, held the office of Grand Master of the Artillery at the battle of Montcontour, and is now Lieutenant General of Picardy and of our good town of Paris, Governor of the Ile-de-France, and the oldest member of the Council of State, and a knight of Saint Michael and the Holy Ghost. His son, the Marquis de Coeuvres, is of a pattern with his worthy ancestors.

"For these considerations, having regard to Caesar as much as to the person of the said lady, seeing that Caesar must reap the advantages which his mother receives, and that the latter has bought the manor of Beaufort and the barony of Jaucourt, and that to these lands belong all the rights, tokens, and qualities necessary for the upholding of the name and the title of honor and dignity of a duchy of France, we hereby raise the manor of Beaufort and the barony of Jaucourt to a dukedom, depending directly in faith, homage, and justice on the court of the Parliament of Paris alone.

"And seeing that it is a question of the person of our natural and legitimate son in the future, and of the Marquise de Monceaux in the present, it is for us to designate the rank as that of the duchy of Beaufort, and to order that it is our wish that this duchy take equal rank with all dukes and peers of the realm, as would have been the case had the duchy of Beaufort been created and raised immediately after the duchy of Montmorency, except that by this present erection and the edicts of July 1500, and of May 1579, in default of heirs male this duchy may revert to the crown, a condition and derogation without which the said lady would in no wise accept our liberality."

The King had made careful preparations during his trip to Paris to insure that the formalities would be observed without delay. Obviously, a copy of his letters patent was in the hands of faithful followers in the Parliament, for the decree was registered only four days later, on July 10. And the Court of Accounts, acting with unprecedented speed, validated it on August 1. In both bodies the vote of approval was unanimous.

Gabrielle had not only been made a duchess, but stood directly below the Constable, the hereditary First Duke of the realm. Noble noses of ancient lineage must have been put out of joint, and more than one proud duke must have sniffed discreetly. The only rung on the ladder that remained to be climbed was the long step toward the coronet of a queen, and even Isabelle de Sourdis, who had spent a comfortable spring and summer at her Paris town house, must have been satisfied with her protégée's progress.

Not only had Gabrielle been elevated to a high perch, a seat which would go to her son at her death, but her father had become one of the most influential lords of the country. His post as Lieutenant General of Picardy had been given to him the previous year, but the lieutenant generalship of Paris and governorship of the Ile-de-France, either of which automatically would have assured him a place on the Council, were new. Thanks to his wayward daughter, he had skyrocketed to political positions of the greatest power and importance; only the Constable's influence was greater.

De Brissac, ever a realist, wrote to his wife from the camp at Amiens, "Do you visit the Marquis d'Estrées, and win his favor, while I, for my part, shall ingratiate myself anew with Her Grace of Beaufort. Their smiles open all doors to the chamber of the King, and their frowns bar access to the throne."

The new duchess was unable to change her style of living after her promotion, and continued to pound her shifts and corsets between rocks on the banks of the Somme. No matter what her rank, she was Henry's woman, and continued to share his tribulations until the Lily flag once again flew over Amiens.

Biron sent a letter to the Constable in mid-July, confidently anticipating her return to Paris in the immediate future, and Montmorency wrote to the King early in August, asking when she might be expected. The King replied that he hoped she would travel with a convoy of wounded led by Sieur Armand de Nevers, but the lady had other thoughts and refused to budge. She believed that when Henry was in trouble, her place was at his side, and neither the dictates of common sense nor blunt royal commands caused her to change her mind.

Diane de Balagny, acting upon the advice of her Aunt de Sourdis, planned to give a ball in honor of the new Duchess when the weary but triumphant King and his mistress finally returned to Paris after Amiens had been relieved and the campaign won. But, Diane reveals in her *Memorial*, the party was canceled at Gabrielle's own request. She wanted no celebration, she told her sister, because she was pregnant again, and needed time to recuperate from the strains of camp life.

15: THE SILKEN GLOVE, 1597–98

After the Spanish threat to France had been removed, Henry was free to turn to the most vexing of his domestic problems, his relations with the duchy of Brittany. The ruler of this virtually sovereign state was Philippe-Emmanuel, Duc de Mercoeur, the brother of Dowager Queen Louise, widow of Henry III. Mercoeur and his haughty wife, the enormously wealthy Marie of Luxembourg, had long been a thorny goad in the royal side. Only now, after exercising patience for years, was Henry in a position to deal with them.

The situation in Brittany was an inherited problem that had been caused by the impulsive and foolish generosity of Henry III. Blithely turning a deaf ear to the advice of his Council and even daring to ignore the admonitions of his mother, he had, with so little forethought that his act seemed almost deliberate, created a knotty problem for the crown.

The handsome, dashing, and inordinately greedy young brother of Queen Louise had been known as the Marquis de Noményé when he had arrived at the court of Henry III, and the two blades had discovered they shared the same interests: women and stag hunting. The weakling King had made his brother-in-law Duc de Mercoeur, and in 1576 had arranged his marriage with the wealthiest girl in France, Marie des Martigues, the only child of the Duke of Luxembourg and Penthièvre. Not satisfied with forming an alliance that undermined his own security, Henry III had insisted on making Mercoeur Governor of Brittany in spite of the fact that the bride's family had long claimed the duchy as their own.

Philippe-Emmanuel and Marie had deserted their monarch at the start of the last, turbulent year of his reign, joining the League in the hope that France would fall apart and that they could then establish their own independent kingdom. They had been violently opposed to Henry IV from the time he had succeeded to the throne, and neither force of arms nor persuasion had affected them.

De Brissac had been made Lieutenant General of the duchy by Henry, but his appointment was meaningless, as Mercoeur's troops turned Henry's royal regiments back at the border. Queen Louise was on the friendliest of terms with Gabrielle and Henry, and with good reason: her financial position was so precarious that, in the early summer of 1597, Gabrielle invited her to make her home at Monceaux, and to live there, rent free, for the rest of her days. Louise tried to show her gratitude by twice visiting her brother and drowning him with letters in which she begged him to yield to royal authority.

Mercoeur paid no attention to the pleas, and instead rallied his forces, which were considerable. The Parliaments of Rennes and Nantes voted unanimously to support him, and the nobles of the duchy, though fearing reprisals by Henry, contributed money to Mercoeur's treasury and men-at-arms to his field forces.

In October 1597, soon after Henry's return to Paris, he sent de Brissac with a few token regiments to demand that the duchy surrender and that Mercoeur take an oath of fealty to the crown. But the Marshal, having been ordered to avoid open warfare, had turned back when Mercoeur met him at the border with an army several times the size of his own.

Henry's patience was exhausted, and he decided to crush the last of the rebels, brushing aside as tenderhearted the advice of Gabrielle, who argued at Council meetings that the same end could be accomplished peacefully. In spite of royal rebuffs, she refused to abandon her argument, and the Council became divided on the issue. The majority, of course, supported Henry, and among those who voted with him was Antoine d'Estrées. But the Constable believed Gabrielle's position was sound, and so, of all people, did Sully.

Henry, however, had made up his mind to wreak military vengeance, and began to assemble a new army for the purpose of reducing Brittany. The prospect alarmed many nobles of the duchy, who had never met the King, having been isolated in Mercoeur's miniature "kingdom" for years. They were relieved when affairs of state that had accumulated during Henry's long campaign at Amiens forced him to postpone his march. Philippe-Emmanuel and Marie breathed more easily, too, and the Duke notified the Parliaments of his cities and towns that Henry was afraid to attack him.

The confidence of Mercoeur vanished early in January 1598, when Marshal de Brissac began to assemble a huge army of eighty-five thousand men, which included regiments of cavalry, heavy and light infantry, and siege and assault engineers. It was obvious that the King was in earnest.

The nobles of Brittany, who had believed for years that Henry was a fire-eating monster, lost their nerve, and the Parliaments became panicky when they learned that the King intended to lead his troops in person.

Finally, on February 8, 1598, all was in readiness, and Henry dispatched identical letters to the ambassadors representing him abroad: "I set out today for Brittany in answer to a summons from my good subjects of the said country, who, being weary of the tyranny of the usurper, the Duc de Mercoeur, are desirous of putting themselves under my protection and showing me their obedience. This, indeed, the people of my town of Dinan are now beginning to do, the same who, assisted by my town of Saint-Malo, have driven out the garrisons of the said Duke, and are now their own masters and ready for my service."

The pregnant Gabrielle insisted on accompanying Henry into the field, even though the winter weather was severe. "His Majesty," Louise de Guise writes in her *Adventures*, "made every effort to persuade Gabrielle that she would be in better health and would enjoy greater safety if she remained at the Hôtel d'Estrées, but she would not heed his advice, and he, notwithstanding that all of France save Brittany was now beneath his benign yoke, bowed his head to her will."

He was in little personal danger, so Gabrielle could not have feared for him, as she had at Amiens. But she was not accompanying him on a whim. "She confided to me," Louise adds, "that she had not abandoned her hope that a peaceful settlement of the estrangement between His Majesty and their graces of Mercoeur could be arranged."

Henry and Gabrielle joined the army near the border of Brittany, and the King took command. De Brissac remained as his deputy. The cold was so intense that the royal foot came down with a thud and Gabrielle was not permitted to set up housekeeping in a tent. Instead, Henry demanded that she occupy the château of Angers, which was located just inside the town wall, and she countered with a request that he make his headquarters there. On the basis of this compromise, they went together to Angers.

Fortunately for Henry, the tide had begun to turn in his favor. Deputations from the cities of Nantes and Rennes, as well as from various towns called on him at the château, promising that if he entered the duchy peacefully, the gates would be unbarred for him.

Word had filtered into Brittany ahead of the advancing army that Gabrielle favored solving the rebellion by negotiation, and many nobles came to Angers hoping she would intercede on their behalf with the King. The role was one long familiar to her, and she willingly played it again. The King was delighted with the results and, prolonging his stay at the château, agreed to receive the rebellious lords in audience.

According to an account written by Scipion Dupleix in his *History of Henry IV*, the great hall of the château was crowded when the King, surrounded by his usual detail of armed guards, arrived for the interview. Elbowing each other and shouting, the nobles rushed forward to gain the ear of the monarch they dreaded, who would be inclined, or so Gabrielle, Duchess de Beaufort, had told them, to accept their oaths of fealty.

In their enthusiasm, the lords almost swept Henry off his feet, and the alarmed captain of the guard called out, "Gentlemen, you press His Majesty too hard with your importunities."

"No, no," Henry declared. "My nobles cannot press me too hard, nor do they ever importune me. If they approach me it is because they love me. It is with their help that I hope to put my enemies to flight."

The nobles made their peace with him on the spot, and were soon followed by others who traveled to Angers by devious routes in order to avoid the cavalry patrols Mercoeur had sent out to intercept them. The Duke's strength was waning, but he continued to hold firm, and it still seemed unlikely that an open conflict could be avoided. In past years Philippe-Emmanuel and Marie had been on the defensive many times, and had shown themselves to be expert in the devious art of procrastination. They had instituted talks with Henry's representatives, showing every reasonable sign of a willingness to cooperate, and then had allowed the discussions to bog down in a morass of delays.

The wily Duke and Duchess tried the same tactics again, Marie sending an emissary to Gabrielle. Henry was willing to let the discussions take place between the women, and a messenger was immediately hurried from Angers to Pont-de-Cé, where the rulers of Brittany maintained a castle. During the last two weeks of February 1598, couriers seemed to be on the road daily, but eventually it became clear that Mercoeur and his wife were merely playing a variation of the same game they had used to such good effect in previous negotiations.

Henry went off to inspect the troops in the field, leaving Gabrielle at the château. There, on the last day of February, Marie de Mercoeur, a princess by birth and a duchess by marriage, came to see her. Gabrielle, as disturbed and angry as Henry, ordered the gates of Angers closed in her face. And for good measure she ordered the drawbridge raised.

The fuming Duchess de Mercoeur "was put entirely out of countenance," according to Dupleix, and retired to Pont-de-Cé. Never had anyone treated her with such a complete lack of respect. An unverified legend, still popular in the eighteenth century at the court of Louis XV and repeated by Voltaire, had it that she paced the ramparts of the ducal castle in impotent rage for three days and three nights.

Gabrielle acted completely on her own initiative in the incident, and even though she was annoyed at the time, apparently her intuition and common sense remained in good working order. "Her Grace of Beaufort," Dupleix reports, "was not surprised to receive from the Duchess de Mercoeur, on March 4th, a letter offering apologies for slights inadvertently administered. On that same day Her Grace wrote a reply noteworthy for its warmth."

Unfortunately, neither document has survived. Nevertheless, it is clear what happened. When Marie recovered from her fury, she realized, as did her husband, that they were dealing with people whose patience was exhausted. Henry and Gabrielle were their peers, and if there was to be a reconciliation, Philippe-Emmanuel and Marie would have to make the first move. If they stood on their pride, they would be forced to take the consequences, and patrols must have brought word that the King's strength grew with each passing day.

So Marie swallowed a large slice of humble pie and wrote a letter of apology. Gabrielle, having won, smiled sweetly and wrote a bland reply. The women must have understood each other, nonetheless, for rapid action followed Henry's return to the château at Angers on March 6.

It may be that Marie received advance notice from Gabrielle of Henry's return, for she made a second journey to Angers, arriving a few hours after Henry rode into the town. Gabrielle went out to meet the chastened Marie and, with a guard of honor escorting them, they drove to the château in the same carriage. They were so deeply engrossed in conversation that they remained in the coach for some minutes after it reached the courtyard, and it was natural that their talk aroused considerable speculation on the part of the courtiers.

Feminine planning had to wait on the realities of power politics, however, and the first step was the surrender of Mercoeur and his wife to the King. Henry received the penitent Marie in the great hall of the château, sitting on a throne that had been carried all the way from Paris for the purpose. Gabrielle made the presentation and remained during the interview that followed; no one else was present.

At the end of the talk it was possible to see daylight ahead in the long tunnel of clogged negotiations, but Henry remained wary, demanding performance rather than accepting mere promise. That night he sent a letter to the Constable, summing up his impressions: "If the deeds of the Duc de Mercoeur in any way correspond to the fair words offered to me by his wife today, our business will soon be over. I mean to have done with it as soon as possible, and to stop at nothing short of my due."

A group of royal negotiators accompanied Marie to Pont-de-Cé, and the King's supporters took heart. One member of the party was the hardheaded Soffrey de Calignon, Chancellor of Navarre, a trusted aide who had never been known to concede even a minor point to a foe.

It was assumed that Mercoeur would be forced to pay dearly for his long and intractable opposition to the crown, but news that leaked out a few days later put a somewhat different light on the relationship. It was said that a marriage was being arranged between four-year-old Caesar and Françoise, the daughter of Philippe-Emmanuel and Marie, who was approximately six months older than the prospective bridegroom.

The courtiers now knew the subject of conversation that had occupied the two ladies seated in the closed carriage.

Gabrielle had been the author of the idea, but the liaison was advantageous to both sides. Mercoeur and Marie would obtain the royal pardon they needed if they were to keep their duchy, property, and heads, and Gabrielle and Henry would be marrying their son to the only child of one of Christendom's wealthiest couples.

Everyone realized Henry could reach the same financial end by confiscating the lands that belonged to Mercoeur, but that was not his system. He would have offended Mayenne, the de Guise family, and other relatives of the powerful house of Lorraine, on Philippe-Emmanuel's side. And had he deprived Marie of her property, there would have been a wild scramble for the duchy of Luxembourg which she had inherited. It was far simpler to absorb everything into his own household by legal means.

On March 11, as negotiations at Pont-de-Cé were drawing to a close, the King sent another letter to his Constable, saying, "I am convinced I could not do better for Caesar, for it would be the greatest marriage in my kingdom."

But first steps had to be taken first, and nothing could be done until the treaty of peace was announced. Its terms were bald. All citizens of Brittany who had supported Mercoeur were required to recognize the authority of the King and to submit to that authority, and the entire government of the duchy was to be surrendered into Henry's hands. Officers appointed by Mercoeur were allowed to keep their commissions on condition that they took a new oath of fealty to Henry and received new commissions from him. And Henry allowed a gentle preamble to be included in the document, in which he granted a royal pardon to Mercoeur and his followers for all time, thus making it impossible for some future monarch to punish any of the rebels for past sins.

By the end of the month the rebellious Duke and all of the nobles who had held out against the crown had capitulated, and on March 30 Mercoeur finally summoned the courage to pay the King a visit. Henry wrote about it the following day in a letter to his Constable, declaring, "Cousin, the Duc de Mercoeur, my cousin, came yesterday to see me at Briolé, where I was dining. As I have received from my said cousin all the submission I could wish for, I gave him to understand how agreeable his recognition of my authority was to me, and the share he had thereby acquired of your good graces.

"This victory, achieved without the loss of blood, belongs entirely to the Duchess de Beaufort, and I wish it made known through publication of notices to be posted throughout my good town of Paris and the lesser towns of my realm that the wives and mothers of my soldiers are forever in her debt."

The King's wishes were obeyed, notices were published, and everyone in France learned that Gabrielle had achieved a victory in which no shot had been fired.

On April 2, Henry and Gabrielle left Angers for Nantes, and were received in the city by a wildly enthusiastic crowd. On the following day, a Friday, letters patent which had been drawn up by the royal notaries of Angers, men named Guillot and Lorry, were made public, and it became obvious that Gabrielle had not been content to rest on her laurels while the final negotiations with Mercoeur had been taking place.

"The King," the letters patent read, "has seen fit, by reason of his affection for his son, Caesar, and by reason also of the projected marriage with the daughter of M. and Mme. de Mercoeur, which will be affected as soon as he comes of age, but without this marriage being the condition of the gift, to bestow on Caesar, by deed of gift between living persons, the duchy of Vendôme in the county of Vendôme, together with its appurtenances and dependencies, in whatsoever they may consist; fiefs, demesnes, vassals, advowson, rights of appointment to the ordinary and extraordinary offices enjoyed by the former Dukes of Vendôme, forests of full-grown trees, meadowlands and all other manorial rights in general, without exception."

Caesar, then, had been raised into the stratosphere of the nobility, receiving a duchy that long had formed part of the crown property. The gift seemed magnificent on the surface, but, in reality, many of the manorial lands of Vendôme were mortgaged, and as a result the revenues of the duchy were small. Presumably Philippe-Emmanuel and Marie were as well aware of this unfortunate situation as were Henry and Gabrielle, for the King promised that within four years he would recover the manorial properties that had been sold and pay off the debts on the rest. He swore, too, that he would give Caesar funds to purchase new lands and manors if former portions of the duchy could not be recovered.

He further stated that he had "deprived and dispossessed himself" of the duchy in favor of his son, who would from that time forward be called Duc de Vendôme. And if Caesar died without issue, the duchy would revert to Gabrielle's other children by the King, male offspring receiving preference.

Princess Catherine must have joined the family at Nantes, for she ratified and approved the gift, and her signature appears beside that of her brother, both being sealed with the dark green wax that was reserved for royalty.

A scant forty-eight hours later, on April 5, a marriage contract was signed on behalf of Caesar, Duc de Vendôme, and Françoise de Mercoeur. In it the fathers engaged in a weird financial contest, each trying to outdo the other in displaying generosity. Henry promised to settle on Caesar the enormous though odd sum of eight hundred twenty-six thousand, six hundred and sixty-six écus, payable either direct to him or to his mother on his behalf. Philippe-Emmanuel settled on his daughter an income of ten thousand écus per year, in addition to the annual revenue of the duchy of Penthièvre and the municipality of Mercoeur. And he further promised that when the marriage was consummated he would give his daughter one hundred thousand silver crowns and jewels worth an additional fifty thousand écus. Henry further contracted to grant Philippe-Emmanuel the sum of two hundred thousand écus, which were to be spent on the acquisition of properties which the bride would bring with her into the marriage.

The financial arrangements were staggering, but there were political considerations equally important. Mercoeur declared that he delivered the government of Brittany into the King's hands, "to be invested, if so it pleases him, and as he himself begged in all humility, on the said Duc de Vendôme, his future son-in-law." So, for all practical purposes, Brittany, one of the wealthiest duchies in France, had become crown property.

A special clause of the contract took note, in a delicate way, of Gabrielle's unwed state and the touchy question of whether, in spite of royal decrees, she could leave property to her son. "There was also present," the document said, "in order to agree to and sanction the said terms, the high and mighty Dame Gabrielle d'Estrées, Duchess de Beaufort, mother of the Duc de Vendôme, who said that she held him for her true and principal heir, following the letters patent of His Majesty, verified by his consent in Parliament and the Court of Accounts at Paris, and in witness of the great affection she had for him, she had given, in favor of the said marriage, by deed of gift between living persons, unconditionally and irrevocably, to become effective upon her death, the duchy of Beaufort, the manor of Vandeuil, and the estates of Assy and Saint-Lambert." Gabrielle's signature appeared directly below that of Henry.

Members of the court were called from Paris and other parts of the realm to a betrothal celebration at Angers, Gabrielle being too far advanced in pregnancy to travel to the capital. A cardinal performed the betrothal ceremony in the presence of scores of great lords and ladies, and later the entire company sat down to a banquet, which was followed by a fireworks display, a ballet, and a concert. Caesar and Françoise were considered too young to attend these adult festivities, and were sent off to bed.

Gabrielle watched from a divan, attended by the foreign ambassadors accredited to Henry's court. The King had made certain there would be no international repercussions by inviting the members of the diplomatic corps to Angers, and these gentlemen not only signified by their presence that their governments approved, but took good care to be attentive to Gabrielle, the heroine who had achieved a bloodless coup and had delivered Brittany and its enormous revenues into the hands of the King.

The impending birth of another child must have been a secondary consideration to Gabrielle, who was now completely involved in the most important project of Henry's reign — the reconciliation of Catholics and Protestants. It is surprising that the King found time for these negotiations while peace in Brittany and the betrothal of Caesar were being arranged; it is miraculous that Gabrielle could concentrate on them, even though they were vitally important. The indisputable fact remains, however, that both of them were making strenuous efforts to bring together the two factions.

Like Henry, Gabrielle had mastered the art of juggling several balls simultaneously. The nobles who came to Angers found themselves participating in serious discussions on religious issues, and the diplomats were summoned to other meetings, equally important, to assist in working out the details of a final treaty of peace with Spain.

Gabrielle, whose constitution modern women might envy, was active in all of these talks. The Catholic and Protestant leaders adjourned to Nantes immediately following the betrothal celebration in order to escape from court gossips. On April 8, Henry and Gabrielle quietly followed them, occupying the château there, and several events took place in quick succession.

A royal decree, dated April 9, named Caesar captain of the Nantes château and governor of the city. His father's favorite name for him thereafter was "Captain Caesar."

The Edict of Nantes, the most important attempt to reconcile Protestants and Catholics since the Reformation had split them, was issued on April 13.

And a scant four days later Gabrielle gave birth to her third child, a son, whom Henry grandly named Alexander, Chevalier de Vendôme. The King must have been frantically busy, but he took time to write a joyous letter to his Constable announcing the event, and ordered his legal advisers to draw up letters patent similar to those following the births of Caesar and Catherine Henriette.

Neither peace between warring religious factions nor a formal end to hostilities with Spain could prevent the careful Henry from making sure that his youngest child would be rendered legitimate.

Gabrielle spent several weeks enjoying a well-earned rest from affairs of state. "The door of my sister's chamber was barred to those gentlemen who wanted His Majesty to modify the Edict granting religious freedom to the Huguenots, and to those who believed that they had received too little liberty," François-Annibal d'Estrées writes in his *Memoirs*.

There is no record, either, that she took any further part in the talks that led, some weeks later, to the signing of the Treaty of Vervins with Spain. But Henry refused to leave her side, and stayed with her at Nantes, which became the temporary capital of the kingdom during one of the most important periods in its history. The King maintained a heavy correspondence with subordinates in every part of his realm, and couriers were arriving or departing at virtually all hours of the day and night.

Gabrielle apparently did absolutely nothing for a period of about one month. She was wise to gain fresh strength, for she must have realized that the promulgation of the Edict of Nantes was the beginning rather than the end of a viciously bitter struggle.

16: THE EDICT OF NANTES, 1598

The decree written by Henry IV that granted religious freedom to the Protestants of France did not spring full-blown from the head of a Zeuslike monarch, but was the end result of years of hard labor, bitter dispute, and compromise.

It would be too much to blame Henry, the mediator, for displaying a sanguine attitude when he wrote from Nantes on May 5, 1598, to the Duc de Caumont la Force, "As for my news, I have to tell you that, having reduced this province to obedience, as soon as I have made a tour as far as Rennes, Dinan, and Saint-Malo, whither I am now about to set out, I shall return by the borders of Picardy, hoping to reach Paris by the end of the month. I have put an end to the matters concerning religion, and on that side my spirit is at rest."

Gabrielle did not share his optimism. Dupleix, a staunch admirer of the King, in whose eyes Henry could do no wrong, indicates that her attitude was infinitely more realistic. According to his *History of Henry IV*, she sent a letter to Princess Catherine only twenty-four hours after Henry had expressed the belief that the religious problems of France were at an end.

"The King," Gabrielle declares in her letter, the original of which has not survived, "receives from all who see him solemn promises that they will obey the Edict and will enforce its provisions within their domains. Nonetheless I have reason to fear that those who have so strongly opposed the Edict have not relented.

"No visits have been made to Nantes by the magistrates, upon whose compliance so much depends. Should these

Catholic worthies stand firm in their courts of law and in the Parliament of Paris, all that we have achieved may again be lost. I am faint when I think that it may be necessary for us to begin our labors again.

"The King laughs and does not share my fears, saying he will force compliance, but in this he may be crossed. Men who are obedient to His Majesty in all other things have defied him in the realm of the spirit, and may do so again."

Gabrielle's letter was written to a colleague, for Catherine had worked equally hard to set up conditions that would enable both religious factions to accept the Edict. The farsighted Henry had realized he could not compel his subjects to swallow a decree that was abhorrent to them, and consequently had used the two women closest to him, his mistress and his sister, to prepare the way for a reconciliation. Perhaps he was justified in feeling that further compromise was unnecessary. Brittany had been conquered, a final treaty of peace with Spain was being worked out, and he had arrived at the peak of his powers. He was to discover, however, that in questions of faith men would become blindly obstinate, and that in the months ahead he once again would call on Gabrielle and Catherine for help.

The roots of the problem were deep, and had originated in the so-called Huguenot Conspiracy of 1560, when the era of religious wars had begun. At that time the Protestants had plotted to reduce the power of the Guise family, who had struck back, through Francis II, to convince the people of France that a war against the house of Guise was a war against the Catholic Church.

The first truce in the vicious struggle had been arranged in 1577, when Henry III had issued the Edict of Poitiers, a decree which had assured the Calvinists of civil freedom, liberty of conscience, and, within narrow limits, a measure of freedom to worship as they pleased. But Henry III had been no champion of religious tolerance; fear of Huguenot power had been the only reason he had signed the Edict of Poitiers, and when the adherents of the League found they could ignore it with impunity, it became a totally worthless scrap of paper.

When Henry of Navarre came to the throne of France, he inherited a seemingly insoluble problem. His Protestant cohorts were shouting that their time had arrived at last, and they were prepared to make the most of their opportunities. The Catholics loyal to the crown were fearful; Henry had no desire to alienate them and send them racing into the camp of his enemies.

He announced at the time of his accession that he considered the Edict of Poitiers valid, that it was a fair declaration of state policy, but neither of the antagonistic groups was satisfied. The Huguenots, who were specifically barred from holding official positions in the country, were clamoring for posts, and the Catholics angrily retorted that if this should happen, they would bolt and join the League.

Henry began his reign by appointing trusted Protestant followers to positions of responsibility, but made no specific announcement that he had established a new policy. As a result, both Huguenots and Catholics remained dissatisfied. It must be kept in mind that the bigots on one side were as greedy for power as their counterparts on the other, and that neither would be satisfied until their religious foes were driven out of France.

The King was determined to allow no repetition of the St. Bartholomew's Day Massacre, however, and in his attempt to play the role of mediator caused great apprehension in both groups. In July 1591, he issued a brief decree known as the

Edict of Mantes, which later became confused with the famous order of 1598. The former merely reaffirmed the principles of the Edict of Poitiers, and required the parliaments of the various cities and towns to ratify it. By 1595, every city and town in the realm had accepted the Edict of Poitiers, Paris being the last to comply.

In May 1593, shortly before Henry's conversion to Catholicism, the Catholic lords of the realm issued a public declaration which was calculated to soothe the Huguenots, but actually succeeded only in infuriating them, for it was at best a patronizing document, and at worst seemed to promise that conditions then existing could not and would not be changed.

The Huguenots had legitimate cause for complaint, although their lot had improved. It was true that they enjoyed civil rights and could no longer be persecuted for their religious beliefs, but they were specifically forbidden the right to hold religious services in forty towns, each with a population of more than eight hundred, and in seventeen country bailiwicks, each with a population of more than three hundred.

Henry had no part in drawing up the distasteful declaration of the Catholic lords, which emphasized that "the safety of the kingdom" made it necessary to restrict Protestant worship. Nevertheless, some of his old associates, among them d'Aubigné, accused him of being a party to the statement.

The actual conversion of the King to Catholicism caused only a mild ripple in most Huguenot circles, and the old suspicion that Henry's abjuration was merely an act of political expediency rises once again to confront the modern student. Did the man who allegedly told Gabrielle that "Paris was worth a Mass" give secret assurances to his Protestant friends that he was, at heart, still one of them?

The question has vexed historians for centuries, and cannot be answered with a flat affirmation or denial. There is no evidence in memoirs, letters, or official correspondence to indicate that the King was playing a double game, in spite of the claims of the austere, or right-wing Calvinists and their Catholic counterparts. But no adequate explanation has ever been offered for the fact that not one prominent French Huguenot nobleman deserted the King either at the time of his conversion or thereafter. The very few who severed relations with him were gentlemen from Navarre, and he permitted them to live where they pleased in his realm, write letters and tracts attacking him, or otherwise disturb the peace.

In any event, by 1597 only the unexpected Spanish assault on Amiens prevented the Huguenots from pressing their claims vigorously. They made two demands: they wanted the right to worship where they pleased, and they wanted the legal right to hold any office in the country, arguing that if Henry died, his successor might reverse his policy and dismiss all Protestant officials whom he had appointed.

Henry knew the time had come to take action, and sat down with a small group of advisers, among them the Constable, Sully, Chiverny, and Villars, to work out the details of a new royal edict. The details of the decree would mean nothing without a broad acceptance of the principles, and Henry turned to Gabrielle and Catherine for diplomatic support. It was Gabrielle's task to persuade the Catholic lords to accept the inevitable with good grace, while Catherine urged the Huguenots to speak less stridently when making their demands.

"Madame and the Duchess de Beaufort have begun their formidable task of reconciling the unreconcilable," Montmorency said on October 17, 1597, in a letter to his cousin, the Archbishop of Bordeaux. "They will need to exercise their command of the arts of persuasion to the utmost and to utilize the natural charms with which they are endowed, for surely no two women have ever undertaken a more difficult task. There are some in the Council who feel that the King would prosper more readily if he performed himself the task he has assigned to Madame and the Duchess, but I do not agree. No man dares to refuse the King's bidding when commanded in person by His Majesty.

"The ladies have sufficient authority themselves to remind their hearers that they speak for the King, but they will speak more softly. I pray God grant them the ability to soften hard hearts."

All through the autumn of 1597 and the winter of 1597–98, Catherine received a stream of Huguenot visitors at the Tuileries, and the pregnant Gabrielle sent out invitations to Catholic lords, who came to her salon at the Hôtel d'Estrées. There she was able to maintain the flimsy fiction that it was she, and not Henry in the nearby Louvre, who was pleading for greater tolerance.

"In the week before Christmas," Diane de Balagny writes in her *Memorial*, "my sister entertained more than fifty members of the gentry, and over a cup of wine argued the cause of religious liberty with them."

François-Annibal adds an undated postscript on the subject in his *Memoirs*, writing, "My celebrated sister, the Duchess de Beaufort, was so earnest in her attempt to obtain converts to the King's cause of granting liberty of worship to the Calvinists that His Majesty became concerned for her health."

Gabrielle and Catherine continued their efforts when they went, separately, on the expedition to Brittany, and many nobles who hadn't conferred with them in Paris were invited to the château at Angers.

"Gabrielle was held in high respect by the gentry who made the pilgrimage to the King's château," Louise de Guise writes in her *Adventures*. "Those who scorned her, saying that the mistress of the King knew nought of spiritual matters, were reminded by the bishops who attended His Majesty that it had been she who had persuaded His Holiness, the Pope of Rome, to grant absolution to His Majesty. And so they listened to her pleas."

There is no record of how many Catholics changed their stand after Gabrielle spoke to them, but Henry paid tribute to her powers in a letter written to his Constable on March 20, 1598, in which he declared, "My mistress has become an orator of unequaled excellence, so fiercely does she argue the cause of the new Edict. Those who come here [to Angers] because they fear to disobey her summons return to their own homes believing, as do we, that spiritual peace will be established in the realm only when the Calvinists are granted new rights."

The order that was to become known as the Edict of Nantes had been written, rewritten, and refined by the time the King left for Brittany, and Henry was awaiting the right moment to make his public announcement. Most members of the Council had read the paper in one draft or another, and had contributed their own ideas to it. Only Biron had been excluded from the royal conferences, which was strange, as he held the titles of Marshal, Admiral of France, and Lord Governor of Burgundy. No reason has ever been offered for Henry's failure to take the warrior into his confidence, but it is believed that he expressed strong opposition to the Edict. In any event, he began to conspire against the crown during the summer of that same year, opening negotiations with Savoy and, a little later, with Spain.

The Edict, in its final form, granted many new rights to the Huguenots, but still deferred to the Catholics. In all, it was the best compromise that Henry and his advisers could work out in a country where hatreds remained intense. Judges of the higher courts were allowed complete freedom of worship for themselves, their vassals, and all persons they wished to admit to their châteaux, with no limit placed on the number who could attend such services. The judges of the lower courts, however, could not receive more than thirty strangers, but religious services could be held for that number in their châteaux or homes.

Huguenots in every bailiwick were granted the right to perform their acts of worship, without hindrance, anywhere. Equally important, the royal treasury was authorized to pay the wages of Protestant clergymen, as it did those of Catholic clerics, and the King specifically authorized the Huguenot ministers to receive donations and bequests.

On the other hand, Calvinist worship was forbidden in those ancient towns of the League that had stipulated for its exclusion in the treaties of peace and submission they had signed with the King. Such worship was also forbidden in such towns where there were no Protestants, and in any place which, in the opinion of the crown, would be disturbed by the holding of Huguenot services. For all practical purposes, this last clause was meaningless, as Henry had granted Huguenots the right to hold worship services wherever they wished, provided they applied to him. He had also given private assurances to the Protestants, through Catherine, that he intended to continue the practice.

One of the most important clauses of the Edict ordered that the Parliaments of all cities and towns be reorganized on a new basis, in which Protestants would be granted equal representation and thus be assured of the administration of impartial justice. Most members of the Parliaments were lawyers, and the function of these bodies was, in the main, of a legal nature. It was their duty to ratify or veto the decrees and edicts issued by the crown, its governors, and local representatives. Only on rare occasions was the King himself defied by the Parliaments, but in local affairs the deputies often exercised their authority. Therefore, the willing compliance of the lawyers was essential to the success of the decree.

Finally, members of the Reformed Church were declared capable of acting in every civil capacity and most military capacities. Only the posts of Constable, Grand Marshal of the Army, Grand Admiral of the Navy, and a handful of lesser key positions were reserved for Catholics.

The nobles and clergy had been persuaded to accept the inevitable before the publication of the Edict of Nantes, so the battle was half-won. But enormous opposition was expected from the Catholic members of the Parliaments who, religious grounds aside, were certain to protest vehemently at the prospect of seeing their own ranks cut in half. There was little that the Protestant Princess Catherine could do to convince these worthies that their cooperation was essential to the safety of the kingdom, so Henry again sought and received the assistance of Gabrielle.

In May 1598, the King made a tour of Brittany, taking Caesar with him, and everywhere received protestations of loyalty from the towns he visited. Meanwhile, Gabrielle lolled at Nantes, regaining her strength after the birth of Alexander, and in June returned to Paris with her two younger children, joining the King and Caesar there. She threw herself into the struggle with the Parliamentarians at once, displaying the energy that had become characteristic of her since her own personal reformation.

Even Henry was surprised at the uncompromising hostility to the Edict shown by the Parliaments in every city and town of his realm. Red-robed deputies stood in assembly halls everywhere from Normandy to Languedoc and shouted that they would not obey an order that not only deprived them of their own rights but that, in their august opinions, would endanger the safety of the country by allowing Protestants to fill public posts. Governors of provinces and towns were ordered to seek the compliance of the lawyers, but the opposition continued to mount, and by midsummer even the Constable began to wonder whether the Edict had been a major policy mistake.

"The aldermen and lawyers will not listen to reason," he wrote to Henry after making a tour of the northern provinces and duchies. "I fear the outbreak of civil war unless they can be made to change their minds."

Henry knew it would be useless to compel the lawyers to obey him, even though he now had the means — the Treaty of Vervins had been signed with Spain; France was at peace with the world; and a large army, ready to do the King's bidding, could have been sent into every town with orders to force the Parliaments to heed the decree.

Instead, he decided to see what Gabrielle could do. He would bring leaders of each Parliament to Paris and expose them to her influence.

When they arrived, Gabrielle held court privately several days each week, discussing the situation, explaining the need for tolerance, and soothing the fears of the disturbed politicians.

Gentle persuasion and the soft, feminine touch were not her only weapons. When necessary, she reminded the lawyers of the King's power, and calmly explained that men of authority and rank who opposed his will might suffer personal punishment for their audacity; on the other hand, those who cooperated might expect suitable rewards — there were a large number of posts open in the royal government, and those who accepted the Edict could apply for a variety of positions on behalf of their sons, brothers, or nephews.

Her tactics were effective, and gradually the opposition to the Edict began to melt away. Nevertheless, a hard core of recalcitrants remained firm in their opposition, and in early December 1598, a group headed by President André Séguier of the Parliament of Paris, the only "national" council, demanded an audience with her.

Gabrielle received the deputies in the great hall of the Hôtel d'Estrées, and every detail was recorded by Dupleix and other historians of the period. In her earlier meetings, she had received the Parliamentarians informally, personally serving them wine and chatting freely with them. On this occasion, however, she was expecting trouble and was prepared for it.

Sentries clad in the black and silver of the royal household guard were on duty at the entrance, and two stood at either side of a low dais. There, in a chair that bore a suspicious resemblance to a throne, Gabrielle sat in splendor, wearing all of her glittering jewels and dressed in a gown of "d'Estrées red," the off-shade of royal purple that was her own version of regal attire.

She greeted the Parliamentarians with a curt nod, and the astonished lawyers bowed low before her, some dropping to one knee, as they did before the King. Gabrielle could not have received them with a greater show of pomp had she been Henry's legal wife, Queen of France.

The confounded men were stricken silent, and Gabrielle opened the conversation by saying, "You wanted to see me. I am here, as are you. What will you?"

The uncomfortable silence continued, and several of the deputies looked hard at President Séguier, their spokesman. Finally, he stepped forward, began to speak, and, warming to his theme, made an impassioned declaration. He insisted that the country would fall into evil hands if Huguenots were granted places in the Parliaments, and he finally said that as the Edict would not become the law of the land until it was ratified by the Parliament of Paris, the King could expect failure.

Gabrielle made no move until Séguier was finished. Then she began her reply, and Dupleix says that although she did not raise her voice, she pounded an arm of her throne-chair for emphasis. "I know full well what is the King's wish in respect of the Edict of Nantes," she told them, "and that he will not do otherwise. He will accept no compromise, and defeat is unknown to him.

"Nor do I myself see any good reason for wishing to prevent those of the Reformed religion, who have been good servants to the King, from entering into the States and other Parliaments, seeing that he allowed this right to the Leaguers, who had taken arms against His Majesty."

At least half of the company had been supporters of the League, according to Dupleix, and Gabrielle's shaft struck to the marrow. It was unnecessary for her to add that men who had been followers of the League were in no position to deny the extension of royal tolerance to others. They themselves were in a tenuous position, and if Henry wanted to prosecute them for treason, he could have them thrown into prison, tried, and beheaded without creating much of a public outcry.

"The Duchess de Beaufort," Dupleix concludes in his account related in the *History of Henry IV*, "then made other remarks appropriate to the occasion, and the Parliamentarians withdrew." Unfortunately, no record of these comments has been preserved, but they must have been similar to the portion of her address that Dupleix has quoted, for opposition to the Edict collapsed overnight.

Chastened deputies returned to their own towns, and absolute silence pervaded the halls of the Parliament of Paris. President Séguier dropped his opposition to the Edict, and when the document was presented to the Parliament of Paris on February 25, 1599, it was registered by unanimous vote.

To what extent Henry was responsible for Gabrielle's tactics at the December meeting cannot be determined, but it certainly was his sword that she held over the heads of the reluctant deputies. She did not even need to add her own opinion, and her contemporaries gave her full credit for winning a smashing victory.

Two days after she had confounded the delegation, she received a visit from Godfrey, Duc de Bouillon, titular leader of the Huguenots since the time of Henry's conversion. He expressed his thanks and the gratitude of other Protestants for her speech, and presented her with a "token," an emerald and diamond ring, which she was pleased to accept. There seemed to be no question in the minds of the Calvinists that she was responsible for routing the opposition.

Had Henry followed his habit of the past, he would have given Gabrielle more than a token gift. But he bought no new estates for her, gave her no new manors or titles, and issued no public proclamations praising her work on his behalf.

She was expecting no such rewards, and could not have been disappointed. By 1598 the stakes had soared, and the King, like his mistress, wanted marriage.

17: A KING, A QUEEN, AND A PAWN, 1598

No biographer of Henry IV has ever been able to determine precisely when the King made up his mind to marry Gabrielle d'Estrées, and many of the details are clouded by the accounts written by that master distorter of history, Sully. The Duke was not entirely to blame for the falsehoods and exaggerations perpetrated in his name, however. Late in life, after he had suffered many personal and official disappointments, he dictated to a battery of secretaries a remarkable account of his stewardship under Henry, which was called the *Economies Royales*. The secretaries themselves made errors, and other authors, who subsequently extracted the *Memoirs* from the *Economies*, put words into Sully's mouth that he had never spoken.

The difficulties of distinguishing the true from the false are compounded by these circumstances, particularly as Sully set himself up as the authority on Henry's domestic relations in the year 1598, and wrote more than anyone else on the subject.

The most famous of Sully's stories, in which truth and fabrication are freely intertwined, concerns a conversation of more than three hours' duration which took place between the King and his faithful Superintendent of Finances in the garden of the royal château at Rennes early in April 1598. There is no reason to doubt the major premise of Sully's account, that Henry declared his need for legitimate heirs capable of succeeding him on the throne and carrying out his policies. Then he proceeded to discuss the eligible princesses of Europe, and found something wrong with each of them.

He dreaded marriage to a shrew or a vixen, he supposedly said, and would marry no one but a woman who fulfilled three conditions: "She must be beautiful, of an agreeable temper, and capable of bearing me children."

It was obvious to Sully that his master was hinting, and wanted his Superintendent of Finances to mention the name of Gabrielle. But Sully, jealous of her, pretended he didn't understand.

Eventually Henry's patience allegedly wore thin, and he said, "O, the clever animal that you are! You could know quite well if you liked. You could even read my thoughts, for it is not as if you had heard no rumor of anything. But I know quite well what you mean by acting the ignorant clown in this way. You mean to make me name her myself, and I will do it, for you will have to confess that all these three conditions are to be found in my mistress."

The King then demanded to know what Sully thought of the idea, and the Duke replied carefully, taking care not to arouse the royal ire. If his *Memoirs* may be believed, he presented a series of objections that certainly were valid. Many people would find fault with a king's marriage to a woman who had given herself to him as a mistress. Caesar was the issue of the adultery of both parents, Catherine Henriette and Alexander of the adultery of only one. And later children, should there be any, might take precedence over their older brothers and sister, at best a tangled situation that could lead to political disputes and possible civil war.

The interview continued at great length, and was finally terminated when Henry declared that he was determined to marry Gabrielle, no matter what the obstacles or how great the opposition, either in France or at the Vatican. With this the Superintendent was forced to be content.

Regardless of whether the King and Sully actually spoke together in the garden at Rennes, certain facts are known. The most important of them is that, in the busy spring of 1598, Henry was taking steps that would enable him to marry Gabrielle. His always steady correspondence with Margot, who was living in semi-isolation at her lonely château outside Usson in the Auvergne, once again broached the subject of divorce, which had lain dormant for several years. And Cardinal d'Ossat, the most reliable of Henry's ecclesiastical diplomats, undertook a new journey to Rome to sound out the Pope on the possibility of granting the King a divorce so he could marry his mistress.

Margot had written a divorce petition somewhat earlier in 1598, signing it at Usson on February 3, which raises the question that Henry may have been thinking of marriage to Gabrielle even earlier than anyone suspected. In any event, that document arrived at the Louvre on February 9, the day after Henry's departure for Brittany. But apparently he had expected to receive it, for a special emissary, Brulart de Sillery, carried it for him to Rome, along with a private message in Henry's own hand, addressed to the Pope. Queen Marguerite's petition may be seen in the archives of the Vatican, but Henry's private letter to the Pontiff is not on file. It therefore must be assumed that the King wrote a very private letter indeed to the Holy Father, and that the Pope treated it accordingly.

Rather than speculate on the nature of this mysterious communication, it is safer merely to say that Henry had every reason to hope he would be granted a divorce. Never had his relations with the Vatican been better, and he stood in such high favor that Clement had intervened with Spain, exerting pressure on Philip II to make his peace with France.

Margot had been pressing for a divorce since 1593, when Henry had first mentioned the subject to her, and when a royal messenger, one Sieur de Erard, had visited her in the spring of that year, she sent an anxious letter to a friend at court, saying, "The Sieur de Erard will communicate with you on the matter, and will give you all the information you may require. And if you would so far oblige me as to take in hand the completion of what has begun so well and on which depends my peace of mind and even the safety of my life, you would earn my undying gratitude."

In the autumn of 1593, de Erard carried a letter from the King to Margot that indicated considerable progress. She wanted two hundred and fifty thousand écus to pay her personal debts and an allowance of an additional fifty thousand écus per year for the rest of her life. Her price was high, but she was the daughter of a King of France. Henry's reply was cheerful: "My Friend, since Sieur de Erard is about to depart, my letter must be short. I can only think that by my last letter you will have seen how pleased I was to hear what he had to report concerning you. In accordance therewith I send him back to you, furnished with the necessary provision, of which you spoke to him. Believe me, I beg, that I will omit nothing that I can think of, as being likely to induce you to give your consent, either now or in the future."

There were several other exchanges in the same spirit, but the attempt to obtain a divorce failed because Pope Clement, still supporting the League, refused to believe that Henry's conversion to Catholicism was sincere.

Through the years Margot continued to ask for a divorce, but Henry evaded the subject. He was not thinking of remarriage, and he knew that divorces were expensive. Margot's debts were mounting again, and he realized he would have to pay considerably more than the two hundred and fifty thousand écus he had given her in 1593 in order to clear her with her creditors. Furthermore, he was paying her a mere thirty thousand écus per year, and obviously would be compelled to increase that sum, too. So, always niggardly, he did nothing until it suited his own convenience.

Margot's situation was becoming desperate, and by 1597 she was confronted by grave problems, both financial and personal. She lived like the wife of a King of France and daughter of a King of France, spending far more than the allowance Henry gave her, and even Sully, who considered himself her close friend, says in his *Memoirs* that, as he reported to the King, her debts amounted to more than five hundred thousand écus.

But money was the least of her worries. A nymphomaniac and consequently promiscuous, she had given birth to at least one illegitimate child, probably the son of one of her gardeners. So many romantic myths have grown out of the story of Margot, last of the Valois, that it is difficult to separate fact from fiction, but there can be no doubt that she was the mother of a child sired by one of her servants.

The punishment prescribed by law for a Queen of France guilty of such an indiscretion, even an uncrowned Queen who was separated from her husband, was death. And Margot, as aware of Henry's love for Gabrielle as she was of his former difficulties with Pope Clement, could feel the ax of the executioner at her throat. Henry, she knew, could solve his domestic problems by having her put to death, and no one would be in a position to blame him.

In her desperation, Margot searched for allies in the cold, friendless, distant center of power, Paris, where Henry was omnipotent. Perhaps she had learned of Gabrielle's desire to succeed her as Queen; if so, there is no letter to that effect in her surviving correspondence. Or it may be that a combination of feminine intuition and logic convinced her that the woman who was the mistress of the King and the mother of his children would understand her desire to obtain freedom from an unwanted marriage.

In any event, Margot had been reduced to a state of frenzy. She had spent the better part of two decades living in a remote château far removed from the city she loved. Few visitors came to see her, and even those who pitied her and went out of their way to call took care to say and do nothing that might offend the monarch in the Louvre. The château at Usson had become a prison, and no matter how recklessly Margot spent money on refurnishing her mansion, buying exotic foods, and throwing herself into love affairs with servants and tradesmen, her life was miserably lonely.

So it is not surprising that, on February 24, 1597, she opened an extraordinary correspondence with Gabrielle, to whom she sent a friendly, even affectionate letter, in which she begged the royal mistress to act as her intermediary with the King in settling her affairs. This extraordinary communication was written with great care, Margot repeatedly assuring Gabrielle that she was not going behind her potential successor's back, but knew that "your desires conform entirely with the wishes of the King, as they do with my own."

The three members of the triangle, it seemed, were one in their thinking. All wished for the divorce. After the separation of the King and Queen was made permanent and final by Pope Clement, a financially and legally solvent Margot could return to the Paris that she loved and Henry and Gabrielle could marry and live happily ever after.

"I speak of you and His Majesty in the same breath," Margot wrote, "knowing you to be so bound together in ties of love that in conforming to the wishes of one, I conform also to those of the other. But I do not envy you the King's confidence that you enjoy; knowing from my own experience that he can be the most tender of living men, I rejoice with you in the good fortune you have earned. All France sings your praises, and I lift my voice with those of others, albeit a feeble song of praise from the hills of Usson cannot be heard clearly in the grand salons you frequent."

Margot was laying on the flattery with a heavy hand, but even in her most calculating mood could not refrain from expressing her wistful longing for the palaces of Paris.

She continued, "I speak freely to you, as to a sister, whom, after the King, I honor and esteem above everyone." Gabrielle, whom she had never met, must have read that statement with some astonishment.

"I have such confidence in your assurances of love for me," Margot added, not explaining how she had gleaned this information, "that I wish for no other defender of my interests with the King. I should myself only weary him with my importunities oft paper, but were they to come from your lovely mouth, I know they could not but be well received. Greatly would you oblige me, therefore, if you would do me this service.

"It is my most fond hope that you will reply soon to this plea from her who calls herself your sister."

The letter was entrusted to the care of a priest from Navarre who, for unexplained reasons, had made a long detour and had stopped at Usson en route to Paris for conferences with Margot's confessor.

Gabrielle was stunned when she received the letter, "and scarce knew what to make of it," according to Chiverny's *Memoirs*. "Dame Gabrielle and her confidantes studied the missive with the greatest of caution, suspecting trickery," he added, meaning that he and Isabelle de Sourdis had gone over every comma with care. "At last she decided that the Queen was sincere in her protestations, and the letter was laid before the King." In other words, Henry was not told of the communication until Aunt Isabelle and her lover had reached the conclusion that such a move would not be harmful to Gabrielle's interests.

"His Majesty," Chiverny continues, "retired to his own chambers, there to ponder on the missive. Thereafter, the Marquis de Coeuvres, acting upon his instructions, was sent forthwith to Usson to speak in private with the Queen."

That Gabrielle's brother should have been chosen for the mission was a shrewd move, and apparently François-Annibal carried a verbal reply to the letter, for he says in his own *Memoirs*, "I carried word to the Queen from my sister, and spoke with her at length, remaining three days and three nights at Usson."

Guesswork is necessary here in order to fill in the blank spaces. The verbose François-Annibal becomes tight-lipped, so it may be fair to assume that Henry told him what to say, but ordered him to pretend he was carrying a message only from Gabrielle. Common sense would indicate that this, in all probability, is what happened.

The likelihood increases when it is kept in mind that, at this juncture, Gabrielle hoped to marry the King, and Isabelle de Sourdis was exerting every effort to place her niece on the throne, while Henry had not yet made up his mind. Gabrielle and her scheming relative were placed in an uncomfortable position by Margot's letter, for if too enthusiastic a reply had been written, Henry might have taken offense.

So the whole matter was placed in his competent hands and, as always, he used the incident to his own advantage. Certainly he knew that Margot was anxious to obtain a divorce. Among his many accomplishments was his reorganization and modernization of French intelligence services, so he could not have been ignorant of his wife's enormous debts and probably had been told, too, of her illegitimate child or children. His own honor and sense of compassion undoubtedly prevented him from taking unfair advantage of her plight, but it may be that he saw no loss in allowing her to rid herself of tensions by corresponding with Gabrielle.

It is impossible to imagine that he was unaware of Gabrielle's high hopes. Even though he had not yet decided to make her his Queen, he would have been less than human had he failed to encourage her by telling her he was trying to solve the problem. Countless other husbands have utilized the same limp but effective excuse when trying to fend off eager mistresses.

It would have been dangerous for Gabrielle to commit herself to paper, as anyone reading a letter from her would have leaped to the correct conclusion that it had been sent with the King's knowledge and approval. So Henry used the technique of sending a courier to deliver a verbal message. And there was no one whose word Margot would have been more likely to accept than that of Gabrielle's own brother, who himself had received so many royal favors.

Margot wrote a second letter to Gabrielle on May 21, 1597, saying, "I am heartened by the knowledge that my sister and I make a joint cause, and that the King has opened his ears and

257

his heart to your sweet importunities. May God grant you every success in this high endeavor."

Henry himself entered the negotiations either that winter or in the spring of 1598, and from that time forward the atmosphere changed. The King had decided he wanted to marry Gabrielle. Now it became vital to obtain a divorce from Margot, and royal messengers began to make frequent journeys to Usson. With Henry in charge, sparks flew, and more was accomplished in a few busy months than had been achieved in many dreary years.

Even when the King wanted something badly, he drove a hard bargain, and Margot must have been dismayed when she learned that her husband insisted she pay a price for freedom and the end of a long exile. According to Dupleix, in his *History of Henry IV*, the Béarnais readily agreed to satisfy Margot's creditors and to increase her allowance. But "His Majesty required, in return, that the Queen also make certain concessions."

Those "concessions" constitute one of the more amusing incidents in the reign of Henry the Great. In the summer of 1598 a group of royal attorneys made the long journey from Paris to Usson, and early in November it was announced that Queen Marguerite had given a magnificent gift to Gabrielle, Duchess de Beaufort. That gift was the duchy of Étampes, one of the most lavish wedding presents that one woman could bestow on another. It is true that Étampes was poor and its revenues small, but it was, nevertheless, a duchy, and Gabrielle was entitled to add the name, Duchess d'Étampes, to her string of titles.

According to the bland royal proclamation, issued somewhat prematurely on November 9, 1598, "Her Highness, Marguerite, in respect of her great friendship to Dame

Gabrielle, Duchess de Beaufort, has made a gift, free, unencumbered and of her own will, of the duchy of Étampes to the said Dame Gabrielle."

Two days later Margot signed the papers that transferred the property, her signature being witnessed by notaries named Portail and Mathurin.

Perhaps a few gullible men were fooled by Henry's announcement, but every woman in France, including the illiterates, knew that no member of their sex would willingly give to her successor property she had inherited. Margot's pride must have suffered, though she may have thought Étampes a small price to pay for freedom and the opportunity to return to Paris, but in any case she had no real choice in the matter.

She carried out her part of the bargain with her head high, pretending to the whole world that she really wanted to give the duchy to Gabrielle. She was so convincing that she confused many historians, who actually believed that she and Gabrielle had become close friends. But the views of posterity were not her chief concern; like Gabrielle and Henry, she hoped the divorce would be granted in the immediate future... The triangle had become a single, straight line aimed at Rome.

During the months that the complicated negotiations were being held, Henry managed to keep himself in the background, writing, as far as is known, only one letter. It was sent to Sully on October 15, 1598, and indicates that the King expected a rapid solution of his marital problems. The letter said:

M. de Rosny, — M. de Silery [*sic*] has been commanded to hold himself in readiness for the journey to Rome which I wish him to make in regard to the dissolution of my marriage, as soon as Sieur Langloise, sometime Provost of my town of Paris, returns from Usson with the necessary procuration, in accordance with the resolution of the Council, at which meeting you yourself were present. This is a matter that as you know I have very much at heart, and I write to beg you to see that all is in readiness for the journey of the said Sieur de Silery [*sic*], in order that he may set out immediately after the return of the said Sieur Langloise.

I have commanded M. de Villeroy to keep you informed of the progress of the affair as long as the Sieur de Villeroy is at Rome.

I pray God, M. de Rosny, to keep you in his good and holy custody.

Henry

Cardinal d'Ossat, it appears, did not go off alone to fight the King's battle at the Vatican, but was being assisted by a number of high-ranking nobles. Henry was leaving nothing to chance; before the end of the year cardinals who were thought to be close associates of Pope Clement were besieged by members of the French community in Rome and by visitors from Paris who pleaded for a royal divorce.

In the early months of 1598, Henry's plan to marry Gabrielle remained a well-guarded secret, but by the autumn the entire country had heard the news, and people talked of little else. D'Aubigné, whose admiration for Gabrielle had been completely restored, sent a letter to a friend in Geneva that soon afterward found its way into print and was widely copied. He said: "The Duchess de Beaufort makes but a modest use of her power over the King, but not so her relations.

"This occasion [her pending marriage to Henry] invites us to discourse on this amour in terms of respect and decorum. It is seldom that the mistresses of our Kings fail to call down upon themselves the hatred of the great; those who do not worship them gradually come to lose favor in the eyes of the King, while everything is done for their relations, their debts paid, their services recognized, their insults avenged.

"It is a marvel how this woman, whose great beauty is entirely free from sensuality, has lived more like a Queen than a mistress for so many years, and with so few enemies. The necessities of the State alone have been her enemies."

Had Henry wished no publicity, the authorities in Paris and the smaller towns would have seized the cheaply printed copies of the letter, but they circulated freely, which meant that the King was not displeased with his former friend's analysis. He may have enjoyed d'Aubigné's blunt attack on Isabelle de Sourdis in the opening sentence, for like all Gascons, he liked crude humor, especially when it revealed the truth.

Memoirs of various people indicate that Paris was filled with rumors. Some stories said that Margot had changed her mind, and was refusing to accept a divorce. Others pretended to know on the best of authority that the King recently had received portraits of Marie de Medici and the Infanta of Spain and that, until he decided which of them he wanted, he was letting everyone believe he intended to make Gabrielle his bride.

The gift of Étampes quieted the tongues and halted the flying pens of the gossips. Even those who could scarcely tolerate the prospect of the King marrying his mistress had nothing more to say. And Henry let it be known through members of his Council that he had granted Margot the right to call herself Queen and Duchess de Valois after the Pope dissolved their marriage. This, according to Dupleix in his *History of Henry IV*, convinced even the doubters that Henry was in earnest.

Gabrielle made no secret of her belief that she would become Queen of France in a short time, and in the latter part of 1598 the court treated her as though she had already mounted the throne. Henry assigned a permanent detail of royal household troops to guard her, and she went nowhere without an escort. In either August or September she gave up the inconvenient practice of staying at the Louvre only when Henry was there, and moved all of her belongings into the palace. Isabelle de Sourdis, her constant companion for so many years, did not accompany her there, but called at the Louvre daily.

New furniture was ordered for the future Queen, and Gabrielle, at last casting aside all pretense, directed that chairs and divans be upholstered in royal purple. Dressmakers started to work on purple gowns, and although several were finished before the end of the year, according to Diane de Balagny's *Memorial*, Gabrielle did not wear them. Not even Henry was willing to defy tradition by allowing her to appear in royal colors before the actual wedding ceremony was performed.

For that reason Gabrielle was attired in her own special shade of red at the baptism of Alexander, which took place at Notre Dame. But in all other respects that occasion was a ceremony performed for a prince of the blood. The Comte de Soissons was the baby's godfather, and Diane de France, the gracious and popular Duchess de Angoulême, a lifelong friend of Henry and his family, was the godmother.

Sully notes in his *Memoirs* that Gabrielle wore a coronet of diamonds to the cathedral, which may or may not be true; he is the only observer to make that comment. Many others, however, noted that she rode in a carriage on whose doors the Lily crest of royalty was emblazoned, and when she arrived at Notre Dame, a carpet of purple was unrolled before her as she mounted the steps.

Gabrielle had become the first lady of France in everything but title, and even Princess Catherine, now the Duchess de Bar, stood aside to let her enter the reception hall at the Louvre for the party that followed the christening. As Dupleix says, "The charms of this lady were so attractive and so powerful that the King's passion grew with its gratification (a thing unusual in love), and he became more and more a slave to it every day."

In November 1598, soon after Margot had relinquished the duchy of Étampes, only one step short of the marriage itself remained, and Gabrielle took it. She moved into the official Louvre bedchamber reserved for the Queen. The date was November 17, Henry's birthday and the anniversary of the Battle of Ivry, and the move was noted by everyone in Paris who wrote memoirs or letters.

For Gabrielle the etiquette that custom decreed appropriate to a Queen of France began to be observed from that time. Her sisters were in attendance on her, and when she arose in the morning, they curtsied and dressed her in her underclothes. Great ladies vied with each other for the privilege of fastening her gowns, combing her hair, and applying rouge to her cheeks. Louise de Guise boasts in her *Adventures* that she won the competition, and intimates that she was the closest of the future Queen's friends.

Two archers in medieval attire stood at attention behind Gabrielle's chair when she sat down to a meal, and the ladies of the house of Guise waited on her at table. Another regal distinction was distinctly unpleasant, however. An official wine-taster sipped every beverage placed before her to make certain it had not been poisoned.

The heir-apparent to the throne was ten-year-old Henry, Prince de Condé, the son of a gallant Huguenot general who had been one of the King's cousins. The boy was unpopular at court, in part because his ambitious mother, the former Catherine de la Trémouille, was believed to have poisoned her husband. Further, the suspicion that the little Prince was not Condé's son caused dismay in conservative circles, while Council members were alarmed because he showed strong feminine tendencies, delighting in dressing himself in girl's clothing. The most that could be said for him by the great lords was that he had been baptized a Catholic.

The Prince was entitled to be addressed as "Monsieur," the official name given to the heir to the throne, but Gabrielle's capture of the court was so complete that virtually every noble who was in attendance at the Louvre called Caesar de Vendôme "Monsieur." According to Dupleix's *History of Henry IV*, neither the King nor Gabrielle corrected anyone who fell into this error. Catherine, Princess de Condé, retired to her town house and made no appearances at the court, consoling herself by curling her son's hair and rubbing rouge on his cheeks.

Gabrielle and the Princess happened to arrive simultaneously at a pre-Christmas party given by the Constable, and for a moment neither gave ground. Then Gabrielle said something to her adversary in an undertone, and the mother of the heir-apparent reluctantly dropped a curtsy. Montmorency asked Gabrielle what she had said, but she apparently had no desire to magnify her social victory, and merely smiled. She was in a position to smile.

Christmas 1598 was celebrated at the Louvre with great pomp. For the first time within living memory the country was at peace, both abroad and at home, and a new era of prosperity was dawning. Parisians stood outside the palace in large crowds, cheering the King and Gabrielle whenever they appeared, and nobles, clergymen, and Parliamentarians from every part of the realm came to the city to pay their respects to Henry and his mistress.

There was a striking difference between the informal atmosphere that had been prevalent at the court prior to the Spanish attack on Amiens and the newer spirit of great dignity. Henry, seated on his throne, received his guests in friendly but formal audiences. Gabrielle invariably occupied a place on his left, and sat in an armchair covered in purple velvet. Only the Lilies were missing from the upholstery, according to Dupleix, but it was common knowledge that other bolts of cloth had been made, and were being stored until Henry and Gabrielle could be married.

A special reception was held for foreign diplomats, and even the envoy from Tuscany, who hoped to prevent the marriage in order to further the cause of Marie de Medici, paid Gabrielle the honors due a Queen. Diane de Balagny writes in her *Memorial* that the representative of the Vatican was indisposed and did not attend the affair, but at the time no one suspected that his illness was of a strictly diplomatic nature.

In short, Gabrielle's last Christmas saw her at the height of her glory.

18: LADY OF FRANCE, 1598–99

Gabrielle d'Estrées enjoyed far more than the outer trappings of royalty. Her power was real, and by 1598 she was exercising the actual influence of a Queen of France in much of Henry's realm.

She acted as the King's deputy for Beaufort and Étampes, of course, but these demesnes were small, and her real strength lay in the authority vested in her as Caesar's guardian. Her son had become governor of Brittany, and she administered the province in his name; she also was in charge of the duchy of Vendôme, and surprised Sully, among others, by functioning as a governor herself. Her father was the crown deputy for Picardy and the Ile-de-France, her brother-in-law was Lieutenant General of Normandy, and her influence extended into every portion of the country.

Gabrielle happily accepted responsibility, and threw herself into her work with astonishing enthusiasm. Henry, it seems, had taught her his secret of storing and utilizing energy, and she bewildered her sister, Diane, by engaging in a heavy correspondence with provincial officials. Four secretaries were permanent members of her staff, and Diane comments in her *Memorial* that "they were as sore driven as the secretaries who occupied places in the household of His Majesty."

The power exercised by Gabrielle at the court was that of a queen, too, as is illustrated by the influence she exerted when Mayenne's son, Henry de Lorraine, was married to Henriette de Nevers. Mayenne himself, in a letter quoted by Dupleix and mentioned in numerous memoirs, thanked Gabrielle at length for obtaining the elevation to a duchy of his son's estate,

Aiguillon. A woman who was able to create new duchies was almost as powerful as the King, and everyone in France knew it.

In fact, the Huguenot leaders decided to give her a pension of ten thousand francs per year, and announced, when making the gift, that "this sum is being settled on this friend of the King who is at heart a Protestant."

The Jesuits held a different opinion. Believing her to be a devout Catholic, they petitioned her for the right to resettle in France. According to Dupleix, she took the matter to Henry and it was discussed in the Council. The King and his advisers, however, were opposed to the project and it was dropped. Here Gabrielle failed, but at least she tried, and on a subject that others would not have dared to open.

A letter written by Gabrielle and quoted by Dupleix demonstrates the firm grip she established and maintained in her relations with those whom she governed. It was addressed to the mayor, aldermen, and citizens of Vendôme, and was sent in her capacity as Caesar's guardian:

Gentlemen,

I was very much surprised at the death of Monsieur de Vignolles, and can assure you that the King has lamented his loss, and greatly regrets him, in that he considered him full of affection and faithfulness in his service and in that of our son, the Duc de Vendôme. You, too, have good reason to regret him, for I know that his aim and intention was to keep and preserve you from harm.

I hope that you may find a worthy substitute in the person of Monsieur de Harambure, gentleman-in-ordinary to His Majesty's bedchamber, to whom His said Majesty has given the post of governor of the town of Vendôme and the surrounding country, and at whose hands you may expect good and gentle treatment, as you too must render him all due

267

honor, respect, and obedience, which I am sure you will, right willingly, and give him all the satisfaction he has a right to expect. I myself have accorded him the captaincy of the château, which fact should bear witness to you how I too esteem him.

Had I not full knowledge of his worth, I should have opposed him, but on the contrary I do desire him for the post more than anyone in the world. And for this reason I exhort you afresh to dispose yourselves to admit him and honor and respect him as you should, and resting assured that you will do so I will say no more, praying God, gentlemen, to keep you in His safe and holy keeping.

Given at Paris on the 20th of February 1599.

D'Estrées

It was in no sense accidental that Gabrielle had established her authority throughout France. Chiverny, speaking bluntly in his *Memoirs*, declares, "The Duchess de Beaufort worked hard to establish her influence wherever she could, with such good result that, in a very short time, there were to be found in each of the provinces many people, of high rank and noble birth, established there for this very purpose. Her desires were always at one with those of His Majesty, and in serving herself she served his cause. For herself she sought nothing save the affection of the people; for His Majesty she sought willing compliance with his laws, under which all were governed for the good of the realm and his subjects."

Members of the aristocracy were not her only supporters. She had made great progress since the days when she had lived a sheltered life at Coeuvres, isolated from the world, and presumably had not only listened to Henry on the subject of obtaining the approval of ordinary citizens, but had seen for herself the importance of that approval when she had lived for months at a time with the army in the field.

The foot soldiers who had formed the bulk of the army were now artisans and peasants, and she cultivated them assiduously, driving through the poorer districts of Paris in her coach. She made it a habit to visit the food markets, where she wandered from stall to stall, often commenting on produce and, occasionally, buying something. If her purchases were infrequent, it was because she had learned stinginess from Henry. "My sister, who was once a spendthrift," François-Annibal notes in his *Memoirs*, "became like the King in her last years, parting with coppers only when it was needful."

The mission undertaken at Rome by Cardinal d'Ossat was producing no results in spite of the happy plans Henry and Gabrielle were making, and the cheers of the citizens of Paris when Gabrielle waved from her coach did not mean that Pope Clement intended to permit the marriage. Apparently neither the King nor his mistress realized that the Vatican was actively opposed to such a union for political purposes, the Pope having decided that a marriage between Henry and Marie de Medici would better serve the interests of international peace.

Brulart de Sillery, the King's special envoy, had returned to Paris shortly after the start of the New Year, and on January 20, Henry sent him back to Rome carrying a humble message to Clement:

Most Holy Father,
    This letter is not only written in my own hand, but proceeds straight from my heart. I will bring to your notice a special fact that will also be laid before you by the Sieur de Sillery, which is of greater importance to my person and my country than anything that has occurred since it pleased Your Holiness to receive me into your good graces and grant me your holy blessing.

269

I beseech Your Holiness with the greatest possible earnestness, to grant me the mercy I would ask of you. I would esteem it no less than if you were to grant me my life anew, so great is my desire to gain consolation at your hands. I promise Your Holiness to use such consolation so that God may thereby be glorified to the aggrandizement of His most holy Church, and that Your Holiness may win from me such feelings of gratitude that I shall for ever bless those whom you love as tenderly as I bless those who touch me more nearly.

Your devoted son,
Henry

The King's desire certainly was no secret to Clement, who had listened to the pleas of Cardinal d'Ossat and de Sillery, the diplomatic courier. But Henry was a worldly man and proposed to deal in worldly terms. De Sillery carried with him a verbal offer to transfer the marquisate of Saluces, which lay on the border of France and Savoy, into the hands of the Duke of Savoy. Both countries claimed the area, and no lasting peace could be achieved between them until the dispute was settled.

Gabrielle had a stake in this matter, too. She was keeping the bargain she had made with the Duke of Savoy when she had accompanied Henry to the border to escort Cardinal de Medici to Paris. The King apparently had promised her the marquisate as a gift, but she was happy to relinquish it in exchange for a crown, and had told the ruler of Savoy she would use her influence to persuade Henry to give up the property. It must be presumed, in return, that the Duke pledged the support of the two cardinals of his realm for the proposed marriage.

The situation was complicated by the interests of other nations. Tuscany opposed the transfer of the marquisate, as the marriage of Gabrielle to Henry would kill the hope that the Grand Duke's niece, Marie, would become the Queen of

France. Spain, on the other hand, favored the bargain, in part because Saluces would be given to Savoy, thereby diminishing the size of Henry's realm, in part because Philip and his advisers believed that a marriage to Gabrielle would weaken Henry's position, both internally and abroad.

Henry obviously was convinced that the news from Rome would be favorable, and on March 2, about one month after Sillery's most recent departure, he publicly announced that the wedding would take place on Easter Sunday. The citizens of Paris celebrated in the streets, and members of the nobility tried to outdo each other in giving banquets and other entertainments for their future Queen.

Gabrielle's attitude was serene, too, and with good cause. According to M. Desclozeaux, she had made a secret deal with de Sillery prior to his departure, promising him the Council post of Keeper of the Seals if he succeeded. Therefore she felt certain he would exert every effort on her behalf.

She erred in making this offer, and her slip was not typical of the caution with which she usually exercised power. Perhaps the prospect of becoming Queen in the near future made her giddy and caused her to forget the devotion of those close to her. Chiverny already held the position of Keeper of the Seals, in addition to his place as Chancellor, and although he would remain as a member of the Council if deprived of the former place, he would not look with favor on the woman who had robbed him of an office.

The excuse she offered to Chiverny was a feeble one, according to M. Desclozeaux's account. Henry, she said, had long wanted to appoint someone else as Keeper of the Seals, and only her devotion to the Chancellor had kept him in the post. But now Henry was determined to replace him, and under the circumstances she had chosen a man who could do her a good turn.

It was true enough that Chiverny was elderly, that he had been overworked and was tired, but he did resent Gabrielle's move, and so did Isabelle de Sourdis. But there was no effective protest that either could offer; Gabrielle's power had become so great that both Chiverny and Isabelle were forced to swallow a bitter pill and pretend they didn't mind. A woman strong enough to offer a Council post to a supporter could become a deadly enemy, and Isabelle de Sourdis must have been stunned by the realization that she herself was now dependent on the whims of her protégée.

The breach was healed rapidly, Chiverny giving a banquet for the King and Gabrielle in mid-March, and Madame de Sourdis storing in her own house the new royal furniture that had been ordered for the future Queen, after some members of the court had been heard to comment on the questionable taste of keeping it at the Louvre before the wedding ceremony was actually performed.

Sensitivity to gossip caused a change in Gabrielle's mode of living, too. It was reported to her, according to Diane's *Memorial*, that some nobles were criticizing her for having moved prematurely into the Queen's suite at the palace. So she compromised again, and only stayed at the Louvre when Henry was in residence. When he was away from Paris, she reverted to her former practice and moved back into her family's house. But it is significant that her bow to convention was a shallow one: when she slept at the palace, she continued to use the King's suite, and when she stayed at the Hôtel d'Estrées, even for a night, the pomp and ritual of royalty were observed.

Regardless of where she stayed, her anterooms were crowded with nobles, Parliamentarians, and common citizens seeking favors. A simple nod or smile from Gabrielle could win a position, obtain a pardon, or settle a longstanding grievance. "My sister," François-Annibal says in his *Memoirs*, "was more powerful than the King at this time, His Majesty's faith in her being so great that he left in her hands many matters that otherwise would have required his personal attention."

According to a popular legend which cannot be verified, two bankers of substance who owned adjoining properties had been squabbling for years about the boundaries of their respective lots. They had spent large sums of money in the courts, and neither had been satisfied with the verdicts handed down by the magistrates.

In April or May of 1598 they had appealed to the King, asking him to examine their respective cases and promising to abide by any decision he made. Henry, reluctant to set a precedent in civil disputes of this nature, yet equally hesitant to turn down the appeals for assistance from two loyal subjects, had resorted to the procedure, unusual for him, of procrastinating.

The two men therefore wrote a joint letter to Gabrielle, who replied that she would interview them. This she allegedly did, made her decision and, when it was written by a secretary, sealed it with a blob of royal dark green wax.

If this document truly existed, it has been lost. But what is important is the story, not its verification. People living at the end of the sixteenth century believed that Gabrielle d'Estrées, an obscure noblewoman from Picardy, was usurping the power of magistrates and making her decisions binding by using royal wax.

"The Duchess de Beaufort," Louise de Guise writes in her *Adventures*, "had become the living symbol of France itself."

That simple statement sums up Gabrielle's position; only Pope Clement remained unimpressed.

Henry, eagerly looking forward to the wedding, had no presentiment of disaster. On the day the marriage plans were announced he gave Gabrielle a diamond ring in the presence of the entire court, first holding the gem over his head so everyone present could see it and understand its significance. It was the same ring with which he himself had wed France on the day of his coronation.

On the same day he presented her with two other dazzling gifts. One was a heavy statue of solid gold, depicting a king with a lion crouched at his feet. The statue, which had been presented to Henry by the city of Lyons, was so valuable that neither the memoir writers nor, apparently, the court jewelers were able to estimate its worth.

He also gave her a chased box of silver which contained a polished piece of rare amber, weighing more than four pounds. It had been presented to him by the city of Bordeaux, and according to the Constable, whose provincial capital was Bordeaux, it was worth "many thousands of écus, the box alone being the handiwork of an Italian craftsman and worth more than one thousand écus."

Gabrielle found time each day to stand for her dressmakers, who had been forced to set aside the extensive new wardrobe they had been making for the future Queen. The due processes of nature had caused a slight but not unwelcome change in the plans of the sewing women: Gabrielle was pregnant for the fourth time.

Apparently neither Henry nor his mistress was disturbed at the prospect of the bride walking down the aisle of Notre Dame carrying an unborn child. No hint of concern or even of embarrassment creeps into the King's correspondence, nor even into the memoirs of Gabrielle's chroniclers. It can only be assumed that all France had grown to accept Gabrielle's pregnancies as normal, natural, and inevitable.

Henry was far more concerned about something of infinitely greater importance: the possibility that he might die in the next year or two and that Gabrielle would be forced to act as regent until Caesar came of age. The King was in the best of physical health, but appears to have fallen victim to depression. He brooded for days, lost his ebullience, and alarmed the Council by refusing to attend several meetings. His meals were served to him in private, he canceled audiences and saw no one but Gabrielle, who dropped all of her other activities to be near him.

To an extent, the problem was real. If Henry should die after the wedding, there were princes who would claim Caesar had no right to sit on the throne, and unless a strong man stood between them and their ambitions, the country would be plunged into a new series of civil wars.

The King was not one to worry purposelessly, and as soon as he analyzed the situation, he took steps to correct its weaknesses. He decided that Biron, a first-rate soldier who was young and ambitious, was precisely the man he needed, not realizing that his lieutenant was a shade too ambitious, and was already dickering with the Spaniards.

In any event, according to Dupleix, the two men reached a private understanding. Biron, on his part, agreed to uphold Gabrielle and her children if the King should die. Henry, in return, promised Biron he would succeed Montmorency as Constable, and in the meantime made him a gift of a large sum of money and two counties, Périgord and Bigorre. In order to bind the soldier still more closely to Gabrielle, Henry arranged a marriage between Biron and Françoise d'Estrées, the youngest of Gabrielle's sisters.

Actually, Françoise was only a half-sister, having been the natural child of her mother's lover, but it was understood that, for purposes of the marriage, Antoine d'Estrées would recognize the girl as his daughter. Françoise herself was not consulted, having just turned fifteen.

Word of the secret understanding soon became public, and Biron became a power in France overnight. Henry was still dissatisfied with his arrangements, feeling that the soldier needed a strong supporter whose loyalty to Gabrielle could be taken for granted. François-Annibal d'Estrées fitted the role perfectly, except that he commanded no strength in his own name, so the King started casting about to find him the right wife.

Ever mindful of the past, Henry could not forget that the de Guise family was capable of creating grave problems, so it seemed a natural solution to marry François-Annibal to the lovely and talented Louise de Guise. "The lady surprised me," François-Annibal writes in his *Memoirs*, "by accepting the union." The other members of the de Guise family, all of them in Gabrielle's debt, heartily endorsed the idea. The future Queen would be protected by powerful alliances.

But Henry was not yet finished. According to M. Desclozeaux, he proceeded to spin an intricate web of deceit and countersubterfuge worthy of the Tuscan de Medicis.

It was Henry's private intention to render the little Prince de Condé harmless by giving him an appointment as a bishop, and eventually elevating him by nominating him for a cardinal's red hat. Such plans, however, would have to wait until the boy reached his sixteenth birthday; in the meantime, it was necessary to deceive his scheming mother. So, acting behind the scenes, Henry arranged for a marriage between young Condé and Mademoiselle de Mercoeur, the betrothed of Caesar.

As the girl was only five years old, it was easy enough to make such provisional plans for her, and ostensibly Henry knew nothing of them. Actually, however, as Caesar would become heir to the throne as soon as his parents were married, the daughter of Philippe-Emmanuel and Marie de Mercoeur was no longer important enough to become his wife.

Henry acted swiftly, and it was arranged that as soon as Caesar officially became heir to the throne, the alliance agreed upon at Angers would be renounced. A few weeks later the people of France would be informed that Caesar would marry the daughter of the Duke of Savoy, who had agreed to such a union in secret diplomatic bargaining.

By Lent the final arrangements were completed, and Henry considered the future secured. At last he was in a position to relax, but as time passed he found it increasingly difficult to sit back and admire what he had done — for there was still no word from Rome.

Not until long after Gabrielle's death and his marriage to Marie de Medici did Henry learn that Tuscany and Venice, in league with the Vatican, had been working toward that end for years.

From the time Henry had first entered Paris as King of France, Tuscany had maintained an agent there. Canon Francesco Bonciani acted as a secret representative of the Grand Duke until 1596 or 1597, pretending to be a clerk on the staff of one or another high-ranking prelate. Finally he appeared in the open as the agent of Tuscany, a position he maintained until early in 1599. During his entire stay in Paris, a period of almost five years, his sole mission was that of negotiating a marriage between Marie and the King.

His letters to his master are filled with tales of Henry's love for Gabrielle and the hopelessness of his own task, but occasionally he deluded himself into believing — or at least wishing — that the prospects had become brighter for his candidate.

"There is reason to fear that *something inconvenient* may take place if the King can free himself from the Queen of Navarre," Bonciani wrote on March 29, 1596.

On December 18 of that same year, he soothed himself, saying, "The King speaks no more of annulling his marriage; whereas his liaison with Madame de Monceaux is creating a scandal."

The christening of Catherine Henriette shortly thereafter caused the Tuscan agent to change his tune and all of his old fears were revived. "A grander christening could not have been accorded to an heir to the crown. The King's love for his mistress grows greater. It soon may become an incurable evil!"

On April 9, 1597, Bonciani argued against an alliance between Marie and Henry, declaring that Henry "is in great need of help, which it would be right to send him were it not for the fact that no reliance can be placed on his life, nor on his succession." The only guarantee he could make, Bonciani declared, was that the affection of the French people for their monarch and his mistress was great.

On April 28, gloomier still, he described his mission as extraordinarily difficult, "in the first place, because the Queen of Navarre is still living, but more particularly because of the King's great love for Madame de Monceaux, which would prevent him from marrying our Princess."

The papal legate hinted, late in 1597, that it might be possible to obtain a dissolution of Henry's marriage to Margot if the King would agree to marry Marie. Bonciani's hopes rose accordingly.

But on March 14, 1598, the agent lost all patience, and in his sharpest letter to the Grand Duke, asked if some way could be found to induce Pope Clement to interfere and "put a stop to the detestable life which the King is living with Madame de Monceaux in the sight of all the world. It would cause a grievous scandal were the King to take this woman to wife."

The Grand Duke seemed to feel he was beaten and abandoned the idea of his niece marrying Henry. Enough, apparently, was enough. Bonciani, obviously realizing he would be out of work if his master did not change his mind, wrote at length about the Peace of Vervins, pointing out that an alliance between France and Tuscany would protect Florence for all time from the Spaniards.

The project was revived, and, judging from Bonciani's letters in the late summer of 1598, it seems clear that Pope Clement would have granted Henry a divorce immediately, provided he intended to marry Marie.

The agent's last letters give up the cause. Henry, he declares, is determined to marry his mistress, so he himself is resigning his place and returning to Florence. He mentions, too, that Francesco Contarini, the ambassador from Venice, shares his views and believes it inevitable that Henry intends to let nothing prevent him from marrying Gabrielle.

But Rome remained unyielding, and Cardinal de Gondi, the Bishop of Paris, was placed in a difficult situation. Henry was becoming increasingly impatient and, according to M. Desclozeaux, twice called the Cardinal to the Louvre. At the first interview, both men maintained at least a pretense of civility. Henry asked if the Vatican was delaying purposely, and de Gondi replied that, to the best of his knowledge, there was no deliberate procrastination on the part of the Pope. Henry then requested the Cardinal to dissolve his marriage to Margot. The Cardinal, still polite, replied that he could not take such action on his own authority, but would be pleased to act if the Pope granted him the necessary powers.

At their second meeting, the King was in a foul mood and abruptly commanded the Cardinal to dissolve his marriage. De Gondi, who was probably the only man in France who could stand up to the irate Henry, refused with equal bluntness.

"His Eminence," writes Dupleix in his *History of Henry IV*, "was in a great rage when he returned to his litter and ordered his bearers to carry him to his own palace. But his anger was not near so great as that of the King, who shouted so loudly that many in the Louvre heard him swear that no power in Heaven or on earth would prevent his marriage to the Duchess de Beaufort."

It is tempting to speculate whether Henry was intending to follow the course taken by his English namesake who had left the Church so he could marry whom he pleased. There is no evidence to substantiate this theory, however, and it seems more likely that the King intended to find a prelate whom he could bend to his will. The memoirs of the period are filled with rumors to the effect that one or another cardinal or archbishop had been chosen for the unsavory assignment.

One fact is certain: Henry allowed neither the silence of Pope Clement nor the obstinacy of Cardinal de Gondi to sway him. He had announced that he intended to marry Gabrielle, and plans for the wedding went forward as smoothly as though the Vatican had already granted the King his divorce.

19: THE DEATH OF GABRIELLE, 1599

The *Memorial* of Diane de Balagny is a lively, intimate journal that takes pains to avoid the spectacular, but one of her dated observations, in itself a rarity, indulges in sheer melodrama. On January 31, 1599, she writes, "On this day, the last of the month, when all the world is talking of the marriage of my sister to the King, a Piedmontese named Bizacasser, who is seldom at fault in his predictions, said to an old friend, who has repeated it to me, that he was willing to stake his life that this marriage would never take place, and, what was more, that my sister would never again see Easter Day."

If Diane actually made the entry on January 31, Gabrielle undoubtedly heard the dire prediction immediately thereafter, and in all probability sent for the Piedmontese fortune-teller with the pseudo-Eastern name. She was in the habit of consulting soothsayers, often shopping around until she found one who told her what she wanted to hear. So, it may be presumed, if she received Bizacasser — and if he dared to repeat his grim warning in her presence — that she dismissed him immediately.

By late March, however, premonitions of disaster began to haunt her, despite her glowing health and the fact that she had encountered no problems when she had given birth to her first three children. She wept frequently, and Henry became so concerned that two royal physicians were attached to her household. Her unusual state of mind can be understood readily if it is remembered that Henry had just recovered from depression and that despondency, like other neurotic tendencies, may be sympathetically communicated to one close to the sufferer.

Dupleix and other historians of the period solemnly relate that Gabrielle began to endure nightmares so dreadful that she awakened every morning before dawn, either screaming or sobbing. The reader is not told how these authors gleaned such intimate details, and neither she nor anyone close to her is quoted.

Nor is any authority cited for a lurid story that appears in many memoirs as well as histories, and which, in the period following her death, seems to have been generally accepted. According to this tale, Gabrielle was warned by unnamed fortune-tellers that she would dream of terrible misfortunes that lay ahead for her, and these dreams would be warnings from Heaven. One night shortly before her death, according to the story, she dreamed that a huge fire was raging around her; gradually it crept closer, hemming her in, and she was unable to escape from it.

The account was further embroidered. Henry dreamed the same thing, and in his dream watched Gabrielle die. Their fear was so great that both awakened, and, after telling each other their nightmares, were unable to go off to sleep again.

Subsequently, even some reasonable, thinking men accepted such stories. Pierre Matthieu, a distinguished magistrate and author of several books on Henry's reign, writes in his *Henry the Great*, "The soothsayers whom idleness and curiosity kept as welcome guests at the Court foretold that a child would prevent the d'Estrées from realizing her hopes. One of these told me what he had gathered from the facts concerning her nativity, adding that it was infallible, but that God was above all. I believed this more sincerely than he, but seeing that the stars had foretold the death of a great lady and that their

282

predictions had in many instances proved true, I cast the burden of my doubts upon the bosom of God."

But Chancellor Chiverny was too intelligent a man to believe in the occult, and in his *Memoirs* relates only the facts, as he himself knew them, concerning the period immediately prior to Gabrielle's death. He says, "As the time of the Easter Festival approached, the King, wishing to be alone, dismissed all of us members of his Council, bidding us celebrate the Festival in our own houses."

Chiverny is also responsible for giving the most sensible account of the reasons why Henry and Gabrielle separated for a short time before Easter. According to his story, Father René Benoit, the King's confessor, suggested to the future bride and groom that they should be parted for a short time. His argument was that Gabrielle, as the future Queen, owed a good example to the people of France after setting so many bad ones. Therefore, he advised Henry to send her to Paris from the palace at Fontainebleau, outside the city, where the couple and their children were staying. The confessor further advised that Gabrielle should offer prayers in her own parish church.

Henry seemed to accept the suggestion; actually he was engaged on another front: With the likelihood that Pope Clement would grant a divorce becoming increasingly dim, Henry secretly made arrangements that would compel one or another member of the French ecclesiastical hierarchy to dissolve his marriage to Margot and to perform the ceremony that would make Gabrielle Queen of France.

Gabrielle's gloom deepened. Her anxiety, combined with the excitement of preparing for the ceremony that would make her Queen, were exhausting, and her physical condition was further complicated by her pregnancy. Henry apparently thought Father Benoit's counsel was timely and urged her to accept it. She could deny him nothing, and in spite of her fears, finally gave in.

She left Fontainebleau on the morning of April 5, 1599, her health so precarious that the physicians would not let her ride in a coach. She was carried in a litter, with Henry acting as her escort at the head of a large party. They halted at Melun for dinner, then resumed their slow journey, and reaching Savigny at dusk, spent the night in the small royal château there. The following morning Henry accompanied his mistress to the bank of the Seine, where a boat was waiting to carry her to Paris on the opposite shore.

A large group preceded Gabrielle onto the boat. There were poets, clowns, and jugglers to entertain her on the short trip across the narrow river; cooks to whip up a delicacy if she became hungry; and a half-company of royal household guards to protect her person. Caesar had made the journey from Fontainebleau with his parents; Catherine Henriette and Alexander were considered too small to travel, and had remained behind at the palace.

Henry and Gabrielle conferred on the riverbank, and Caesar then kissed his mother goodbye. The boy was taken back to the King's waiting escort, and the time of parting had come for Gabrielle and Henry.

At this moment, M. Desclozeaux reports, Gabrielle completely lost her courage. Apparently abandoning all self-control, she burst into tears and Henry could not console her. After a time her hysteria spent itself, but her gloom remained unabated. She told Henry repeatedly that she was sorry she had taken his advice, and she said loudly that she was certain they would not see each other again.

She made such a scene that Henry offered to take her back to Fontainebleau, and the pair stood for some time, unable to reach a final decision. Then they embraced, and Gabrielle clung to the King, giving him lengthy instructions about the children and for those servants who were not accompanying her, and, above all, telling him of her concern for his welfare.

Finally there was a last caress, and the soldiers escorted Gabrielle onto the boat. She landed in Paris at about three o'clock in the afternoon, stepping ashore on a quay that was part of the property belonging to the official arsenal, where Marshal de Balagny and Diane made their residence. Both were on hand to greet her, as was François-Annibal. Hordes of friends were also there, including Louise de Guise and her mother. There was no lack of company had Gabrielle chosen to spend the rest of the day being consoled.

"My sister was too weary to accept offers of entertainment," Diane says in her *Memorial*, "and withdrew to my private apartment, there to refresh herself. I carried word to those assembled that she begged to be excused, and they departed. Wanting to escape from the fawning and curious, she then betook herself to the house of Zamet for dinner."

At first glance Gabrielle's choice seems odd; it certainly was not prudent. A woman intending to set a good example to the people of France should have thought twice before going to the mansion of a man who enjoyed a well-deserved reputation for being a lecher and reprobate. There is no reason to assume, as Sully and others subsequently did, that Gabrielle had some immoral purpose in mind when she decided to accept the hospitality of Zamet. A physically tired woman well advanced in pregnancy and fearing for her life could not have been searching for sinful pastimes, particularly when she expected to become Queen of France within a week.

Sully later made the assertion that she had spent the night at Zamet's house, but M. Desclozeaux flatly contradicts this assertion, saying she dined there in order to achieve privacy, precisely as Diane states in her *Memorial*. Then, instead of going either to the Louvre or the Hôtel d'Estrées, she retired to the town house of Isabelle de Sourdis, who was not in the city. Again, the choice seems strange, but Diane's statement is the key to the way Gabrielle felt. Had she gone to the Louvre, scores of people would have insisted on seeing her, and the crowds would have been only slightly smaller at her father's house.

The best method of insuring privacy for the night was to go where she was not expected. In any event, she did not behave immorally, Sully to the contrary, for she was accompanied by at least a dozen members of her staff, all of whom were examined by royal magistrates following her death. These servants told substantially the same story: she had eaten a lemon at dinner, and was suffering from indigestion. She went to her aunt's house, where a skeleton staff was on duty, and the place was opened for her.

Then, before going to bed, she wrote to Isabelle, saying she was ill and begging her aunt to join her. A messenger was dispatched to Chartres, and the curtains that surrounded Gabrielle's bed were closed for the night.

Her actions thereafter were public knowledge. The following morning, a Wednesday, she was carried in a litter to the church of Petit Saint-Antoine, where a sacred concert was being held. The commander of the household guard marched beside her litter, a full company of royal archers acted as her ceremonial escort, and a large number of ladies, including Mademoiselle de Guise, followed her to the church in their coaches.

Spring had come to Paris, the weather was warm, and crowds lined the streets to greet their future Queen, who looked sallow and drawn. In spite of her ill health, however, she responded to the cheers, repeatedly smiling and waving. Obviously she knew what was expected of her and played her part.

The large crowd gathered outside the church roared its approval so lustily that Gabrielle bravely left her litter and walked a short distance so that everyone could see her. Every pew in the church was filled, and Gabrielle was conducted to a chapel that had been reserved for her. At her request, Louise sat beside her, and the two young women chatted at length before the sacred concert and during an intermission.

Louise writes in her *Adventures* that Gabrielle, although wan, had recovered her good spirits, showing her friend two letters she had received from de Sillery, who promised her unequivocally that her desires would soon materialize. It is interesting to note that the shrewd Louise observed no evidence to substantiate his claim that Pope Clement would be granting Henry and Margot a divorce in the immediate future.

Gabrielle also showed her friend two letters from Henry, delivered to her earlier in the day by a royal courier. Louise writes that "they were full of tenderness and expressions of the keenness of his desire to see their marriage celebrated."

There were so many people in the church that the atmosphere soon became stuffy. Gabrielle complained of the heat, but remained in her seat until the service ended. Then she informed Louise that she intended to return at once to her bed at her aunt's house and, displaying fear, begged her friend to join her there. Louise promised she would do so, and they left the church.

Crowds again cheered Gabrielle as she was carried through the streets. She made occasional, feeble efforts to wave, but many who saw her realized that she was ill. By the time Louise arrived at the house of Madame de Sourdis, Gabrielle was standing in the center of her bedchamber, her hands pressed to her temples, frightened servants clustering around her. Louise immediately took charge, telling the maids to undress Gabrielle and put her to bed. Gabrielle complained of a splitting headache, and Louise sent the captain of the guard for the royal physicians, who should have been in constant attendance on her, but for unexplained reasons happened to be elsewhere.

Almost as soon as Gabrielle was placed in bed, she fainted. Aromatic spirits were waved under her nose, burning feathers were held an inch or two from the soles of her feet, and several other remedies, all equally popular at the time, were tried without success.

At last the physicians arrived, and one of them forced the unconscious girl to swallow an elixir, holding her tongue to prevent possible choking. By this time a large throng of relatives, friends, and court sycophants had gathered in her chamber, hampering the doctors, but it occurred to no one that the patient might desire privacy.

"Within the hour," Louise writes, "Gabrielle recovered, and all who were present rejoiced at seeing the cheerfulness of her countenance."

Cheerful she may have been, but she was too weak to leave her bed, and two dinners that had been planned in her honor that evening, one by Marshal and Diane de Balagny and the other by Zamet, were held without the presence of the Duchess de Beaufort, who dined on cold mutton, slices of cold fish, and mead, all prescribed by the physicians.

That night the curtains that surrounded her bed remained open, and the doctors took turns guarding Gabrielle. She slept peacefully, and on Thursday morning seemed to have recovered her strength. The physicians happily gave her their permission to dress, eat breakfast, and carry out her normal schedule for the day. As it happened, she was planning to attend High Mass at the church of Saint-Germain-l'Auxerrois, which was so near her aunt's house that she needed neither a litter nor a carriage to get there.

She walked the short distance, accompanied by the royal guard, attended Mass, and walked back to the house. Except for a loss of appetite, she seemed completely recovered. Then, suddenly, at about two o'clock in the afternoon, she again felt violently ill and was put to bed. Her baby was not expected for another three months, but at four o'clock she began to feel labor pains, and for the next four or five hours suffered agonizing spasms, fainting at least three times, according to Louise de Guise, who remained at her bedside.

That night was deceptively calm, but the labor pains continued, depriving her of sleep, and by Friday morning she was in a very weak condition. The physicians decided to assist in the delivery of the infant; the child was stillborn, but Gabrielle had no idea of what was happening. Throughout the day her pain increased, and by six o'clock Henry IV's beloved mistress had lost the powers of speech, hearing, and sight.

Two surgeons and three apothecaries and a priest had been called in to assist the royal physicians, but no one could do anything to help, and at about five o'clock on Saturday morning, April 10, 1599 — thirty-six hours from the time she would have become Queen of France — Gabrielle d'Estrées died.

The physicians and surgeons conducted a post-mortem examination, and later announced that her liver and one lung were diseased. The primary cause of death, however, they solemnly declared in their report to the King, had been the lemon she had eaten at Zamet's house. The fruit, they said, had been "corrupt."

The actual cause of death, according to modern medical science, appears to have been puerperal convulsions.

In any event, the reign of the uncrowned queen ended with sudden and dramatic finality.

20: AFTERMATH

Paralysis and confusion attacked nobles, personal servants, and members of the royal bodyguard during Gabrielle's last hours. Large crowds of curious citizens gathered in front of Madame de Sourdis' house on Good Friday, when the people of Paris learned that the King's mistress was ill, and by that evening someone had discovered that the door was unlocked and that there were no sentries on duty. People wandered in and out of the house at will all night, stealing bric-a-brac and even furniture. According to M. Desclozeaux, some of the bolder citizens actually wandered into Gabrielle's bedchamber, where the chaos was so great that no one bothered to order them out.

Louise de Guise admits in her *Adventures* that she fainted when Gabrielle died. A short time later Isabelle de Sourdis arrived home after a long and grueling journey. She seemed calm enough when she received the news, and retained sufficient presence of mind to have the house cleared. Then she, too, fainted.

In midmorning on Saturday, Madame de Sourdis, her strength recovered, and Diane de Balagny, who had spent all of the previous day and night with Gabrielle, invited the Venetian ambassador, a long-time family friend to bless the deceased with holy water. Soon thereafter it was announced that Gabrielle's effigy would be placed on a couch, and that her body would be taken to an abbey near Meaux, where a chapel would be built to receive the coffin. Order at last had been restored.

The question arises, as it did in the days immediately following Gabrielle's death: why was Henry not at her side?

On Thursday, April 8, Gabrielle became sufficiently alarmed about her condition to write a letter to Henry, which was taken to Fontainebleau by a nobleman named Puipeyroux. Gabrielle begged Henry to let her return to him at once, and expressed the hope that, for the sake of their children, he would be able to marry her before she died.

The letter alarmed Henry, who ordered Puipeyroux to see to it that the royal barge was made ready, so he could return to Paris without causing too much commotion in the city. The order was carried out, and the King left Fontainebleau before dawn on Friday morning. Receiving word from a royal courier that Gabrielle's condition had grown worse, he changed his mind about the boat and decided to ride straight to the city. He set out at a gallop.

The story of his activity is picked up by François de Bassompierre, later a Marshal of France, who had joined the court in 1598 and had already become a favorite of both the King and Gabrielle. "On Good Friday," Bassompierre says in his *Memoirs*, "when we were at church at Saint-Germain-l'Auxerrois, La Varane, a member of the household of Madame de Beaufort, came to announce to Marshal d'Ornano that Madame had just passed away and that it would be advisable to prevent the King from coming to Paris. He begged the Marshal to go out to meet the King, who was already on his way, traveling by diligence, and stop him from entering the town.

"I happened to be by the side of the Marshal, and he begged me to come with him. We found the King close by at Villejuif, riding posthaste for Paris. Notwithstanding the news, he wished to go to Paris and see the Duchess as she lay dead."

He was dissuaded, according to Bassompierre, by several of the gentlemen accompanying him. They used a number of arguments, stressing that he could do no good, that he had to think of his royal dignity and of his reputation; all of them, it appeared, were motivated by the fear that he might break down. The crushed Henry allowed himself to be taken back to Fontainebleau, admitting that he was too weak and grief-stricken to look at the body of his beloved Gabrielle.

The error committed by La Varane seems natural. Everyone in the de Sourdis house, including the doctors, was hysterical, and it is reasonable to assume that the steward jumped to a premature conclusion. In any event, according to Bassompierre, Henry "called Heaven to witness that never had accident so pierced him to the heart before or brought him such affliction. 'I acknowledge,' said he, looking up to Heaven as he spoke, 'that God loves this country and has no wish to destroy it.'"

When Henry arrived at Fontainebleau, he went straight to a pavilion set in a pine garden, where Caesar was playing. The King burst into tears again as he told the story and tried to comfort the child who was weeping too. Bassompierre, who witnessed the scene, says the five-year-old child seemed to understand that his mother's death would make it impossible for him to succeed his father on the throne. Henry's great grief stemmed in part from the lonely future he saw ahead of him and despair over the combination of tragic circumstances which had separated him from his beloved in her final days.

The Constable, who was spending the holidays at a château he owned near Fontainebleau, came to the palace at once to offer the King consolation. Montmorency had lost a wife under similar circumstances a short time earlier, and the two lonely men went into a private chamber together, closing the door after them. There is no record of what they said to each other.

By the following day Henry had recovered sufficiently to write several letters ordering that an inventory be made of the jewels in Gabrielle's possession at the time of her death. Most of her gems were at Fontainebleau at the time, fortunately, for Diane de Balagny, who immediately instituted a search after receiving Henry's command, was shocked to discover that several rings were missing from Gabrielle's fingers. (La Varane, the steward, was later sent to prison, along with his wife, after being found guilty of stealing some of the missing pieces of jewelry.)

On Easter Sunday the King went into black in mourning for Gabrielle, an unprecedented act on the part of a French monarch, who traditionally did not wear black even when his legal wife died. Henry wore black for a week, then changed to violet and remained in mourning for three months. The court, of course, followed his example.

Princess Catherine wrote a letter to her brother on Easter Sunday, April 11, saying, "My dear King, — I know well that to your bitter grief words can bring no remedy. Therefore I will only use them to assure you that I feel your loss as deeply as I feel the great love I bear you, and as the loss of so perfect a friend itself compels me, I long to be by your side. That it may please God, my King, to lessen your grief with the years, I pray with all my heart; and on this, my dear, good King, I kiss you a thousand times."

One week later Henry replied, "My Dear Sister, — I received much consolation from your letter. I have great need of it, for my affliction is as much without equal as was she who is the cause of it; regrets and lamentations will go down with me to the grave. Yet since God has sent me into the world for my country's sake and not for my own, all my powers and my energies will be employed solely to the advancement and preservation of this, my realm. The roots of my love are dead, they will never spring up again; but those of my friendship for you will be ever green, my dear sister, whom I kiss a million times."

On the Tuesday following Gabrielle's death, Henry returned to Paris, bringing his three motherless children with him, and went into residence at the Louvre. His first official act was to order a state funeral held on the following Saturday, April 17, and he directed that Gabrielle should receive honors befitting royalty.

For the next four days an effigy of Gabrielle, made of stucco and wax, reposed on a huge bed in a chamber at the Hôtel d'Estrées under a canopy made of cloth of gold. The figure was made in a sitting position, and was clad in a ducal coronet and a golden cloak. At one side stood Gabrielle's father, brother, and sisters, all in black; on the other side priests offered prayers unceasingly at two altars that had been erected for the purpose.

At the foot of the bed stood two royal heralds, wearing black armor, on which Lilies of France had been painted in gold. It was the heralds' duty to offer holy water to the princes, great lords, and other nobles who came to pay their respects to Gabrielle. The chamber was lined with magnificent tapestries belonging to the King, and the entire royal household staff remained on duty at the Hôtel d'Estrées during this period. The coffin containing Gabrielle's body was placed under the bed, Isabelle de Sourdis' quick thinking in announcing its removal to Meaux having prevented damage by curiosity seekers.

A custom peculiar to the fifteenth and sixteenth centuries was followed with great care. Four elaborate meals were prepared each day, and the dishes were offered to the stucco and wax figure on the bed. Princesses and other great ladies who were present at these hours presented the food, and a pretense was maintained that Gabrielle was still alive.

While this pantomime was being carried out, Henry was engaging in serious conversations at the Louvre with Cardinal de Gondi and other high-ranking members of the clergy. According to Bassompierre, whose *Memoirs* are the authority for these discussions, the King wanted the funeral service held at Notre Dame. De Gondi and the other clerics pointed out to him gently but firmly that this could not be done. Henry had not married Gabrielle, and funeral services were held at Notre Dame for no persons of lower rank than a king or queen.

The weary Henry had fought long enough for his mistress, and when he finally realized he could not win this last point of honor, he consented to allow the funeral to take place at the church of Saint-Germain-l'Auxerrois. The principal mourners were Henry and Caesar, who sat alone in a pew reserved for them. Virtually every nobleman and lady of consequence in France was present, as well as the whole diplomatic corps.

After the funeral the entire assemblage rode in carriages to Saint-Denis, where another, shorter service was held, and then the mourners rode to the convent of Maubisson, where Angélique d'Estrées, Gabrielle's sister (who had not yet become involved in scandal) was the Abbess. There, after another brief service, the casket was placed in a church vault pending a decision regarding a final resting place.

Henry glumly returned to Paris with his children, and within a few days the rumors were flying. It seemed inconceivable to many people that Gabrielle could have died from natural causes only a day and night before the date set for her highly publicized wedding. Everyone, including Henry himself, was suspected by the gossipmongers, some of whom pointed out that the King had been saved great embarrassment and loss of prestige as, his divorce not having been granted, he would have found it necessary to postpone his marriage.

Scurrilous handbills flooded Paris, most of them written in doggerel, according to Dupleix, who says in his *History of Henry IV* that all those who had possible reasons for poisoning Gabrielle had been listed. He adds that when the usually tolerant and good-natured King read one of these innuendo-laden papers, there was a violent explosion of the royal temper.

A new section was being added to the Louvre, and the angry Henry stalked out into the open, clutching the paper. Shouting so loudly that hundreds of stonemasons, carpenters, and passing pedestrians heard him, he swore he would obtain vengeance and promised to execute, with his own hand, those who had written, printed, and distributed the foul document.

The handbills, Dupleix states, disappeared overnight, and the subject of poisoning was dropped. It was revived many years later, and Sully speculated on the matter at length in his *Memoirs*, even going so far as to hint, in his neurotic hostility toward Gabrielle, that he himself had conceived the idea and that the deed had been performed by persons in his pay.

Bassompierre does not mention the possibility of poisoning in his *Memoirs*, nor do Diane and François-Annibal. Even Chiverny, who was afraid that he would be sent into complete retirement now that his protectress was gone, does not raise the thought in his *Memoirs*. It appears that, after a brief period of speculation, France calmly accepted Zamet's lemon as the culprit.

Isabelle de Sourdis, according to Dupleix and others, begged the King to grant her the custody of Gabrielle's children, and it is impossible to determine whether she was motivated by love for the children or by a desire to maintain at least some measure of influence at court. Henry appears to have considered the idea, but finally rejected it, keeping his sons and daughter in his own custody.

Immediately after Gabrielle's funeral, Antoine d'Estrées sent heavy wagons to collect his daughter's expensive furniture, and had it carted off to Coeuvres. Under the law he was entitled to gain possession of the property, and although he acted with unseemly haste, no one criticized his greed.

François-Annibal, whose hopes of achieving greatness were at least temporarily dashed, fell ill and spent three months in his bed at the Hôtel d'Estrées. Certainly he was not surprised to learn that his marriage to Louise de Guise had been canceled. The arrangements to marry Françoise d'Estrées to Marshal Biron were quietly shelved, too. No diplomatic letters were needed to call off the engagement of Caesar and the daughter of the Duke of Savoy, both sides tacitly understanding that such a union was now out of the question.

The stucco and wax image of Gabrielle was carried to the King's private apartment at the Louvre, and there was placed in a small chamber which Henry visited daily. Bassompierre states in his *Memoirs* that the dummy was dressed each day in a different gown, and that Henry continued his habit of visiting the room and meditating silently for several years, long after Henriette d'Entragues became his mistress and Marie de Medici won her long battle to be crowned Queen of France.

Caesar, Catherine Henriette, and Alexander were raised at the King's court, and Henry kept up a strong interest in all of them. It is odd that Queen Marie, who meddled in almost everything, allowed Gabrielle's children to grow up with her own sons and daughters. A strong bond of affection tied Caesar, who had almost become the crown prince of France, and Henry's eldest legitimate son; in later years the Duc de Vendôme loyally served Louis XIII.

Diane de Balagny gave birth to several children, none of whom achieved importance. And Isabelle de Sourdis faded into complete obscurity soon after her beloved niece's death. Her husband kept his post as governor of Chartres, and she joined him there, retiring from a life at court.

François-Annibal was by far the most distinguished member of the d'Estrées family, and unlike his father, who gave up all of his high posts and went back to Coeuvres, the younger man remained active in the service of Henry IV. Under Louis XIII he was appointed in 1621 to the post of ambassador to the Vatican; five years later, after returning to active military duty, he received the baton of a Marshal of France. In 1632 he defeated an army of the German states at the Battle of Treves, and in 1636 he returned to Rome as ambassador.

In 1640 he reached the peak of his career, and was appointed Constable of France, holding the second highest place in the realm for eight years. In 1648 he announced his retirement, and became the Duc d'Estrées, but he was not yet ready to spend the rest of his days contemplating his vast collection of silver. Instead, he received an appointment as Governor of the Ile-de-France, and in that position found ways to increase his already great wealth. He married three times, taking his last wife at the age of seventy-three.

Caesar de Vendôme led a pleasant, mildly useful life and, thanks to the property he inherited from his mother, not to mention the sums of money paid to him regularly by his father, was in comfortable circumstances. Caesar married a noblewoman of no distinction, and through her founded a new line. His elder son, Louis, who succeeded to the duchy, married one of the many homely nieces of Cardinal Mazarin, the real ruler of France during the last years of Louis XIII's reign and the minority of Louis XIV. Caesar's second son, François, who became Duc de Beaufort, lived at court and did nothing worthy of note.

Louis Joseph, Duc de Vendôme and Marshal of France, the grandson of Caesar and great-grandson of Henry and Gabrielle, was one of the most distinguished French soldiers in an era of great captains. He won laurels for himself in action from the time he entered the army as a young junior officer, and although his relative, Louis XIV, disliked him intensely, he won his Marshal's baton on sheer merit. He fought with great distinction against the Duke of Marlborough and Prince Eugene of Savoy in the early eighteenth-century War of the Spanish Succession, and achieved a lasting niche for himself in the annals of warfare. Unfortunately, he was the last of his line.

Catherine Henriette de Vendôme, who was her father's favorite during the decade prior to his assassination in 1610, married brilliantly, becoming the wife of Charles de Lorraine, Duc d'Elbeuf, a prominent member of the Guise family. The tragedy of Gabrielle and Henry sprang to life again in the middle of the seventeenth century when Caesar and Catherine Henriette became involved in a long, ugly legal fight over their mother's property. All of the old scandals were revived, much to the amusement of the court, and in the process, the reputation of Gabrielle, already suffering as a result of Sully's widely read *Memoirs*, was further sullied. Neither son nor daughter seemed to care.

Alexander, Chevalier de Vendôme, was the least conspicuous of Henry and Gabrielle's children. Plans were made to enter him in the priesthood, as was so often done with younger sons of a great house, but Alexander showed no liking for a clerical life. Instead, he entered the army, and because of his late father's name was given the rank of colonel. He fought in several campaigns, showing no real merit, and was retired, quietly, with the rank of general. He neither married nor sired children.

Gabrielle d'Estrées was all but forgotten by the generation that grew up after her, although interest in her short life and dazzling career was renewed, briefly, during the quarrel between Caesar and Catherine Henriette. The historians of the eighteenth century rescued her from oblivion, but she sank from sight once again until about a hundred years ago.

Few women of her generation exercised greater power and influence, few have been the object of so much gossip, and few have been more assiduously courted by vast numbers of people. But it appears to have been her fate, through the centuries, to appear briefly from time to time, like a brilliant comet. Strangely, her reputation parallels her life itself.

NOTES

The First Meeting: November 1590
The château of Coeuvres was partly destroyed by artisans and peasants during the French Revolution, but was subsequently restored to its sixteenth-century elegance, and the better part of it still stands. It has weathered well, and looks much as it did when Gabrielle lived there. The initials, G. d'E., which are to be found in the woodwork of the south wall in the bedchamber occupied by Gabrielle, probably were not carved by her, but were the handiwork of a tourist many generations later.

The Early Years: 1573–90
A lively controversy over Gabrielle's birthplace has raged for the better part of four hundred years, and shows no signs of abatement. Desclozeaux presents logical arguments in his monograph which assign the honor to Coeuvres, but Tours, not insensitive to the tourist trade, stubbornly clings to its own claim. For all practical purposes, the site of Gabrielle's birth is unimportant. What does matter is her age, and here Louise de Guise must be accepted as the final authority. Her *Adventures* have proved to be so accurate in other details that she is regarded as a reliable historian.

Henry was mistaken when, in his enthusiasm, he tried to praise the patriotism of Gabrielle's ancestors and declared that Jean d'Estrées served under four kings. Henry actually had a better case than he realized, for Jean served under five. First carrying arms in Italy under the banner of Louis XII, he later fought under Francis I, Henry II, Francis II, and Charles IX,

302

dying peacefully at Coeuvres in 1571, two years before Gabrielle was born.

D'Aubigné's letter praising Gabrielle's virtues was written in 1598 to his cousin, the Huguenot bishop of Bern, who had been one of Henry's first instructors in the Protestant faith. The entire d'Aubigné family turned against the King when he embraced Catholicism, and for several generations thereafter considered him a "traitor."

Marie de Medici, niece and heiress of the Grand Duke of Tuscany, was married to Henry in 1600, following Gabrielle's death, and became the mother of Louis XIII. The de Medicis were somewhat less than comely, but Marie was the beauty of the family, which in part accounts for Henry's marriage to her. He never allowed politics to stand in the way of his appreciation of feminine attractiveness.

Diane d'Estrées, writing in her *Memorial*, never refers directly to her mother's elopement. Obviously the whole family was sensitive on the subject, for François-Annibal always mentions the abandonment obliquely in his *Memoirs*, too. It is likely that Antoine d'Estrées deliberately instilled this attitude in his children, who were not reluctant to write freely about their own affairs.

Henry III was the last male member of the House of Valois. His assassin, Jacques Clément, was a religious fanatic who believed France could be saved only if the King were dead. Whether the Guise family was responsible for his act is still debatable; a living Henry III was less dangerous to them than the energetic Henry IV, who had been named the official heir to the throne. The facts are confused because it was a common sixteenth-century practice to use the services of fanatics rather than those of hired killers to commit political murders.

Henry the Great

There is remarkably little dispute among historians about the life, career, and reign of Henry IV. He himself is largely responsible: he knew from his youth that he was destined for greatness and, constantly keeping posterity in mind, wrote thousands of letters and had copies made of every document he signed. As many as six authenticated copies of some of the papers relating to his reign have been found.

A childhood of relative poverty left a permanent mark on Henry, who spent almost no money on himself and very little more on the women in his life. His personal suite in the Louvre was furnished with old chairs and tables brought up from the cellars, and only rarely did he consent to have new clothes made. According to his Constable, he wore his boots "until they fell from his feet." He was generous only in his treatment of Gabrielle, and even with her often became unpredictably parsimonious.

Rendezvous at Chartres, 1591

Corisande d'Audoins was one of the most verbose royal mistresses in French history. The details of her affair with Henry appeared in many memoirs of the time, and after Henry's death she offered to sell her story, but changed her mind when Queen Marie, Henry's widow, threatened her with imprisonment. The most voluptuous beauty of her day, Corisande remained lovely in old age, and poets praised her when she was over seventy.

The few authentic letters written by Gabrielle in her own hand are preserved in the archives of the National Library in Paris.

Marriage, 1592

It was not difficult for royal propagandists to portray Nicolas d'Amerval as unattractive. Only two miniatures of him survive, both of them paintings of an unusually homely, insignificant-looking man. Incidentally, he sometimes used one of his lesser titles, Seigneur de Cerfontaine.

The Love Game, 1592–93

The national guessing game as to when Henry and Gabrielle first went to bed together assumed staggering proportions. No one dared to ask the King, Gabrielle wisely said nothing, and Isabelle de Sourdis, who undoubtedly knew, confided in no one except Chiverny. Virtually every letter and every memoir written during this period raises the intriguing question. French historians, more persistent on the subject than their colleagues elsewhere, have evolved some complicated theories, most of which cannot be proved.

The name, "Feuillemorte," was given to Bellegarde by Henry after a color then in fashion. The duke was the best-dressed member of the court; in fact, he was the only man in the King's suite who tried to keep up with current styles, other courtiers preferring to copy Henry's manners and wear shabby doublets, breeches, and boots.

The letter from Gabrielle to which Henry refers in his famous epistle to her of late November 1592, has been lost. Numerous forgeries have appeared through the centuries, of course.

The Power Behind the Throne, 1593

In the early days of Gabrielle's power, few people gave her credit for wielding any influence. But everyone in France was afraid of Isabelle de Sourdis, and the League's adherents hired poets to write scurrilous limericks about her.

Gabrielle's famous letter to Catherine, proposing they work together, is quoted in Berger de Xivrey's authoritative biography, *Catherine of Navarre, Duchess de Bar*. The original appears to have been lost, and de Xivrey does not cite his source.

Before the French Revolution of 1789, the States-General was a shadow Parliament with ill-defined powers, and was used by royalty for its own convenience. It was composed of three orders — the clergy, the nobility, and the commoners, mostly lawyers.

The Conversion, 1593

Few statements made by distinguished men have aroused greater storms than Henry's alleged remark to the effect that Paris was worth a Mass. French historians have quibbled for centuries, unable to pinpoint the person to whom he supposedly said the famous words. Through the eighteenth-century reign of Louis XV, the professionals followed religious lines: Catholics hotly denied that he made the statement, while Protestants insisted that he did.

D'Aubigné's almost incoherent letter of August 9, 1593, blaming Gabrielle for Henry's conversion, was written to his brother. It is often quoted, although the original has been lost.

Few assemblies in history ever suffered a more devastating or humiliating collapse than that of the League's puppet States-General. The congress held a final meeting at the Louvre on December 22, 1593, with only a few deputies in attendance, and then quietly disintegrated without being formally dissolved.

Paris in the Springtime, 1594

Charles de Cossé, Comte de Brissac and later Duc de Brissac, was one of the most nimble opportunists in an era when the breed had reduced the knack of fence-jumping to a fine art. He supported the League valiantly, but when he transferred his allegiance to Henry, he served the monarch with a vigor and fidelity that surprised many of his old friends. His wife, who amused some of the ladies of Paris by sticking pins into a dummy of Henry, became a good friend of Gabrielle's, and never again attacked the King in word or deed.

The closest association existed between King Henry and his Constable, Henry I, Duc de Montmorency, whose *Correspondence* (in two volumes) tells so much about his monarch's reign. Why the duke remained loyal to his master is something of a mystery, as Henry IV, who never believed in delegating too much power to any one man, saw to it that the Constable absented himself from his own domain, the Languedoc region, with Bordeaux as its capital. Montmorency didn't see Bordeaux for many years, but seemed content. Both men were Gascons, and therefore were in rapport; no word on the subject was ever reduced to paper, but they achieved an understanding through some form of intellectual and emotional osmosis.

The Divorce, 1594

The most curious feature of Gabrielle's divorce proceedings was Henry's naïve belief that people would accept, at face value, his "coincidental" presence in Amiens — and under the same roof — with his mistress. As he had no real business in Amiens at that time, he kept busy by writing scores of letters on both official and personal subjects. In none of them did he mention either Gabrielle or her legal case. Subsequently he was hurt, or at least professed to be hurt, when it was suggested to him that he had engaged in arm-twisting tactics in order to make certain that Gabrielle obtained her decree.

Sir Walter Raleigh is the authority for the allegation that d'Amerval sired fourteen children. The comment appears in his diary (*Works*, Vol. 2), written in Sherborne, Dorsetshire, in February 1595.

De Brissac, obviously using his wife as his source, states in his *Correspondence* that Gabrielle refused to accept the forecasts of the fortune-teller, "Madame Cozzini." The Comtesse de Brissac, for whom a more cheerful future was predicted, believed what she was told.

The Lady and the Pope, 1594

The curious and convenient royal custom of issuing decrees to render bastards legitimate had become common in the early Middle Ages when, due to the Church's influence, illegitimacy became a stigma. Some royal bastards were recognized as legitimate, others were not; the degree of power wielded by the royal father was usually the determining factor. Technically, such decrees should have been issued by the Vatican, but the French had gone their own way since the days of the Schismatic Popes, and the right of a French king to dub his own bastards legitimate was considered a national prerogative.

Montmorency, who always gave Gabrielle her due when she won a victory, maintained correct relations with her, but they were never really friendly. Apparently each respected the authority of the other, and tried to avoid unnecessary toe-trampling. Many efforts were made to set them against each other, but Gabrielle was too shrewd to be taken in by such maneuvers, and the duke was too wise.

The Lady Diplomat, 1595–96

Balagny was one of the most charming, talented, and

unscrupulous rogues in French history. His marriage to Diane d'Estrées probably was the best thing that ever happened to him, for he settled down and became — for Balagny — relatively sober and honest. In his old age he became involved in several shady financial enterprises, among them the sale of shares in a company that promised enormous returns on investments to be made in the New World. Nothing came of these ventures, and his high rank protected him from prosecution as a swindler.

Gabrielle could have been paid no greater tribute by the citizens of Paris than their calm acceptance of her station. The demonstration outside the Hôtel d'Estrées was the only incident of its kind to occur during her "reign." Few king's mistresses could claim similar, kindly treatment from the volatile Parisian masses.

Mayenne probably was the greatest trencherman of his era. He reputedly made it a habit to spend two hours at breakfast, two to three at mid-day dinner, two to three at evening dinner and, when entertaining or being entertained, at least another at supper.

Keeper of the Keys, 1596

Among the items stolen from Gabrielle on her deathbed were the golden keys that were the symbols of her membership in the royal Council. Obviously, the thief acted without thinking when taking the keys, which were too hot to handle. Henry personally supervised a long and painstaking search for them, but to no avail. The practice of giving such keys to royal advisers was abandoned during the reign of Louis XIII. Incidentally, keys allegedly taken from Gabrielle's chain showed up, at one time or another, for more than one hundred years, and by no stretch of the imagination could all of them been hers. The first did not appear until Henry himself had died; the memento-sellers were taking no chances.

The Crucible, 1597

According to legend, Henry bought the ring for Gabrielle at a later date and presented it to her privately. No evidence can be found to substantiate this tale, which seems to be the product of a romantic author's wishful thinking.

Dupleix, one of Henry's biographers, wrote a play based on Mayenne's heroic intervention against the Austrians. Unfortunately, the actor who played the rotund duke was laughed from the stage, and no subsequent performances of the play were given.

The Silken Glove, 1597–98

Gabrielle was merely tolerated by Mercoeur and Marie because of her power and influence, but they are among the few who did not fall under the spell of her personality. In 1600, after Henry's marriage to Marie de Medici, the haughty duke and his wife apparently thought it safe to snub François-Annibal d'Estrées at a reception being given by Princess Catherine. Gabrielle's brother suffered the insult in silence, but when the story was repeated to Henry, the King ordered Mercoeur to apologize, both verbally and in writing. François-Annibal mentions the incident briefly in his *Memoirs*.

The Edict of Nantes, 1598

Gabrielle's influence in setting the stage to make the Edict possible, together with her subsequent labors to make certain it was obeyed, have been forgotten because, in large part, the ministers of Louis XIV ordered history rewritten. They found the past embarrassing, and when the Edict was revoked by the

Sun King, the promulgation of the Edict by his grandfather was a fact no one cared to recall. Therefore the efforts of Henry, Gabrielle, and Catherine were ignored, and many citizens literally did not know who had been responsible for the decree.

A King, a Queen, and a Pawn, 1598

Sully's relations with Queen Margot were formal and distant, but in his dotage he writes as though they had been intimate friends. She, of course, represented no threat to his power, as Gabrielle had, and in his *Economies* he displays many of the sentimental traits shown by later writers. A conservative count indicates that at least two hundred romantic novels and plays were written about her tribulations.

Those portions of Sully's conversation with Henry that are obvious falsehoods or distortions have not been included in this chapter. Sully writes many pages, quoting Henry and himself verbatim; I have edited his work with a large, fat pencil.

Lady of France, 1598–99

Dupleix estimates that more than five thousand official documents — perhaps half of the total number of papers of one sort or another submitted to Henry in the course of an average year — were read by Gabrielle in 1598. She was not only Queen in all but title, but a working Queen.

The pension awarded to Gabrielle by the Protestants was paid to Caesar for several years after her death. Henry apparently hinted to the Huguenot leaders that he would appreciate the gesture, and the sum was paid annually until the conspiracies hatched by Queen Marie changed the atmosphere of the court.

The Death of Gabrielle, 1599

At the time of Gabrielle's death, no one thought of criticizing her because of her visit to the house of Zamet, where she ate the "fatal" lemon. Eyebrows were not raised until many years later, when Sully belabored the point.

Dupleix and other contemporary historians estimated that the jewels stolen from Gabrielle before and after she died were worth — in modern terms — more than one hundred and fifty thousand dollars. About half were recovered.

Aftermath

When Henry wore black for a week, following Gabrielle's death, he established a new custom.

BIBLIOGRAPHY

Allison, E. E. *Loves of Henry IV*. New York: 1886.

Archives of the French National Library, Paris.

Aubigné, Agrippa d'. *Letters*. Paris: 1611; revised, 1630.

Balagny, Diane d'Estrées de. *Memorial to Gabrielle, Duchess de Beaufort*. Paris: 1615; London: 1721.

Bassompierre, François de. *Memoirs*. Paris: Société de l'Histoire de France, 1877.

Bellegarde, Roger de Saint-Larry, Duc de. *Amours du Grand Alcandre*. Paris: 1622.

Bickley, Francis. *Kings' Favourites*. London: 1910.

Bonciani, Canon Francesco. *Letters and Memoranda*, ed. by Paul Martel. Paris: 1836. Translated by Roger Humphreys. London: 1859.

Bouillon, Godfrey, Duc de. *Memoirs*. Paris: 1618.

Brissac, Charles de Cossé, Duc de. *Letters*. Paris: 1640.

Brown, H. "Mayenne," *English Historical Review*. London: April 1895.

Chiverny, Armand de. *Memoirs*. Paris: 1611.

Colau, P. *La Belle Gabrielle*. Paris: 1816.

Conti, Louise de Guise, Princesse de. *Adventures de la Cour de Perse*. Paris: 1818 (revised).

Desclozeaux, Adrien. *Gabrielle d'Estrées*. Paris: 1887.

Dupleix, Scipion. *History of Henry IV*. Paris: 1612–14, 3 vols.

Estrées, François-Annibal, Duc d'. *Memoirs*. Paris: 1666.

Groulart, Claude. *Correspondence*. Paris: 1622.

Grundy, Rudolph. *Church and State in the Sixteenth and Seventeenth Centuries*. Philadelphia: 1894.

Hauser, Henri. *Sources de l'histoire de France*. Paris: 1906.

Howard, Robert L. *France in the Sixteenth Century*. New York: 1913.

——. *Henry the Great, King of France*. New York: 1910.

Lamotte-Langnon, E. L. *Agnes Sorel, Diane de Poitiers and Gabrielle d'Estrées*. 2 vols. Paris: 1820.

Lindsay, T. M. *History of the Reformation*. London: 1907.

Mariéjol, J. H. *History of France*. Vol. VI. Paris: 1905.

Matthieu, P. *History of France*. Paris: 1631.

Montignani, C. I. *History of the Republic of Venice*. London: 1781.

Montmorency, Henry I, Duc de. *Correspondence*. 2 vols. Paris: 1690.

Poirson, Auguste. *Historie du règne de Henri IV*. 4 vols. Paris: 1862–7.

Raleigh, Sir Walter. *Works*. Vol. II. London: 1829.

Réaux, Tallemant de. *Historiettes*, translated by C. C. Brooks. London: 1718.

Sainte-Edme, A.-F. *Amours et Galanteries des Rois de France*. 2 vols. Paris: 1829.

Street Ballads of the Sixteenth Century, ed. by Jacques Sorel. Paris: 1838. Translated by R. O. Fisher. London: 1859.

Sully, Maximilien, Duc de. *Economies Royalies*, translated by Charlotte Lennox. London: 1756.

——. *Memoirs*, translated by Charlotte Lennox. London: 1856 (revised).

Tilley, A. A. *Cambridge Modern History*. (Vol. II) Cambridge: 1902.

Valois, Marguerite de. *Memoirs, Poems, and Letters*, ed. by F. Guessard. Paris: 1842. Translated by Eric Moulton. Boston: 1890.

Xivrey, Berger de. *Catherine of Navarre, Duchess de Bar*. Paris: 1856.

——. *Letters and Documents of Henry IV*. Paris: 1839–53.

———. *The Marriage of Gabrielle d'Estrées and M. de Liencourt.* Paris: 1862.

A NOTE TO THE READER

If you have enjoyed this book enough to leave a review on **Amazon** and **Goodreads**, then we would be truly grateful.
The Estate of Noel B. Gerson

Sapere Books is an exciting new publisher of brilliant fiction and popular history.

To find out more about our latest releases and our monthly bargain books visit our website:
saperebooks.com

Made in the USA
Middletown, DE
03 April 2022